Remains to be Seen

Archaeological Insights into Australian Prehistory

David Frankel

Originally published in 1991 by
Longman Australia Pty Limited
Designed by Mark Davis S
(ISBN 0 582 87040 2)

Second edition
2014
© David Frankel

ISBN
978-0-9924332-1-5

Contents

Introduction   *vii*
1 Approaches to research   *1*
2 Australian Aboriginal prehistory and society   *15*
3 Burials   *28*
4 Coastal shell middens   *41*
5 Rockshelters and caves   *56*
6 Mounds   *74*
7 Stone structures   *87*
8 Fish-traps   *94*
9 Ceremonial sites   *106*
10 Quarries   *118*
11 Rock art sites   *131*
12 Regional prehistory   *140*
Glossary   *152*
Government archaeological authorities   *153*
Further studies   *154*
Annotated bibliography   *155*
Index   *157*

Acknowledgements

A book such as this owes much to the many people whose work and ideas are incorporated and summarised in it. My debt to colleagues whose work I have used is obvious, while students who participated in my Australian archaeology courses at La Trobe University over the last decade will find arguments and discussions which developed in their classes.

Lena Frankel, Caroline Bird and Peter White read and commented on the book as a whole, while individual sections were read by Ann Brown, Brian Egloff, Colin Pardoe, Mike Smith and Elizabeth Williams.

Introduction

Remains to be seen. All around us are the remains of tens of thousands of years of Aboriginal occupation.

Whether one follows Aboriginal belief that their ancestors and the very landscape itself were produced by the creative forces of the Dreaming, or the scientific view of human evolution and colonisation of this continent, these remains provide tangible links with the past.

We may look at sites of ancient occupation in different ways. They may stimulate emotional, perhaps romantic, feelings; personal responses of identification with past generations. They may provide political symbols, solid evidence of prior occupation and a source of pride in ancestral achievement. They may be used as sources of information, the basis for investigating how people lived in the past. It is this last approach which is the main subject of this book, although the social significance of archaeology provides a subsidiary theme.

Remains to be seen. All around us are ideas about ourselves, and about other people, past and present.

Many of these ideas, especially those about human origins and past behaviour, come from archaeological research. But archaeology, as with all science, is not a simple set of answers, but a constant enquiry. There are answers. Many answers, and always new answers. But which of these, if any, are to be believed, remains to be seen.

This book is not a general prehistory of Australia, describing sites, artefacts, events and developments, although we should never lose sight of these more general aims of our research, or forget the achievements of our discipline in exposing the achievements of the Aboriginal past. My aim is more limited, concentrating on detail and the more practical side of archaeology. I hope that by introducing some of the complexities of archaeological procedures I will be able to demonstrate the challenge, as well as the products, of research.

Although intended for teachers and students in the final years at secondary school, this book will also appeal to anyone with an interest in Australia and in how archaeologists work. Two main elements are interwoven: techniques of archaeological research, and information and ideas about local prehistory. This follows from a basic belief that archaeology is a process of discovery and that the ideas we have are intimately linked with the way we research them.

Building discussion around different types of site or approaches to research gives a series of insights into the nature of our data and methods, and shows what we know, how we know it, and how this can be integrated into stories about the past.

Preface to the 2014 edition

It is now over twenty years since *Remains to be Seen* was published in 1991. Durng that time there have been many developments in Australian archaeology, not the least of which is the increasing importance of an Indigenous voice. This has transformed many aspects of archaeological practice, and in some states the role of Aboriginal communities in managing heritage sites is enshrined in legislation.

Most of the younger generations of archaeologists who have graduated during the last decades are primarily engaged in heritage management rather than 'pure' or academic research. Large-scale mining and other development projects in all parts of the continent have all required archaeological fieldwork to assess and mitigate their impact on heritage. This has led to an massive increase in the number and scale of archaeological surveys and excavataions. Unfortunately the demands of working in this environment often provide little opportunity to follow up the implications of the vast quantities of information gathered and much of it remains largely inaccessible. One of the biggest challenges facing the disciplne is how to manage, and, equally important, how to make use of this constantly accumulating and varied data to develop new views of Australian Aboriginal land-use patterns, economies, and adaptations over some fifty or sixty thousand years of history.

Alongside the flow of new evidence, new concepts and new techniques of dating and analysis also continue to stimulate archaeological debate. Older arguments and ideas are constantly being re-evaluated, and other, perhaps equally temporary, questions about the past now engage archaeologists attention and energy.

In such a context of a dynamic and evolving discipline one may ask whether re-issuing this book is useful, especially as I have made no attempt to bring it up-to-date, apart from adding a few additional references. However, because it deals to a large extent with argument and approach I believe it still has value, encouraging a focus on the ways in which ideas have been developed and alternative views advanced by assessing the available evidence through different eyes. For archaeology is, for me at least, as much a creation of individual researchers as a documentation of surviving remains.

In all of our debates and analyses we should not, however, forget that the material we study was made and used by people whose descendants take pride in their ancestors' culture which forms a part of their heritage, and we should therefore acknowledge the Traditional Owners and their Elders, past and present.

David Frankel
December 2013

Archaeological sites discussed in the text.

Approaches to research: ideas, methods, data

This chapter provides a brief introduction to the more specific case studies on selected sites. These show up a variety of approaches, and should be seen not as guides to how archaeology should be done, but rather as examples of what actually has been done.

Archaeologists confront many issues. Some are technical, others theoretical, some about practicalities of excavation or analysis, others about theories of human behaviour and historical development. In this book much attention is paid to the actual process of research in order to show the interplay between data, methods and ideas about the past.

The context of research

Data, methods and ideas constantly change. Australia is a very large continent, and archaeological research is still new and limited. We must always be ready to adjust to new ideas and information.

Each year new fieldwork or the reanalysis of previously excavated sites adds to our primary data base. Sometimes one site can radically alter what we know. For example, before 1987 the oldest known occupation in arid central Australia was 10 000 BP. One new excavation provided a radiocarbon date of 22 000 BP. Suddenly we

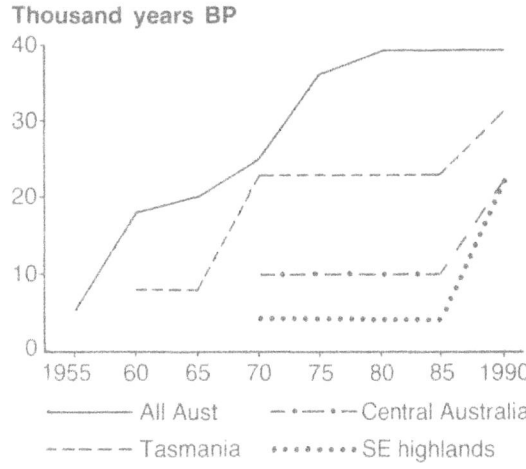

1.1
Each year new research changes our basic information. This is shown clearly by the earliest radiocarbon dates known for different areas at different times over the thirty-five years that this technique has been generally available.

knew that people had been in the region for twice as long, and this opened up a whole new debate on the timing and nature of colonisation of arid lands. Not all fieldwork has so simple and direct an impact, but the accumulation of new information gradually places our previous information into better perspective, allowing reassessment of interpretations based on initial, more limited knowledge.

New methods develop. Some of these are technical. For example, the microscopic examination of residues and use-wear on the edges of tools, or a technique for determining the season of the year in which shellfish were collected. Others are more abstract, such as different statistical approaches to describing or comparing material. Re-examination of standard ways of doing things allows us to see more clearly problems inherent in our work, and challenges us to overcome them.

New ideas are as important as new data. Changing views about how societies function and develop can also prompt the reassessment of old data to give new insights into what happened (or may have happened) in the past.

In addition to all this, the social context in which we work changes. Not only are there more archaeologists now than ever before, but they do different kinds of things. Twenty years ago almost all archaeologists worked in universities and were primarily concerned with sites as resources for research. The majority now work in areas related to heritage management, concerned with assessing the cultural significance of sites and regions and protecting or managing them in a more conservation-conscious world. Perhaps the most significant change comes from the growing influence of Aboriginal communities. Many communities now have legal rights and responsibilities for archaeological sites and material and are increasingly involved in decisions on management of sites and research.

The types of questions we ask, the ways we ask them and the kinds of answers that satisfy us, all constantly change. If this change is to be for the better, we must clearly understand what we do now.

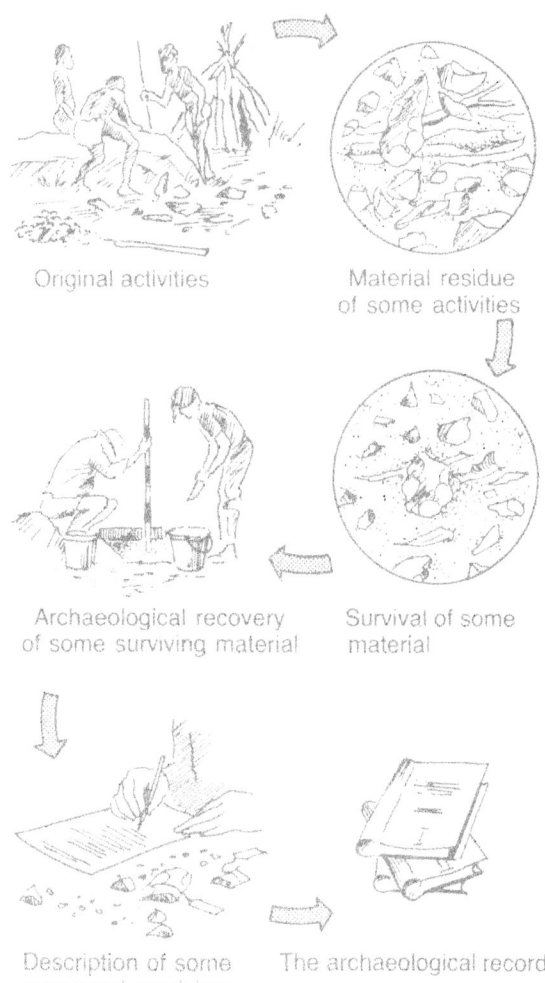

1.2

Archaeological sites develop through series of processes which reduce the objects associated with original activities to surviving remains. Techniques of recovery and selective analysis then transform some of these remains into archaeological 'facts'.

Evidence and survival

Archaeologists deal with material remains. While information about living peoples illuminates our work, the primary challenge is to develop ways of exploring behaviour from physical evidence — the things people made, used and discarded. This is made even more difficult as not everything survives equally well. This limits our information and structures our data base and interpretations.

Stone tools dominate the Australian archaeological record, as wooden dishes, digging sticks, spears, spear-throwers, shields, clubs and boomerangs do not survive. We may be able to determine that stone tools were used for woodworking, but the form of the items made escapes us.

Similarly, animal bones survive while remains of plants do not. But we do know that the diet of hunting and gathering societies included at least as much plant-food as meat.

The following is a summary of the main types of evidence used by Australian archaeologists.

1 Archaeological sites

We can study these in many ways, considering their size, location, age and contents. We know a great deal about excavated sites, but others may be little more than dots on maps, providing a very different quality of information — spatial distributions rather than site-specific detail or chronological sequences. There are many types of sites including:

- camp sites, such as caves and rockshelters, middens, oven mounds, stone houses and, most commonly, scatters of stone artefacts which provide the only evidence of open campsites
- quarries, from which stone for tools, or ochre for painting and ceremonial use were obtained
- facilities, such as fish-traps, both inland and on the coast
- ceremonial and sacred sites, either made by people, or natural features on the landscape
- burials, which can provide evidence of biological variation, health and structure of populations, and burial customs
- rock art, sites with paintings or engravings, in ceremonial or more domestic contexts

2 Artefacts

Stone tools and the discarded by-products of their manufacture are most common finds in archaeological sites, while bone tools are less frequently found and ancient wooden artefacts are extremely rare. Museum collections of wooden artefacts counterbalance this bias, and provide valuable information on the material culture of Aboriginal people during the last 200 years. Artefacts can be analysed in a variety of ways:

- technological studies are concerned with how tools were made
- functional analyses determine what tools were used for and may be based on analogies with modern tools or microscopic examination of characteristic damage to the working edges, or traces of residues on them
- raw material analyses consider the selection of material and may be used to trace distribution of stone from specific quarries
- morphological analysis is used to describe the shape and size of artefacts and to compare them within and between sites

3 Remains of plants and animals

Remains of plants and animals discarded in archaeological sites provide evidence of diet and how the environment was used. Shells and bones are most common in Australian sites, but occasionally evidence of plants can also be recovered.

4 Environmental data

Archaeological and historical information needs to be considered in an environmental setting. Although not totally conditioning how people lived, the climate and available resources are obviously important. While some landforms have changed little, at least over the last four or five thousand years, geomorphological and palynological evidence shows the nature of earlier environments. We can consider variation in:

- climate, in temperature, rainfall, and wind patterns
- rising and falling sea levels, exposing or flooding coastal plains
- water balance, fluctuating levels of water availability, filling and drying of rivers and lakes
- landform changes in coasts and the development of dunefields and river sediments
- vegetation, with changes in response to climatic and other fluctuations
- animals varied with changing conditions, becoming available or locally extinct, or in some cases, totally extinct

Developing research projects

Although archaeologists are generally thought of as excavators, this is only a minor element in archaeological research. Any project starts with the identification of a problem and the definition of the aims and methods to be used, based on a preliminary study of previous work in the region or on similar sites or material. This might include historical or ethnographic accounts dealing with Aboriginal people in the area to illuminate archaeological data. Local Aboriginal communities must be consulted and official approval to carry out fieldwork obtained. When the excavations or surveys are completed, the finds must be identified, measured, classified and catalogued before further analyses can be attempted and general conclusions drawn. Detailed reports on the sites, fieldwork and finds as well as the interpretations need to be prepared and published.

1.3
Geomorphologists drill a core through the sediments in a swamp to obtain samples of pollen representative of the plants in the region at different times in the past.

Fieldwork: survey

Much archaeological work (especially that carried out for environmental impact assessment or for planning heritage management) does not involve any excavation, but is limited to surface surveys. It is increasingly common practice to record all material in the field and not to collect anything for later analysis.

Types of information

- types of sites in region
- relative numbers of sites
- size and density of sites
- degree of preservation of sites
- location of sites in relation to landscape and resources
- contents: types of stone, artefacts, shells, art etc.
- potential for further research or excavation
- cultural or heritage value of sites or regions

5 Ethnographic, historical or traditional information

Ethnographic, historical or traditional information about or provided by Aboriginal people can be used to develop general ideas about how land and resources were used, or to provide analogous examples of artefacts and behaviour to help explain the archaeological record. We need to tread a fine line between using this information to help understand the past and imposing ideas derived from recent societies onto ancient ones.

Issues which can be addressed

- density of occupation
- types of activity in the region
- site location, and the relative importance attached to different resources or landscape features
- access to, or selection of different types of stone
- significance of sites and regions

Advantages

- relatively cheap and quick
- sites need not be disturbed
- a basic knowledge of otherwise unknown areas is obtained
- a regional perspective means that sites are seen as elements in a complex, not necessarily as centres of activity
- an inventory of sites useful for planning management and research

Disadvantages

- observation limited by visibility of sites
- many sites are poorly preserved (and may only be visible because they have been damaged or destroyed)
- not all material survives on the surface
- sites cannot be dated and the material visible on the surface may be from very different periods of use of the site

Basic procedures

Essentially it is very simple; to go out and look for sites, record their location, size, appearance, and contents.

Although specific sites may be located by asking local people for information, in most cases comprehensive surveys to find otherwise unknown sites must be carried out on foot. As this can take a long time, it is often necessary to sample the area – that is, not to look at all of it,

1.4
Archaeological recording: Denise Gaughwin and Gabrielle Brennan document a small shell midden on the shores of Western Port, Victoria.

but at only a part regarded as representative of the whole. It is, of course important to look at all parts of the study-area, even though we would not expect to find sites in some areas. This will ensure that our preconceptions of site location do not bias the results, but are tested in the field.

Various strategies for sampling a study-area can be employed. A random sample, not biased in any way, can be obtained by dividing the whole area into a series of squares and randomly selecting 5% or 10% of them. A more complex procedure (a *stratified sample*) ensures that all different environmental zones are looked at by deliberately sampling each. In practice, however, these ideal sampling strategies often cannot be used. In some heavily vegetated areas it may simply be impossible to see the ground, so that no sites can be found, except where there are roads or tracks. Similarly, very rugged terrain may restrict access. Factors such as these need to be identified and taken into consideration in assessing the results of survey work.

Having found a site, the next problem is to decide what to record about it. The South Australian Aboriginal Site Card illustrated in Figure 1.5 covers the basic information required for documenting archaeological deposits for their State Register. Each of the other State archaeo-

REMAINS TO BE SEEN

CONDITION OF SITE

Causes of Site Damage:

- [ ] Vandalism
- [ ] Camping
- [ ] Foot Traffic
- [ ] Vehicle Traffic
- [ ] Pastoral
- [ ] Animal
- [ ] Natural Erosion
- [ ] Mining/Extractive
- [ ] Urban/Rural Development
- [ ]
- [ ]
- [ ]
- [ ]
- [ ]
- [ ]

Site Exposure:

Vegetation:	[ ] Majority Cover	[ ] Partial Cover	[ ] None
Soil:	[ ] Majority Cover	[ ] Partial Cover	[ ] None
Site Preservation:	[ ] Mostly in Situ	[ ] Partly in Situ	[ ] None in Situ

Description of Site Condition:

Have items been collected from the site?   [ ] Yes   [ ] No.   [ ] Unknown.

Name of Collector:

Location of collection:

ACCOMPANYING DOCUMENTATION:

	Location		Location
[ ] Photos		[ ] Notes	
[ ] Tapes		[ ] Published Ref.	
[ ] Drawings		[ ] Artifact Coll.	
[ ] Aerial Photo		[ ] Charcoal Sample	
[ ] Tracings		[ ]	

PUBLISHED REFERENCES:

RECOMMENDATIONS IN RESPECT OF PRESERVATION/MANAGEMENT:

SIGNIFICANCE OF SITE TO ABORIGINES.   [ ] Historical.   [ ] Mythological.   [ ] Ceremonial.   [ ] Unknown.

Informant's Name:

Address:

Details:

SITE RECORDER   Date:

Address:

1.5

Portion of the South Australian Aboriginal Site Record Card illustrating the range of information that can be recorded about sites during a surface survey. This can be used both for research and management purposes. (Courtesy of South Australian Aboriginal Heritage Unit, Department of Planning and Environment)

1.6
Recording stone structures in western Victoria.

logical authorities uses its own recording form. Individual researchers, with specific questions in mind, may record details which others ignore. Although much of the information collected is similar, there can be significant differences in scope and detail.

Fieldwork: excavation

The classic archaeological activity. Excavations are now less common in Australia than surveys, but contribute disproportionately to our common data base and discussion. This book, too, emphasises excavation-based research, partly as it exposes more problems and issues, and partly because of my own personal interests.

Types of information

- clearly defined, dated assemblages of material
- periods of site use or abandonment
- relative quantities of artefacts
- bones showing exploitation of animals
- distribution of material within sites
- history of sediment accumulation

Issues that can be addressed

- how sites were used
- change through time, within and between sites

1.7
Jill Gallagher, Aboriginal Liaison Officer of the Victoria Archaeological Survey, and a member of the local Aboriginal community discuss the future protection of a midden on the banks of the Murray River near Robinvale.

- in artefacts or raw material use
- in economy
- in site use
- in intensity of occupation or regional activity

Advantages

- detailed analysis of material
- controlled assemblages, suitable for comparison with one another
- dates allowing a view of antiquity and change through time
- specific sequences of development or change
- preservation of bone
- material in clear association, functionally related

Disadvantages

- relatively expensive and time-consuming
- sites are disturbed or destroyed
- a limited view of regional patterns
- a tendency to exaggerate the significance of single sites

Basic procedures

Sites are selected for excavation in order to investigate particular problems, but frequently provide evidence which opens up new questions. Quite simply, if we knew exactly what we would find, there would be no need to dig. Sites are always full of surprises, and excavators have to be flexible enough to cope with a continual series of practical problems.

The greatest advantage of excavations is the potential for dating material. Almost all excavations in Australia have this as their prime concern and archaeologists tend to excavate small, deep holes, to provide a chronological sequence through the accumulated deposits which make up the site. A desire to avoid disturbing sites more than necessary and also to avoid dealing with overwhelming quantities of finds from larger excavations reinforces this tendency.

Many excavations are therefore confined to a few square metres, providing small samples from selected parts of the site which we must assume are representative of the site as a whole.

The strategy of excavation varies from site to site and problem to problem; some of these different approaches will be elaborated in the later case studies. The standard technique of *stratigraphic* excavation is to work down through the sequence, defining and removing each superimposed deposit in turn. Where changes in soil colour and texture allow, these provide the basis for differentiating excavation units.

Many sites in Australia do not have clear markers of this kind and it is therefore common practice to define arbitrary 'spits' to provide vertical control. Over the years people have begun to use thinner and thinner spits, so that where 10 cm and later 5 cm spits were common, many now excavate only 2 to 3 cm slices at a time. As 2 cm depth of soil from a 50 cm × 50 cm square fills about one bucket this is a convenient standard.

Excavated sediments are sieved, and all the

1.8
Excavations in progress at a cave site in South Australia.

stone artefacts, pieces of bone or other material brought into the site by people are collected for later analysis. Increasing attention is given to the nature of the sediments themselves, which can provide clues to the conditions under which the site developed.

The quality of excavated data changes with different styles of excavation. There is a general tendency toward closer control and definition of excavation units and the use of finer mesh sieves and better techniques for collecting material. It is important for us to appreciate how the style of excavation structures the data that we have and conditions the types of questions that we can ask of it. This is another theme that will be developed in some of the later case-studies.

Historical and ethnographic analogies

In this book constant reference is made to recent Aboriginal societies to illustrate or help to understand the archaeological record. The sources of this information vary in quality and scope. Although this data is valuable, its use is not always simple.

HISTORICAL SOURCES

Accounts by nineteenth century European explorers, government officials, missionaries and settlers provide a background to understanding the recent prehistoric record. Their official reports, personal diaries or reminiscences vary in reliability. In using them we must bear in mind when they were written and distinguish between personal observations and later second-hand accounts. We must also consider the experience and preconceptions which influenced how individual Europeans perceived events, in addition to problems of language and communication. Among the most important Victorian sources referred to in this book are the following.

George Augustus Robinson (1788–1866). From 1829 Robinson worked with Tasmanian Aborigines, eventually setting up the ill-fated settlement at Wybalenna on Flinders Island. Between 1839 and 1849 he was employed in Victoria as Chief Protector of Aborigines to mediate between Aboriginal communities and European colonists. Apart from his official reports, his private diaries of travels through parts of Victoria provide invaluable information on aspects of Aboriginal life and the effects of European settlement.

James Dawson (1806–1900). Dawson had a property near Port Fairy between 1844 and 1866. He then lived for a time near Melbourne before moving to Camperdown. From 1876 when he was appointed Local Guardian of the Aborigines he collected reminiscences from Aboriginal informants in the area around Camperdown.

Peter Beveridge (1829–1885). Beveridge settled near Swan Hill in 1845. Over many years he observed and documented Aboriginal life along the Murray, Murrumbidgee and Darling Rivers.

A.W. Howitt (1830–1908). Famous as an explorer, Howitt led the expedition to rescue Burke and Wills. He held a variety of official positions in Victoria and developed a serious interest in Victorian Aboriginal customs between 1877 and 1907, collecting much information from Aboriginal informants such as William Barak.

William Barak (1823(?)–1903). William Barak of the Wuywurrung Clan saw the first European settlers arrive in the Yarra Valley. In his youth he served in the Native Mounted Police. Later in life, while living at Correnderrk, he was not only well respected in his own community, but became the most well-known Aboriginal person in Victoria. He provided much important information to early anthropologists on Aboriginal life and customs.

R.H. Mathews (1841–1908). A land surveyor

in New South Wales who developed an interest in rock art and Aboriginal ceremonies in the 1890s. His accounts are based on personal observation and responses to a questionnaire.

R. Brough Smyth (1830–1899). Brough Smyth was an important official in the mining industry, and prepared many reports and catalogues. From 1860 he was the honorary secretary of the Board for the Protection of Aborigines. In this capacity he collected together information from a wide variety of sources which he included in the two volume *The Aborigines of Victoria* published by the Victorian Government in 1878.

Applications

1 *Source for specific information*
- the use of sites and artefacts
- technology (manufacture of tools, food gathering and processing)
- the range of plants and animals exploited
- social organisation, group composition and relationships
- economic systems

2 *Understanding of site formation processes*
Observations of the way in which sites are formed and how material culture is related to behaviour provide a basis for developing methods of interpreting archaeological material.

3 *A reminder of human diversity*
Illustrations of the complexity and diversity of behaviour, to avoid simplistic interpretations based on limited understanding of patterns of human behaviour.

4 *An image of humanity*
Descriptions of living people and societies allow us to envisage a past with real people in it.

Problems

1 *Uniformity of behaviour*
The use of modern analogues assumes that past behaviour was like that of the present, or that societies far from one another did things in the same way.

2 *Restricting or limited ideas*
Using only modern parallels may limit our ideas to a small number of well-documented situations. For hunter-gatherers these are generally confined to observations of people in more marginal areas who were not affected by colonial expansion until very recently. We have less information on hunter-gatherers in richer environments.

3 *Scales of time*
Ethnographic or historical accounts give details of individual events or people, while archaeology generally deals with long periods of time and broad patterns of behaviour.

Dating

Dates are fundamental to archaeological research. There are three main types of dating: by *artefact type*, by *stratigraphic relationship*, and by *radiometric techniques*.

1 *Artefact type*
Dating by artefact type has limited value in Australia. Few formal tool types can be defined or dated so well that they serve as chronological markers. Although one generally accepted indicator is the appearance of a range of backed microliths after about 4000 years ago, we cannot give even an approximate date to most tools or most surface sites.

2 *Stratigraphic relationship*
Stratigraphic relationships within sites give relative ages. Objects from lower in a sequence are older than those from the later deposits which overlie them. Geomorphological context (for

example, dunes or river terraces) containing or covering archaeological deposits also can provide us with relative dates.

3 *Radiometric techniques*

Radiometric techniques provide the chronological framework for almost all Australian prehistory.

The most important method is *radiocarbon dating*. It is not so necessary to understand the chemistry of the technique as its significance and validity. Charcoal and shell are the commonest material dated, but bone and any other material with some organic component can also be used. Although older dates are theoretically possible, most laboratories can only provide dates back to about 40 000 years ago. Dating is done in specialist laboratories; most archaeologists send samples to commercial laboratories, which charge about $300 for each date. This high cost clearly restricts use of the technique, and we often have fewer dates from sites than we would like.

It is important to remember that radiocarbon dates are not precise, but represent a statistical range. The error levels provided by the radiocarbon dating laboratories are important. A date given as 3000 ± 100 BP means that there is a 67% chance that the true age of the sample lies between 2900 and 3100 years before the present (present is conventionally fixed at 1950). Doubling the error (3000 ± 200 BP) means that there is a 95% chance that the sample is between 2800 and 3200 BP (i.e. 850 and 1250 BC). In human terms this means that a single radiocarbon date refers to a time at least as great as that from the time when your grandparents were born until your grandchildren die of old age. For distant prehistory, where we talk in thousands of years, this level of precision is not as significant as it is when we discuss more recent periods.

There is one further complication. Radiocarbon 'years' are not the same as real, calendar years. Comparison of radiocarbon dates with those calculated from annual growth-rings on trees shows that older radiocarbon dates are significantly younger than they should be. As we go back in time the difference increases. A date of 5000 radiocarbon years is about the same as 5730 calendar years, and 8000 radiocarbon years is equivalent to about 8920 calendar years. We can convert radiocarbon dates to calendar dates for the last 8000 years, but we do not know what happens before that. It is quite likely that the trend continues with the discrepancy increasing the further back in time we go. The fluctuating value of the radiocarbon 'year' is analogous to the fluctuations in the value of the 'dollar', which was worth more twenty years ago than it is today, and worth different amounts in different countries.

Another dating technique, *thermoluminescence dating*, measures the energy stored in buried material since it was last exposed to heat or sunlight. It has the advantages of being useful for sediments and other inorganic material and for much older material. But it is far less precise than radiocarbon dating. The error level is often greater than ± 10% of the age, and so the range of time represented by a single date may be as great as 20 000 years at about 50 000 years ago. Thermoluminescence dates are in calendar years, and so cannot be directly compared with radiocarbon dates. As long as we only use one chronological 'currency' then the difference between dating systems is not of great significance.

Dates are only as good as the samples submitted, and any contamination will affect their validity. Because of this, and the built-in error of the techniques, a series of dates is far preferable to a single one, but all too often the high cost of dating restricts the numbers of samples submitted.

Scales of time

As we will see later, an important problem which needs to be constantly borne in mind is the scale of time with which we deal. Archaeological sites build up slowly, and layers or floors representing specific events can seldom be identified. Mostly we deal with composite layers, accumulated over tens or hundreds of years. While an individual tool may have been made, used and discarded in a single day, other tools found beside it in an excavation may be far older or younger: an archaeological deposit therefore represents the sum of many activities over very long periods, often longer than any one person's lifetime. Similarly, no two sites can be so accurately dated that we can say they were occupied at the same time, unless by 'same time' we mean within one or two hundred years. We therefore deal with long-term processes rather than individual events and with general patterns of behaviour rather than individual acts. While the study of long-term change is one of the great contributions archaeology has to make to understanding how societies function, it is also one of the most difficult problems we have to address.

Creating data

Fieldwork produces vast quantities of finds and information on their context and relationships. Far more time has to be spent working on this material than on fieldwork.

There are two aspects to the analysis of finds: *compilation* and *explanation*. Compilations will provide a basic catalogue of the material found and what it is like. This becomes the primary record of the excavations and finds and serves as the basis for further analysis. Explanation or analysis of data identifies significant features or patterns and gives some meaning to them.

These two aspects are closely linked. The choice of what to record can be affected by the type of explanation which an archaeologist prefers. Conversely, future explanations can be limited or conditioned by the type of information originally recorded.

We need to know how many items come from the site or region, what different types are present, and in what proportions. The structure of each assemblage or collection of material must be described before it can be compared with others within the same site or from elsewhere. The process is therefore one of classifying artefacts or identifying the animal or plant remains. Archaeologists do not, however, always document their finds in the same way.

Just as sites and regions are selected for particular reasons, so too will analyses of finds vary according to the aims and interests of individual researchers. The choices made are partly determined by personal interest and ability and partly by what questions are regarded as important. The basic 'facts' are therefore created by researchers and need to be understood in terms of why and how a site was excavated and why and how the finds were analysed in a certain way.

Individual archaeologists are interested in different things. They may often see very different patterns in the prehistoric record. Sometimes this is because new or better information becomes available. Sometimes it is the result of a clearer understanding of how the archaeological record is formed. Sometimes it stems from a different attitude toward prehistory. The selection of which sites to study and what emphasis to give different elements follows from these differences.

For much of this book the emphasis is on specific sites. Most are selected from a relatively small region of south-eastern Australia and are concerned with relatively recent prehistory. We may look at them individually but must also consider how we can integrate the evidence from these independent studies and the different types of data from each different type of site into broader discussions of behaviour and change.

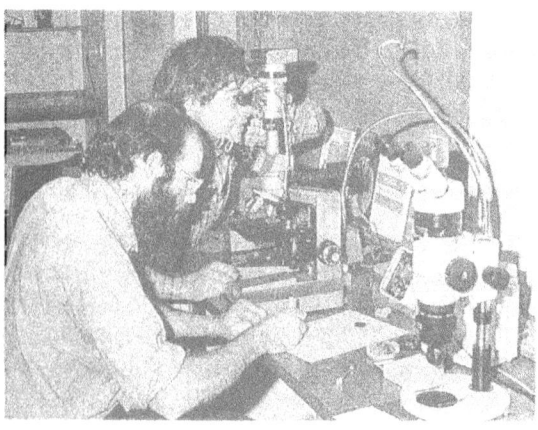

1.9
Microscopes are used to examine the edges of stone tools for evidence of use.

POINTS FOR DISCUSSION

1 What are the main types of archaeological evidence, and what can we learn from each?
2 What are the main differences between the evidence from documents, oral traditions and anthropological studies on the one hand, and archaeological surveys and excavations on the other?
3 Archaeology deals with very long periods of time. Can you imagine what 1000 years, or 10 000 years really means in human terms?

EXERCISE

- Describe what is happening in Figures 1.10 and 1.11.
- List the artefacts and any other animal or vegetable items that you can see or that you think must have been present.

1.10
An Aranda family photographed by W. Baldwin Spencer in 1896. (Museum of Victoria)

1.11
Joseph Lycett 1774 – ca. 1825. Aborigines spearing fish, others diving for crayfish, a party seated beside a fire cooking fish (ca. 1817). (National Library of Australia)

- List those things that will survive in one year, ten years, one hundred years, one thousand years.
- Draw a plan showing each area immediately after people have left it.
- Draw a plan showing each area one hundred years later.

A DEBATE: SURVEYS OR EXCAVATIONS?

A famous British archaeologist, Sir Mortimer Wheeler, once contrasted two strategies of excavation and compared them to having either timetables without trains, or trains without timetables.

In much Australian archaeology excavations give us chronology, or timetables, but limited information on what was happening at each time. Broad-scale regional surveys may give ideas about site location, but with little chronological control — trains without timetables.

Debate the relative merits of these two approaches to research.

Australian Aboriginal prehistory and society

When did people first reach Australia?

The first question that most people ask is 'When did the Aborigines come to Australia?' For those Aboriginal people who believe that as part of the continuous event of the Dreaming they have always been here, this is a meaningless question. The scientific view of human evolution sees the world differently.

Ancestors of all living people may first be distinguished in east Africa three million years ago or more. By one million years ago their descendants had spread out of Africa into Europe and over much of Asia. The continual process of physical development, accompanied by changes in technological ability, led to the development of archaic forms of our present species by 200 000 years ago. 100 000 years ago we find the first evidence of people with similar physical and intellectual abilities to our own. Whether our species (*Homo sapiens sapiens*) developed simultaneously in all areas, or if there was a major replacement of ancestral types by a migration throughout Africa, Europe and Asia, is still unclear. Whatever the process, by 40 000 or 50 000 years ago we can be confident that fully modern people were living in most areas of the world, including island South-East Asia and Indonesia. Some of these people made the first sea-crossing to Australia.

Establishing 'firsts' is always difficult, especially in archaeology, where there is always the possibility that a new find will provide much older evidence. All we can do is to tell our stories according to the evidence that we have today. This shows that people were in Australia about 40 000 years ago. Although earlier evidence may be found, for the present we can only say that the first colonists had arrived by that time, and that within a few thousand years of crossing the sea barrier we find evidence of occupation in many areas of the continent.

Several claims have been made for far older dates, including one based on changes in the vegetation and quantities of charcoal seen in a pollen core from Lake George near Canberra, at about 120 000 years ago. The suggestion here is that increased burning, with its impact on local vegetation, should be attributed to human use of fire. Not only could this change be simply natural, but its date is also problematic. This, and other similar claims are therefore currently not accepted.

A very recent claim of 50 000 or 60 000 years ago for artefacts at the site of Malakununja II in Arnhem Land is based on thermoluminescence dating of sediments. There are a number of problems with this. One is that the error level is such that the date could equally well be 41 000 or 63 000 years ago. The other is that thermoluminescence dates are in 'real' or calendar years, unlike radiocarbon dates (see the section on dating in Chapter 1). A radiocarbon date of about 40 000 years ago may be the same age as a thermoluminescence date of 50 000.

This reminds us that general statements like 'Aboriginal people have been in Australia for 40 000 years' refer to radiocarbon years. We simply do not know what this means in real, calendar years.

2.1
River terrace at Upper Swan.

EARLY SITES IN AUSTRALIA

- *Huon Peninsula (Papua New Guinea) 40 000 BP.* Large flat 'waisted' axes, on the raised coral terraces of the Huon Peninsula. If the stratigraphic associations are correct, they are about 40 000 years old.
- *Cranebrook Terrace (NSW) 40 000 BP.* A few stones, not certainly artefacts, in river sediments. If these and their geomorphological dating are accepted, they provide evidence of occupation by 40 000 years ago.
- *Upper Swan (Western Australia) 38 000 BP.* Stone tools found in river terrace sediments provide the earliest well-accepted evidence of human occupation in Australia.
- *Willandra Lakes (western NSW) 36 000 BP.* Shell middens on the shores of now dry lakes. There is a possibility that some sites are older. Two burials at Lake Mungo previously dated up to ten thousand years later, may also be 36 000 years old.
- *Matenkupkum (New Ireland) 33 000 BP.* Occupation in a cave near the coast of this island west of mainland Papua New Guinea.
- *Nunamira Cave (Tasmania) 31 000 BP.* Occupation in an inland cave in the southern forests of Tasmania.
- *Malakununja II (Arnhem Land) 41 000– 63 000 BP.* Thermoluminescence dates for sediment associated with stone artefacts in a rockshelter.

2.2
Dunes at Lake Mungo.

2.3
Nunamira Cave. (Photo: R. Cosgrove)

Colonisation

Australia is a large continent with many different environments. There are tropical rainforest and wetlands in the north, cool temperate woodlands in the south, and arid deserts in the centre. How, and how quickly, did people move into these different areas and develop appropriate ways of living in them?

Any colonists must have come by sea, crossing such distances that we must consider them to have had well-developed watercraft and an efficient marine economy. Some archaeologists argue that people continued to have a specifically coastal orientation, as they spread around the continental margin before penetrating up the major river systems and settling around inland lakes; only much later did they move into highland and more arid zones — perhaps only after the end of the cooler glacial periods.

The accumulation of new evidence favours a different model, one in which coastal resources play only a minor part in a general move through all the better-watered woodland areas on the margins of the continent. Dates of over 30 000 years found in the extremes of tropical island New Guinea and cold southern Tasmania, and of well over 20 000 years in the highlands of Papua New Guinea, the arid centre of Australia and high country near Canberra, all hint toward rapid, widespread movements and adaptations.

Environmental changes

Not only do we have great diversity in present environments in Australia, but evidence of enormous changes in the past. The climate, landforms and vegetation that we see today are only a general guide to previous conditions.

Among the major changes that we have to bear in mind are the following.

Sea level and coasts

Global temperatures continuously fluctuate. As they do water is either frozen in the polar icecaps, or released, lowering and raising the level of the sea. Over the last 100 000 years these fluctuations have radically altered the shape of the Australian continent, as the continental shelf was exposed or covered. All the coast seen by the first arrivals in Australia is now under water. Tasmania and Papua New Guinea were intermittently joined by dry land to the mainland and cut off by higher sea levels flooding Bass and Torres Straits. The most recent of these major changes was between about 15 000 and 6000 years ago, when the sea rose from about 150 m below its present level.

Rainfall and water balance

Fluctuating temperatures of the 'ice ages' not only affected polar ice and the snow cover in highland areas, but also affected rainfall and rates of evaporation. In a continent as dry as Australia these changes had marked effects. During some periods of high rainfall major river systems developed and inland lakes formed, such as those of the Willandra system in western NSW, which provided a rich environment between 36 000 and 25 000 years ago. The onset of the last major glacial period saw at first a fluctuation in lake levels, and then finally about 18 000 years ago these lakes became permanently dry and have remained so until today.

Wind and sand

Evidence of the development of large dunefields across much of south-eastern Australia between about 18 000 and 15 000 years ago (the height of the last glacial period) testifies to increased winds at this time — which contributed to the harshest conditions ever experienced by people in this continent.

Plants and animals

Such dramatic climatic changes naturally had an impact on plants and animals. The range or distribution of species expanded or contracted, changing local availability. Some species became extinct. The harsh cold, dry period between 18 000 and 15 000 years ago was probably responsible for the extinction of a range of large animals, bigger than those we see in Australia today. Warmer and wetter conditions need not have improved local conditions for people. For example, the spread of cool temperate rainforest inland in south-west Tasmania as conditions became warmer may have reduced or eliminated plants and animals useful to people, leading to the abandonment of the area.

Aboriginal economy and society

Great diversity can be seen in present-day or recent Aboriginal society, economy and technology across the continent. Some of this diversity reflects the environments in which people live. The assessment of the comparative importance of social, technological and environmental factors in structuring how people live is a matter for continuing debate. For some archaeologists the prehistory of Australia is largely a matter of tracing the ways in which people adjusted to different conditions; others place much greater emphasis on cultural processes of change.

At the time of European contact all Aboriginal people in Australia were *hunters and gatherers*. This general term includes a very wide variety of different economic systems. The essential common element is the low investment of energy in long-term manipulation of land and resources. In most circumstances food was no sooner gathered than it was eaten. Sometimes people altered local conditions by the use of fire, clearing out old dead vegetation and opening up land for fresh growth and easier movement. In some areas people ensured that vines were replanted once tubers were collected for food. There was, however, none of the planned working of soil, selective planting or breeding of animals and regular storage of food from one year to the next which characterise farming.

The particular resources used were, of course, limited by availability. But there was still considerable discretion, with choices determined by preference, custom, need and technology. Technology — including knowledge as well as equipment — is the most obvious and easily demonstrated of these, as new methods could enhance the productivity of some resources or open up access to new ones. For example, it is likely that watercraft capable of reaching offshore islands were developed in Tasmania within the last 3000 or 4000 years. These allowed people access to previously inaccessible seals and mutton birds. The development of efficient seed-grinding technology may also be fairly recent, allowing a better exploitation of the grasses of the arid and semi-arid interior and a more intensive use of these areas.

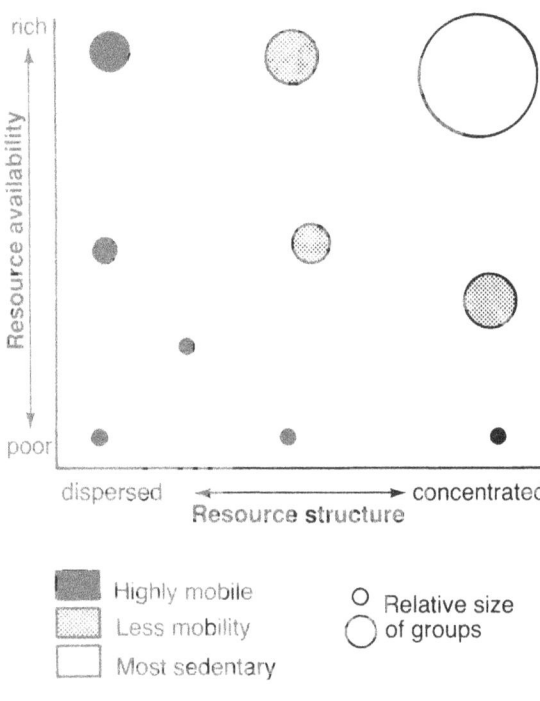

2.4
Hunter-gatherer group size and mobility is closely related to the availability of resources. Resources can be seen in terms of their abundance (ranked from poor to rich along the vertical axis) and in terms of their structure (ranked from dispersed to concentrated along the horizontal axis). When resources are poor or dispersed people break up into smaller, more mobile groups, and scatter widely across the landscape. When resources are richer and more concentrated, people come together in greater numbers, and stay in the one place for longer periods.

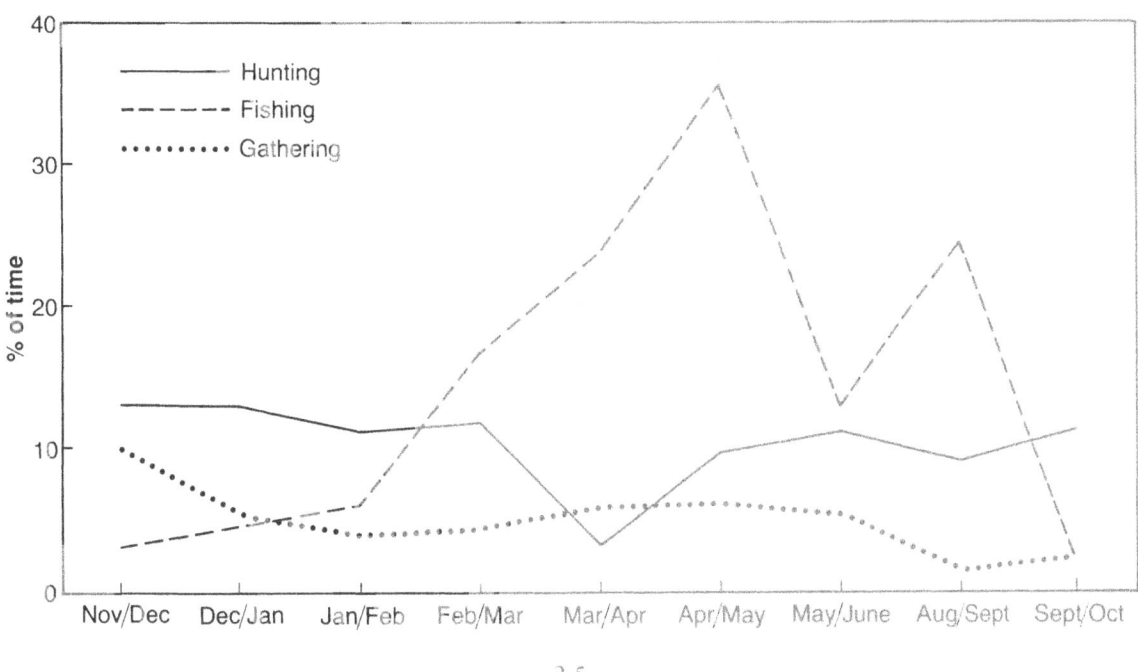

Time allocated to different subsistence activities at different times of the year at Momega Outstation, Arnhem Land, 1979–80. (Data from Altman 1987)

Resource availability is closely linked to population density and structure. Obviously, more people can live in richer areas. The classic image of desert Aborigines, few in number, with light equipment, moving regularly from place to place, is inappropriate when thinking about life in the tropical north or well-watered temperate regions. Here larger groups of people could be supported, staying in the one place for longer, and travelling over smaller distances. In other words, we have considerable variation in the intensity of use of land and resources.

Particular patterns of relationship follow from the richness, and especially the reliability, of resources. Where people confidently expect a regular supply of food, they tend to keep to themselves; where there is more uncertainty, with the possibility of local scarcity, long-distance networks of connections may develop, as people establish relationships by trade and marriage so as to have rights of access to different areas.

Seasonal and local patterns also affect population structure and density. Local patterns of seasonal dispersal and aggregation can be seen. Larger groups collect for longer periods during some seasons or near to specific resources. At other times people break up into smaller groups, and spread out over the country.

Hunter-gatherer affluence?

The standard older image of hunter-gatherers was largely negative. They were seen as eking out a meagre existence, with a constant battle for survival. This was replaced in the late 1960s and early 1970s with a new image which owed

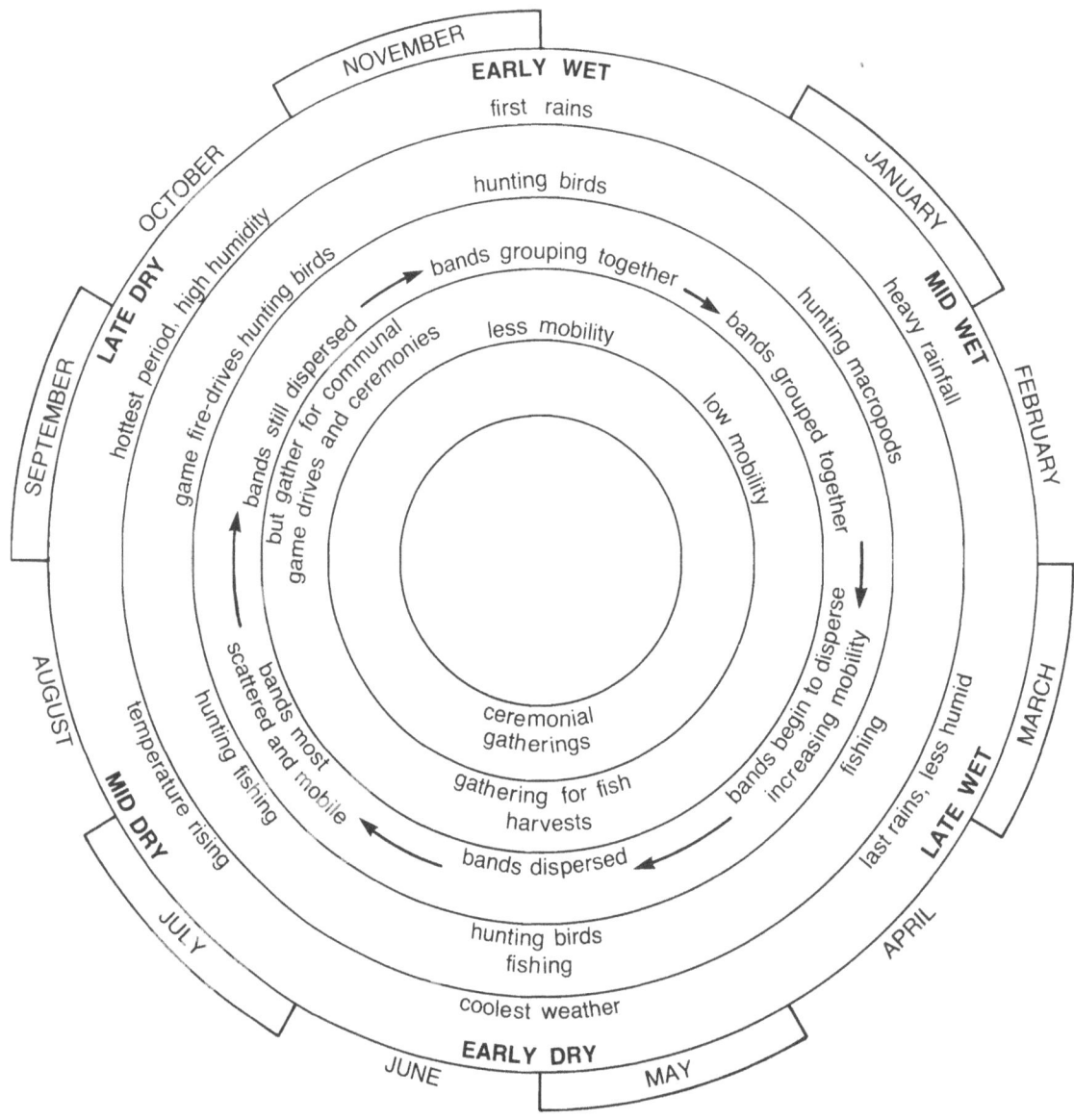

Tropical climate
Momega Outstation, Arnhem Land
(data from Altman 1987)

2.6a

The annual cycle of life in two modern communities in Australia. Group size, degree of mobility, major food resources, and the location and type of settlement all vary with the seasons. a) Tropical environment: Momega Outstation, Arnhem Land. (Data from Altman 1987) b) Sub-tropical to semi arid environment: Robinson River, Gulf of Capentaria. (Data provided by M. Pickering)

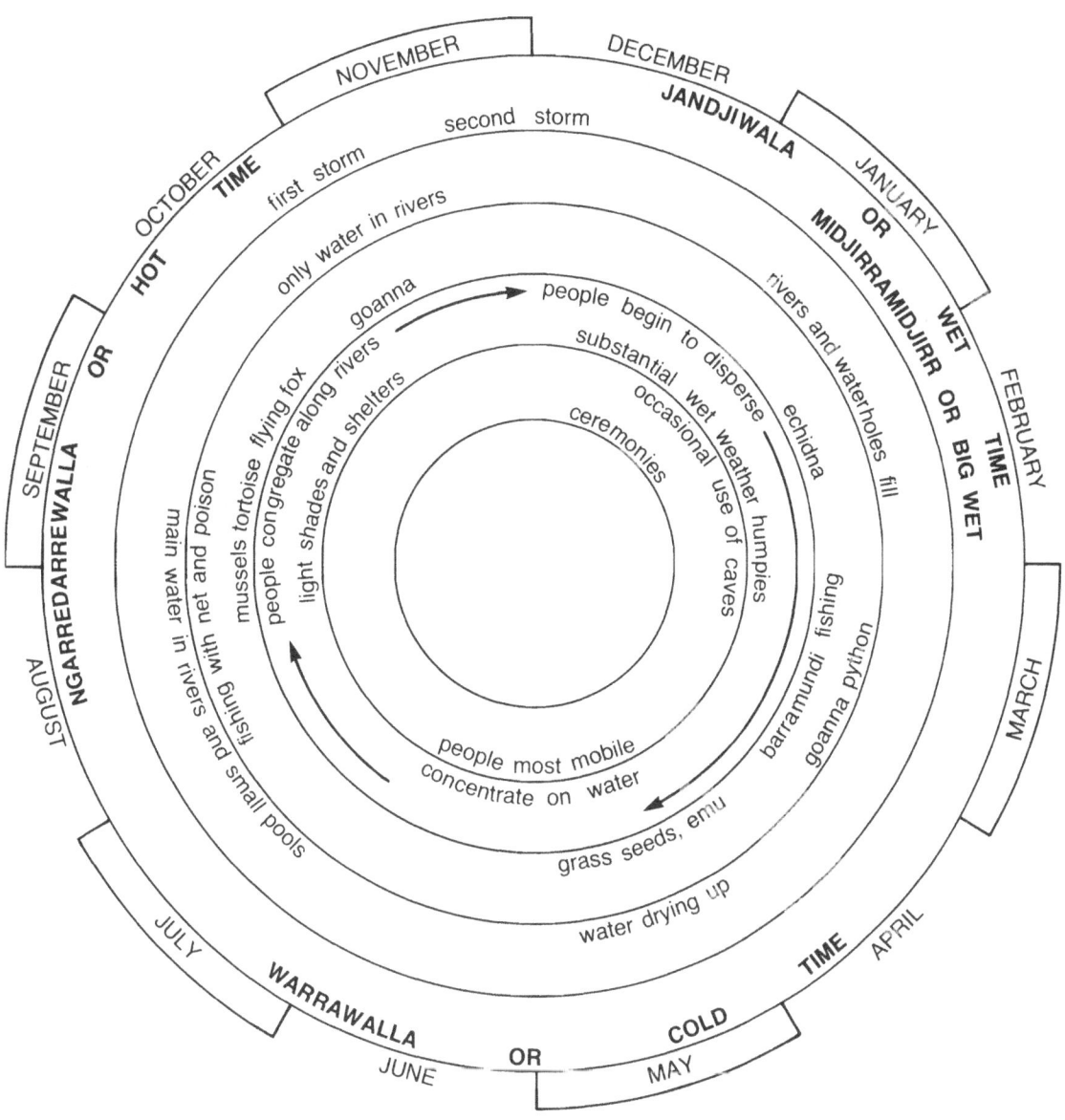

Sub-tropical to semi-arid environments
Robinson River, Gulf of Carpentaria
(data supplied by M. Pickering)

2.6b

as much to a questioning of Western values as to anthropological data. Some evidence collected about southern African hunter-gatherers fitted well with this new concept of 'affluence' measured in terms of satisfaction of wants, rather than material possessions. Here hunter-gatherers, despite living in a relatively poor environment, were seen to work less hard and for shorter periods than previously thought. Later research has modified this over-optimistic view of an idyllic foraging lifestyle. We cannot assume that living as a hunter-gatherer was necessarily particularly easy nor especially difficult. Instead we must attempt to understand more clearly how each different society was organised and approached the basic problems of social and cultural survival.

Women and men in the food quest

Women are often regarded as the providers of the basic, reliable staples, such as plants and shellfish, while men were hunters — a more exciting, but sometimes less reliable activity. Although largely true, such a simple dichotomy obscures more complex behaviour. For example, among the Anbarra people of Arnhem Land men and women working separately contributed about 40% each of all food, and mixed groups the remaining 20%. Most nuts and fruits were collected by mixed groups, but almost all of the important plant staples, such as yams, were provided by women. Most of the meat in this case came from small animals, shellfish and fish. Although men 'caught' most fish, women 'gathered' most shellfish.

Women at Momega Outstation in Arnhem Land produce between 10% and 15% of their daily energy requirements for each hour spent collecting food. Men's productivity is now far more efficient than women's. This may be because men have most access to modern technology (guns, vehicles, boats). But if men used to control the more efficient traditional means of production (fish-traps, game-drives using fire) this may also have been the case in the past.

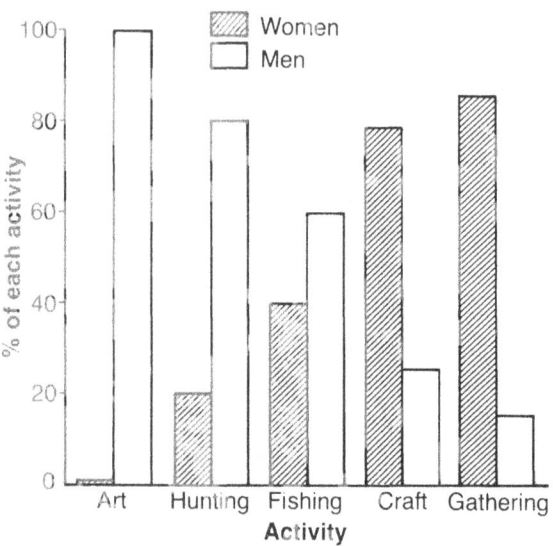

2.7
Men and women in most societies have different tasks, as seen at Momega Outstation, Arnhem Land in 1979–80. (Data from Altman 1987)

What resources were used?

A wide range of foods are available in Australia. In most cases Aboriginal diet was broadly based and people ate at least as much plant as animal food. Not all available food resources were necessarily used. Sometimes the appropriate technology was not available, or people concentrated on tastier or more easily obtained food. Sometimes particular food was avoided because of a specific prohibition affecting the whole community or certain groups within it.

Plants

Plant-foods were always an important part of the diet, providing the most regular, reliable source of food.

Plants vary with climate, so that different types of plant foods were common in the different regions of the continent; roots and tubers in the temperate south-east, fruits in the tropical north, and seeds in the arid interior.

Although most plant-foods could be eaten raw, some, such as seeds, were usually processed. A few required complex processing before they could be eaten. The use of plants is therefore partly conditioned by knowledge and technology.

Land animals

All land animals were eaten, although some might be forbidden to particular groups of people or at certain times.

Once again environmental conditions determined availability. For example, large animals such as kangaroos were hunted in more open country while smaller animals such as possums inhabit scrub and woodland. Although providing large quantities of food at one time, larger animals were rarer than the more easily obtained smaller ones, and snakes, goannas, rats, mice, turtles and a range of other small species were more regularly eaten.

Animals were hunted in different ways. Individuals or small groups might build hunting hides near isolated water sources where they could await and intercept animals coming to drink. Sometimes large numbers of people co-operated to drive quantities of animals into traps and nets. Smaller animals could be picked up more regularly and at any time.

Fish and shellfish

Although shellfish and fish were eaten on most coasts, rivers and inland lakes, there are some important exceptions. Aboriginal people in south-west Western Australia, for example, avoided shellfish, while scale fish, at earlier times part of the Tasmanian diet, were not eaten there after about 3500 years ago. Shellfish were never a major contributor to the diet, although they provided a reliable background staple. Fish were probably never very important in Tasmania or along the Victorian coast, but in northern New South Wales or south-east Queensland seasonal runs of fish were a crucial part of the winter economy.

Fish were caught by a variety of techniques, with spears, nets, hook-and-line and traps. As with different hunting strategies, these different techniques not only reflected local conditions, but also the way in which society and labour was organised. Some people, for example, argue that the development of complex systems of fish-traps was a recent development which not only increased the reliability and productivity of fishing, but also involved a major investment of energy which affected social relationships.

Birds

Birds, particularly waterfowl, were often important. Some species could be individually collected by hand; for example, the mutton-birds taken in large numbers from their burrows on offshore islands. Flocks of other birds were driven into large nets strung across rivers.

Communication and exchange in Aboriginal Australia

Aboriginal communities were in no way isolated from one another. People used to travel long dis-

Table 2.1 Some ethnographically recorded distances travelled

Distance (km)	Place	Reason
200	Lake Hindmarsh	ceremonial
200	Merri Creek	ceremonial
100	Mt William	obtain greenstone
300–500	Bunya nut area, S.E. Queensland	ceremonial
30	Ballina	salmon fishing
150	Townsville	ceremonial
250	Bega	ceremonial
650	Bega	messenger
300–500	Lake Eyre	obtain pituri, ochre
300–500	Coopers Creek	obtain pituri, ochre
500	Flinders Ranges	obtain ochre

(Source: Mulvaney, D.J., 1976)

tances to large-scale gatherings. At these meetings many activities took place and a wide variety of goods were exchanged. People also went on long journeys to obtain particular items from distant sources, while the distribution of some goods show that they were passed from one person to another in a chain of connections stretching over hundreds of kilometres.

Alongside the exchange of material items, people also adopted rituals and mythological stories, some of which are found widespread over many areas. Dreaming tracks, tracing the progress of ancestral creation figures criss-cross the landscape and illustrate routes and interconnections between different groups.

Technology and change

Some changes in technology have already been mentioned. Of the other innovations those in stone tools are perhaps the most easily seen. In some ways there was little change to the basic Australian tool-kit. Most stone tools were not carefully shaped, but some clear types can be defined. Figure 2.8 shows the gradual introduction, at different times, of a range of different tool types.

The appearance between 4000 and 5000 years ago of small finely made microlithic tools (which may have been used as spear barbs) is one of the few clear chronological markers in Australian archaeology. How and why these artefacts were adopted across most of the continent is, however, less clear. Some suggest that these spear-barbs increased hunting efficiency but this does not fully account for either their patchy adoption or later fall from popularity. Partly because their first appearance can be fairly well dated, the introduction of these small tools is often used by archaeologists as a convenient marker with which to link other developments in society and technology.

Many archaeologists have recently argued for significant changes not only in technology, but also in population density and structure in the last few thousand years, with a more intensive use of resources. They suggest that many aspects of Aboriginal society at the time of European contact must have been very different in the past. Obviously, one of our major tasks is to explore each of these developments. Some may only become apparent over periods of thousands of years, but smaller-scale faster changes can be traced, especially at a local scale. In either case, it is unlikely that individuals would ever have been aware of gradual evolution accumulating over many generations.

Biological problems

One continuing debate in Australian archaeology concerns the physical appearance and ancestry of Australian Aboriginal people. Although there may always have been a constant trickle of new arrivals on the northern shores, this debate has concentrated on the earliest colonists.

There are, currently, two conflicting theories. One view, gaining increasing acceptance, is that the Australian population has always been relatively homogenous. Minor variations reflect factors such as the degree of interaction between groups of people at different times.

The alternative view, based on one particular way of classifying ancient skeletons, is that in earlier times there were two distinct races in Australia: one, more heavy-boned and robust deriving from populations of modern form which evolved in Java and another, lighter-boned more gracile group inheriting their physical form from people who evolved in China. According to this view the narrower range of variation in physical form among modern Aboriginal people must show the integration of these two very different types within the last 10 000 years.

Big problems, and little

This chapter provides only a brief glimpse of some of the underlying larger issues and ideas involved in Australian prehistory today. Not all of them can be dealt with in a book of this size. Here we will concentrate on smaller-scale problems — the more detailed questions that arise

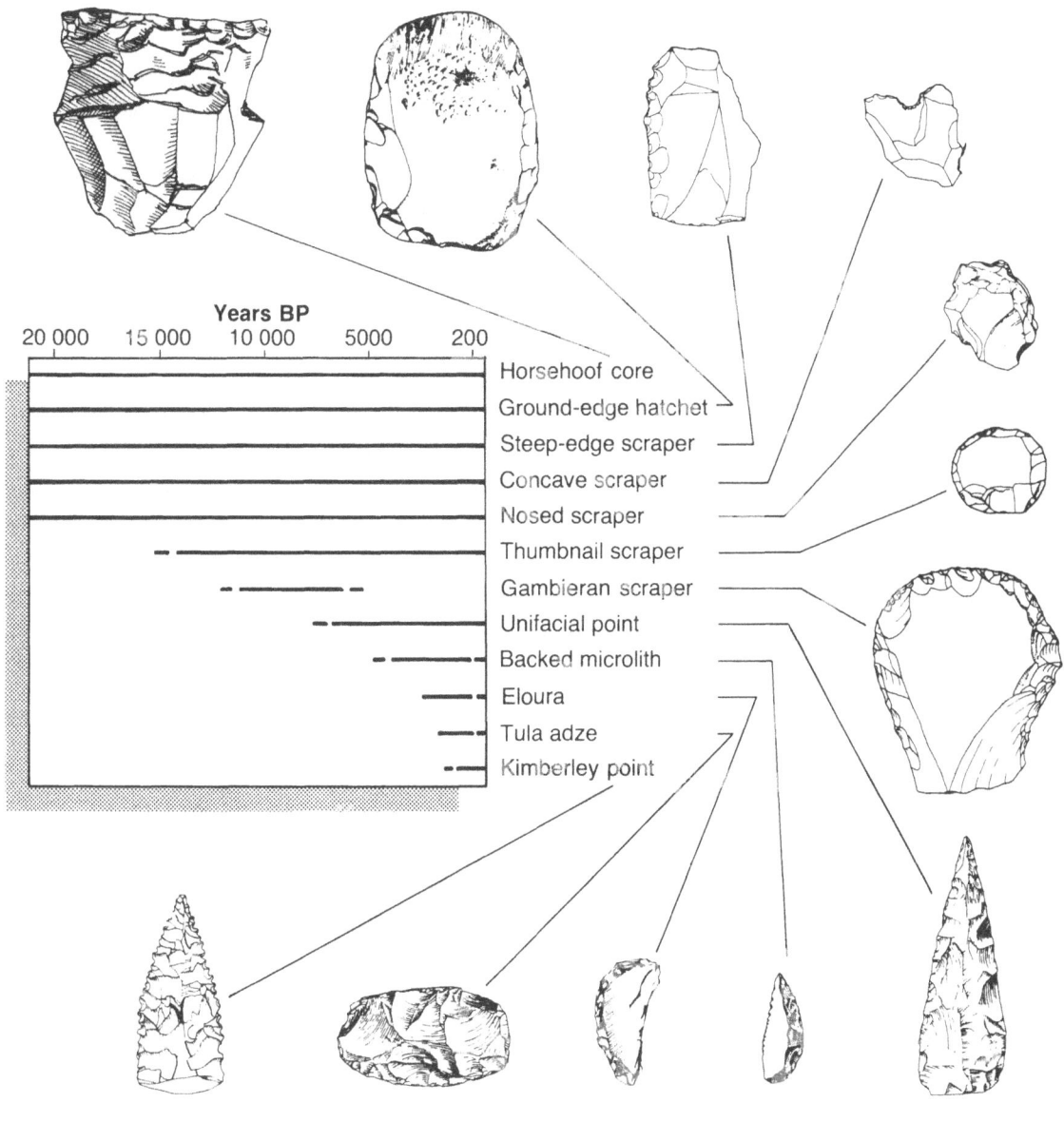

2.8
The chronology of some major tool-types in Australia.

during the process of archaeological research. The ideas we develop in each case are to some extent affected by the attitude we have to broader questions and types of explanation that we prefer, while the specific data that we present feeds back into the larger issues. In each of the case studies that follow, the detail of one site is related to more general questions so that, by the end of the book, we may be in a position to draw these threads together and reassess the changing nature of past societies in some parts of Australia.

Archaeologists debate many issues, sometimes politely. There are alternative views on almost every topic. Some differences of opinion are technical or methodological — how to classify material, organise it into groups, or calculate quantities. Others are differences of interpretation — what significance to give to data, and which of many possible answers is the best. There are also problems in assessing the heritage values of sites.

Some of the more important general questions of interpretation of current interest are:

- When did people first arrive in Australia?
- What does the variation in physical form of early populations mean?
- When and how were different environments first used?
- How much similarity was there between different regions?
- What was the population in different areas and at different times?
- What changes have there been in the environment?
- How much influence did the environment have on society, economy and technology?
- Was there a significant change in economy, technology, population and social organisation in the last 4000 years?
- To what extent are recent Aboriginal societies different from those in the past?

POINTS FOR DISCUSSION

1. Do men and women that you know:
   - use different tools?
   - do different tasks?
   - eat different food?
2. Do you regularly change your residence, daily activities or food at different times of the year? Is this a common pattern among others in your class?
   Do any seasonal patterns leave noticeably different traces, which would reveal this pattern archaeologically?
3. What major changes have taken place in the Australian environment since people first arrived?
   What impact do you think these had on society and economy?
4. What types of food were eaten by Aboriginal people? What archaeological evidence would you expect of each type?
5. How can we be sure when people first arrived in Australia?
6. How many people do you need to establish a viable population in a new land?
   Why did people first sail to Australia and later spread to different parts of the country?

EXERCISE: A VARIED AND CHANGING LAND

Describe the climate and environment in northern Australia, central Australia and temperate coastal regions.

- What differences could you expect in tools and technology, group size and mobility, housing and economy in these different regions?
- What differences might be archaeologically identifiable?

EXERCISE: VARIATION IN TOOLS AND ACTIVITIES

Sites may differ because they are of different ages, were occupied during different seasons, were used by different groups of people or for different purposes.

Harry Lourandos excavated two sites in eastern Tasmania.

Little Swanport is a coastal shell midden beside a large estuary. Crown Lagoon is an inland site in open woodland beside a large lagoon.

Lourandos examined aspects of the stone tools in order to compare the activities which took place at these two sites. He divided the pieces of stone into size classes. Those less than 12.5 mm can be regarded as unusable small chips produced whenever stone tools are made — much as sawdust is produced when working wood. Larger pieces may have been used as tools. This can be seen by close examination of the

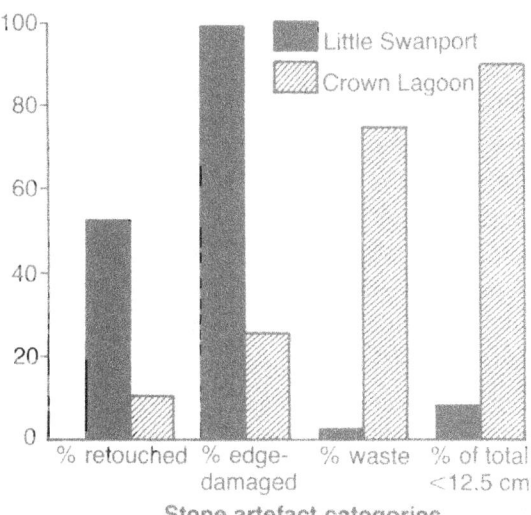

2.9
Relative proportions of stone artefacts at Crown Lagoon and Little Swanport. (Data from Lourandos 1977)

working edge for signs of use-damage. Some flakes are used in their original form, others are modified (or 'retouched') to give them a more specific shape, or to improve their working edge.

The diagram summarises this information on the stone tools from these two sites. What are the significant differences between them and what do you think they might represent? (Lourandos, H., 1977.)

References

Allen, J., 1982, 'When Did Humans First Colonize Australia?', *Search*, Vol. 20, No. 5, pp. 149–153.

Altman, J.C., 1987, *Hunter-gatherers Today: An Aboriginal Economy in North Australia*, Australian Institute of Aboriginal Studies, Canberra.

Frankel, D., 1982, 'Population Trends and Relationships in Prehistoric Australia', *Journal of Australian Studies*, Vol. 11, pp. 3–8.

Horton, D.R., 1981, 'Water and Woodland: the Peopling of Australia', *Australian Institute of Aboriginal Studies Newsletter*, Vol. 16, pp. 21–27.

Lourandos, H., 1977, 'Stone Tools, Settlement, Adaptation: A Tasmanian Example', in *Stone Tools as Cultural Markers*, ed. R.V.S. Wright, Australian Institute of Aboriginal Studies, Canberra, pp. 219–224.

Meehan, B., 1989, 'Plant use in a contemporary Aboriginal community and prehistoric implications', in *Plants in Australian Archaeology*, eds W. Beck, A. Clarke, L. Head, Tempus Vol. 1, pp. 14–30.

Mulvaney, D.J., 1976, 'The "Chain of Connection": the Material Evidence', in *Tribes and Boundaries in Australia*, ed. N. Peterson, Australian Institute of Aboriginal Studies, Canberra, pp. 72–94.

3

Burials

It is appropriate to begin the more detailed examination of site-types with a discussion of burials as these remind us that we are discussing people and not simply sites, artefacts or abstract concepts of society and history.

What can we learn from burials?

Burials provide us with a different form of data from other prehistoric sites. As we will see in later chapters we normally deal with long periods of time and composites of different events involving an unknown number of people. With each burial we have one specific event, perhaps only a few hours long. And we have the remains of individual people, about whom we can learn a great deal of personal detail — their sex, age at death, height, health and sometimes even relationships to others.

In addition we can combine the information from these discrete events to look for more general patterns of two types, biological and cultural. The broader historical and anthropological questions that we can ask include:

- genetic ancestry and relationships
- health and disease
- diet
- population size and density
- burial customs
- social relationships

Respect for the dead

The treatment of burials has become a matter of great concern to Aboriginal communities. Before 1980 little or no attention was paid to Aboriginal attitudes toward research on skeletons or the excavation of burials. Since then Aboriginal people have become increasingly involved in decisions regarding archaeological sites in general and human remains in particular. Some museum collections of skeletons from earlier excavations have been reburied by local communities. They regard the respectful treatment of ancestral remains as more important than their preservation for scientific research.

It is not that Aboriginal people are uninterested in what can be learnt from studying burials, but rather that they wish to determine appropriate treatment of human remains. Increasingly, where burials are turned up by erosion or development, communities will work together with archaeologists and anthropologists to excavate and study the remains before burying them again.

ABORIGINAL BURIAL CUSTOMS

Aboriginal people in different parts of the continent had a wide variety of burial customs. As in any society, these were integrated into a complex network of other religious and social customs. Corpses were disposed of in many ways. Sometimes this might involve several stages, with a series of rites held at long intervals. In some areas bones of dead relatives might be carried for considerable periods before final disposal. The major methods of burial were:

Inhumation. Simple burial in graves. Bodies were either placed in a crouched position or stretched out. Occasionally grave-goods might be placed with the body, and sometimes mounds built over the grave.

Cremation. Sometimes this can be part of a more complex sequence of activities, sometimes the only one. Bones collected after the cremation might later be buried or placed in hollow trees or log coffins.

Desiccation. Bodies were dried out or smoked. They were then often carried around before being disposed of permanently.

Platform exposure. Corpses were placed on platforms or in trees to decay and the bones later collected for final disposal.

Case study 1: Bones and health

Our first case study is concerned with understanding the health of ancient people. Stephen Webb investigated health and related behaviour by a comprehensive study of skeletal pathology. His particular interest was in monitoring the level of stress imposed by the environment, diet, population density and behaviour in different areas of Australia — the Central Murray the Southern and Eastern Coasts, and Desert Areas.

He examined the remains of about 2000 people for signs of dental hypoplasia and cribra orbitalia, and x-rayed over 1000 to look for Harris lines. Some of the data from his work is summarised here.

Childhood illness

The high proportion of long bones with Harris lines in the Central Murray and Southern Coast indicate that most people in those areas suffered at least some periods of deprivation during their childhood. This could be caused by two main factors: disease or inadequate diet. Webb observed a regular spacing of Harris lines on the Southern Coast which he argues is the result of regular seasonal nutritional stress. This had its greatest effect on older children, no longer

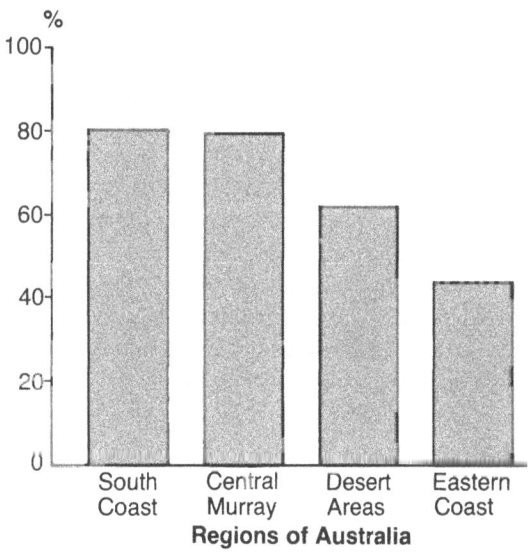

3.1
The percentage of skeletons examined by Webb which show Harris Lines (evidence of interruption to bone growth in childhood). (Data from Webb 1989, Figure 4)

breast-fed but not yet able to forage efficiently for themselves. While there is a high incidence of Harris lines in the Central Murray, they do not appear in bones with the same regularity, so that Webb suggests other, more general causes of stress.

Dental problems

There is also a high incidence of dental hypoplasia in children under about seven. This also means a degree of stress, here affecting growing teeth. In all four areas seen in Figure 3.2 this is slightly higher for boys than girls — a common phenomenon in all populations. The rate of this feature is much lower for older children, and is probably greatest at the nutritionally stressful period when children are being weaned at about the age of four or five.

Anaemia

This is a pathological condition brought on by lack of iron. As Figures 3.3 and 3.4 show it is more prevalent in the Central Murray than the other three areas. All sections of the population were affected to a greater or lesser extent. More skeletons of younger people than older ones were anaemic, and perhaps this contributed to their death at an early age. In all areas, more women than men had this pathological condition, probably because they are more prone to iron deficiency as a result of menstruation, lactation and breast-feeding. The high frequency of anaemia in the Central Murray suggests also the effects of a range of parasites, especially on children in the process of being weaned.

Arthritis

Webb examined the damaging effects of arthritis on bones. This is closely related to the amount of use of different joints. He observed that, in general, arthritis affected elbows more than knees, more men than women and people along the Murray more than anyone else. Left knees were more affected than right and the right elbow more than the left. There were some sig-

---

PATHOLOGICAL INDICATORS

Pathological condition of bones can give information on a variety of aspects of health and behaviour. Several indicators show stress from disease or malnutrition and can be used to monitor:

- the age at which children are most vulnerable
- the persistence of stress
- variation in male/female susceptibility to stress
- general health of a population

Most important of these are:

Harris lines. Serious illness during childhood interrupts bone growth. X-rays reveal the distinctive marks left in long-bones as a result of these stressful episodes.

Dental hypoplasia. Some stress restricts the development of tooth enamel, resulting in thinner bands than normal. The most common cause today is measles. The relative severity of stress can be assessed from the type of hypoplasia, such as lines and grooves or pitting.

Cribra orbitalia. Anaemia (particularly iron deficiency) can lead to characteristic pitting of the frontal bone of the skull. Anaemia can be brought about by poor diet or conditions, or worms and other parasites.

Osteoarthritis. The incidence of arthritis increases with age and with activity. The extent and location of arthritic conditions gives an indicator of how active people were and what type of activities they carried out.

Traumatic damage. The incidence and regularity of broken or damaged bones can also give information on aggressive or other behaviour and insights into lifestyle.

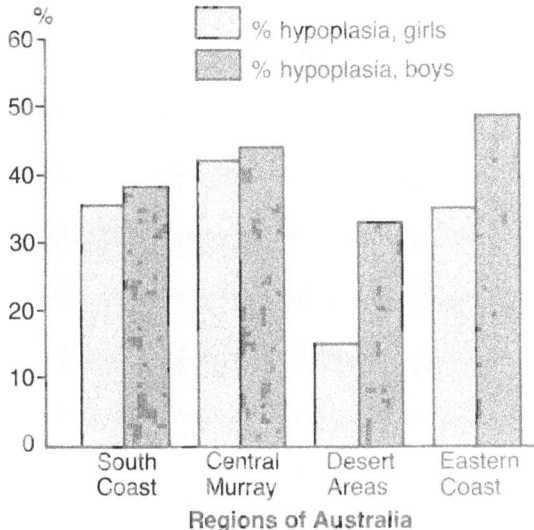

3.2
The percentage of skeletons examined by Webb which show evidence of dental hypoplasia (inadequate deposition of enamel). (Data from Webb 1989, Figure 6)

the high proportion of broken legs in the Desert sample, and their absence along the Murray. Is this to do with regional lifestyle? There is a higher incidence of 'parrying fractures' on the lower left arm among women on the East Coast and men in the Desert. Webb suggests this may reflect greater violence toward women in the one area, and more fighting between men in the other. The unification and alignment of broken bones is generally good, indicating care and skill in treatment.

Cranial traumas — severe blows to the head — were also monitored. There are regional variations in the frequency and type of head injury, and generally women suffered more than men. The Desert areas have a higher rate of head injury than the Central Murray and Webb notes some interesting differences in the position of the damage. In the Central Murray most cases of damage were to the front and left side, indicating face-to-face attacks. In the Desert damage is normally to the back and right, suggesting blows from behind. Can we interpret this information to show a different kind of dispute, or

nificant regional variations, however, which indicate that people in different environments carried out tasks using different parts of the body.

Arthritis of the jaw is also more common in the Central Murray than elsewhere, and is linked to the incidence of tooth-loss. Tooth wear can be caused by chewing fibrous food, by the grit included in food and by the use of the mouth and teeth for holding or biting other things. The high degree of use and damage to the jaw and teeth in the Central Murray is explained by Webb as the result of chewing fibrous bulrush roots to make the twine for the extremely large hunting and fishing nets common in the area.

Broken bones

It is no surprise that people leading an active and strenuous life suffered broken bones. There are some interesting regional variations, especially

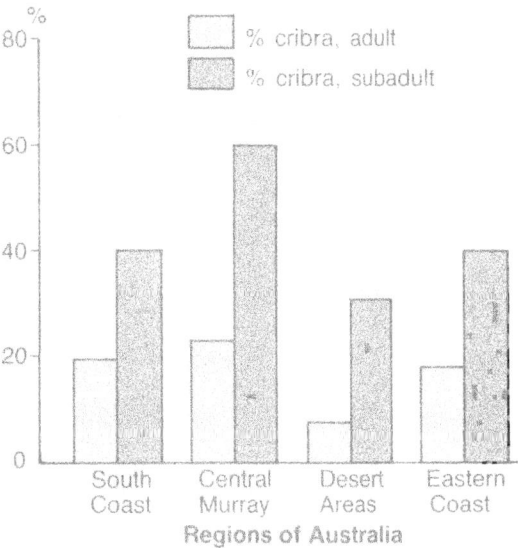

3.3
Proportion of adult and sub-adult skeletons examined by Webb which show evidence of cribra orbitalia (pitting of the skull brought about by anaemia). (Data from Webb 1989, Figure 7)

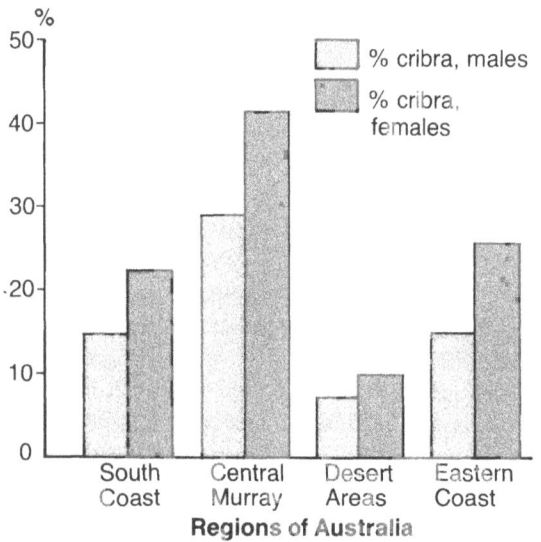

3.4
Proportion of male and female skeletons examined by Webb which show evidence of cribra orbitalia (pitting of the skull brought about by anaemia). (Data from Webb 1989, Figure 2.2)

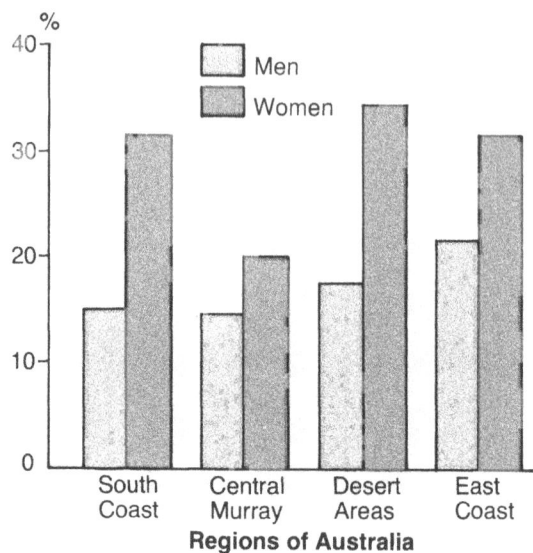

3.6
Percentage of male and female skeletons examined by Webb which show severe blows to the head. (Data from Webb 1989, Figure 7.4)

different behaviour during disputes in these areas?

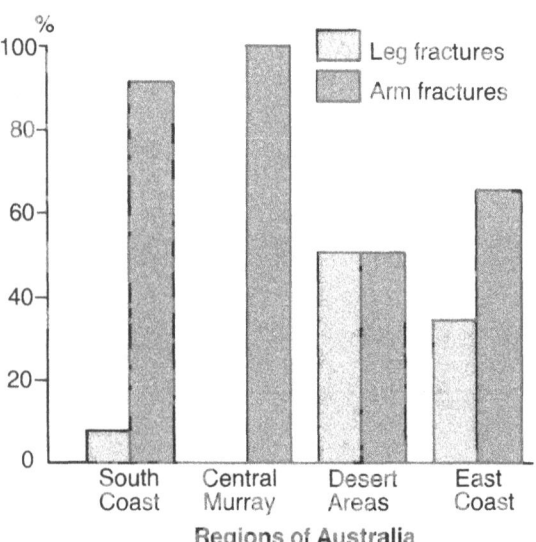

3.5
Relative proportions of broken arms and legs. (After Webb 1989, Figure 7.1)

Implications and regional variation

Webb's study has important implications for our understanding of Aboriginal health and behaviour. It also shows up the variation between different parts of the continent.

The Central Murray

Populations in the Central Murray had a high incidence of stress-related health problems, especially anaemia and arthritis. This is somewhat unexpected, as the area is normally thought to be one of the better-favoured environments in Australia, with ample water and food, which should provide for an easier and healthier life. Webb therefore argues that there must have been a dense population, living a fairly sedentary life. He suggests that the resulting overcrowding not only placed heavy demands on available resources but also led to an 'infectious environment'. Despite the high density of population the low incidence of 'parrying fractures' and cranial traumas associated with interpersonal violence suggests other processes of conflict resolution.

The Southern and Eastern Coasts

In these regions there was less chronic anaemia than in the Central Murray, which Webb takes to suggest less population aggregation. The Southern and Eastern Coasts vary in other ways. Toward the east there are fewer Harris lines per person than in the south. Webb therefore argues that there were more regular seasonal shortages in western Victoria and south-east South Australia. The level of osteoarthritis is greatest among women in Queensland: they must have had to work harder than people elsewhere. The level of aggression appears to be high in these areas.

Desert Areas

The low incidence of anaemia is seen by Webb as reflecting the low population density in arid regions. As in other areas, as children grew older there was less stress on them, and Webb argues that life in these regions was hazardous only for the very young. More people reached an older age in the arid areas than elsewhere but more people, especially women, suffered from aggressive attacks.

Case study 2: Lindsay Island, Victoria

Lindsay River is a side-branch of the Murray which cuts off a large section of flood-plain to form Lindsay Island. Much of the area is covered by red gum and black box woodland, dry for most of the year and only rarely flooded. Sand dunes have developed on the shores of shallow lake beds and a large dune, or meander scroll, runs parallel to the eastern bank of the river near the western end of the island.

Aims and approach

Colin Pardoe carried out work on the Lindsay Island meander scroll as part of an environmental assessment for the Victoria Archaeological Survey and the Department of Conservation, Forests and Lands. The main aims of the project were:

1. to locate and document archaeological sites
2. to assess any threat to them from erosion, stock, rabbits and development
3. to define significant sites or areas and make recommendations about their future management

In this study, as with most similar projects designed to document and assess archaeological significance, sites were not excavated. The area was surveyed on foot to locate sites. These and the material in them were recorded as they appeared on the ground. This can still provide important data useful for research as well as management recommendations.

Only five weeks (thirteen days in the field) were available for the whole project, so not all aspects of the archaeology of the area could be looked at in detail. After discussions with Mark Grist (Cultural Heritage Officer, north-west Victoria) to determine Aboriginal views of relative significance, Colin Pardoe decided to concentrate on burials, a subject in which he has a particular personal interest. Even so, scatters of stone tools, hearths, and small shell middens were also recorded and studied.

Burials and cemeteries

Burials were found eroding out of the surface of sand dunes in several localities. Pardoe divided these into 'cemeteries' and scattered individual burials. This, as we will discuss later, follows from his own view of contrasting burial customs. 'Cemeteries' are defined as clearly distinct areas with large numbers of burials close to one another and with little or no evidence of other occupation.

The one 'cemetery' on Lindsay Island is on 'Cemetery Dune' where sixty-five burials could be seen. Seventy-nine other burials are in smaller, less densely clustered groups or on their own elsewhere along the dune.

Recording and analysis

In keeping with the wishes of the local Aboriginal community, Pardoe recorded as much information about the burials as he could without disturbing them. Not all characteristics could be determined for every burial. The data collected can be used to give some idea of burial practice and population structure.

Date

The main dune ridge developed between 7000 and 4000 years ago. The burials must be more recent than this, and probably all date to within the last 3000 years.

Reuse of the cemetery

If the Cemetery Dune site was regarded as a special burial ground, one might imagine that graves would have been marked in some way. As time went by these markings would have disappeared. The longer the cemetery was in use the greater the chance of a later burial accidently cutting into an earlier one. Examples of this are known from other cemeteries. Pardoe found only one case of disturbance on Lindsay Island. He therefore suggests that the cemetery may have been used for a relatively short period of time, perhaps hundreds rather than thousands of years.

Age at death

An approximate age could be determined for about two-thirds of the individuals. In the cemetery there were ten children and forty-two adults. Away from the cemetery there were two children to fifty adults.

The ratio of children to adults is far lower than one might expect for a hunter-gatherer population as these normally have a fairly high rate of infant mortality. Many societies do not bury children in the same place or in the same way as adults and this may well have been the case here. Pardoe takes this further, and suggests that the higher ratio of children to adults in the cemetery compared with the ratio elsewhere may

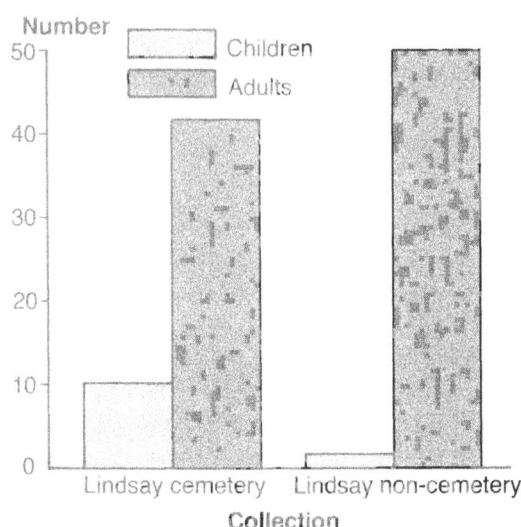

3.7
Comparison of the proportion of adults to children buried on Lindsay Island. There is a higher proportion of children to adults in the 'cemetery' than elsewhere, but in both cases there are fewer children than one might expect. (Data from Pardoe 1989)

indicate some specific family (or lineage) connection, but this is more speculative.

DETERMINING AGE AT DEATH

The age of children up to about sixteen can be fairly accurately determined because the sequence of tooth eruption is reasonably regular. In children and young adults the ends of growing bones are not yet ossified. The age of adults is harder to determine, as local factors can effect criteria such as dental attrition and other degeneration of bones. (See Figure 3.8.)

Sex

It is not always possible to determine the sex of individuals from their skeletons. Pardoe was able to determine the sex of twenty-two individuals in the field, and by analysing measurements was later able to increase the number to forty-two.

	Child	Adolescent	Young adult	Older adult
Milk teeth	▬▬▬▬			
Permanent teeth		▬▬▬▬▬▬▬▬▬▬▬▬▬▬▬▬▬▬		
Dental attrition			▬▬▬▬▬▬▬▬▬▬▬▬▬	
Epiphyseal ossification			▬▬▬▬▬▬▬▬▬▬▬▬▬	
Closure of cranial suture			▬▬▬▬▬▬▬▬▬▬▬▬▬	
Arthritis and other bone decay			▬▬▬▬▬▬▬▬▬▬▬▬▬	

3.8

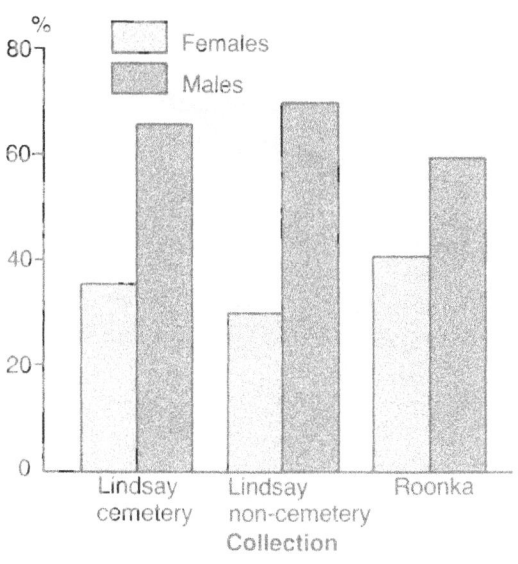

3.9
Comparison of the ratio of men to women buried on Lindsay Island and at Roonka in South Australia. (Data from Pardoe 1989)

Figure 3.6 summarises the ratio of males to females on Lindsay Island. Both in the cemetery site and elsewhere there are about twice as many men as women. A similar ratio is found at the cemetery at Roonka, just over 200 km down the Murray in South Australia. Other cemeteries up the Murray, east of the Darling River, generally have more females than males.

DETERMINING SEX OF SKELETONS

The sex of skeletons cannot always be determined with certainty. 80 to 90% accuracy is normal. Some bones are better indicators than others. The most reliable part is the pelvis as the female pelvis, adapted to childbearing, is generally wider and shallower. The skull is less reliable, especially where only a small number of specimens are available. The types of characteristics used to determine sex include those listed in Table 3.1.

Orientation

It was possible to record the direction in which fifty-six of the bodies were laid. Once again it is possible to compare the Lindsay Island cemetery burials with others on the island, as well as those from elsewhere along the Murray.

These show a general tendency to bury people aligned south-west to north-east. In the majority of cases the head is toward the south-west, but some were the other way around. There appears to be a slight difference in orientation of male and female burials on Lindsay Island, with males headed more to the south but the sample is so small that this cannot be regarded as certain.

Table 3.1

Anatomical feature	Female	Male
Sciatic notch	wider and shallower	narrower and deeper
Subpubic arch	U-shaped	V-shaped
Sacrum, centrum (body of vertebra)	1/3 total width	1/2 total width
Skull	smaller and more gracile	larger and more robust
Other bones	lighter and smaller	heavier and larger

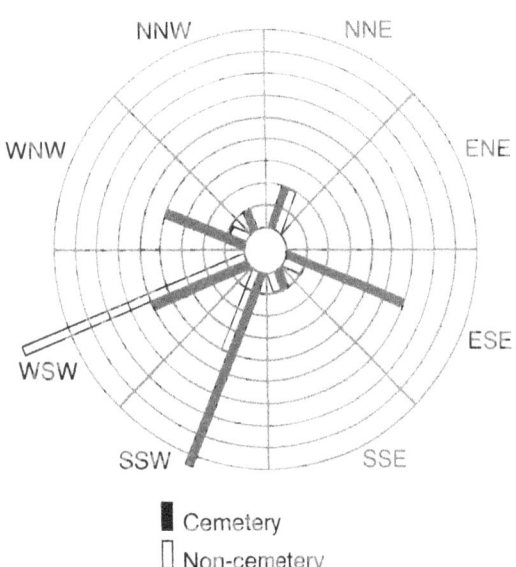

3.10
Orientation of burials on Lindsay Island. Most bodies were placed with their heads to the south-west, with a tendency for those in the 'cemetery' to face more southerly than those elsewhere on the island. (Data from Pardoe 1989)

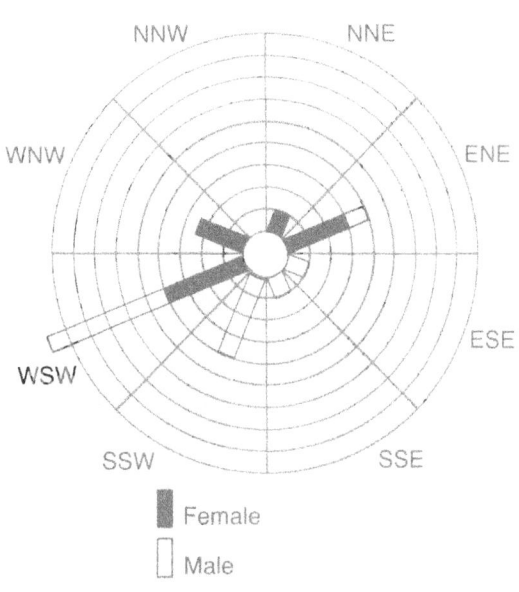

3.11
Orientation of male and female burials on Lindsay Island. (Data from Pardoe 1989)

The orientation of burials in the cemetery can be compared with the other burials. Once again there are some differences, with cemetery burials tending southerly. In addition a larger number of cemetery burials have the head toward the north-east.

These observations show a clear preference for patterning in burial practice. This suggests a long continuity of custom and possibly the association of a particular group of people with the cemetery and other parts of the dune.

In addition, Pardoe compared the pattern of burial orientation of the Lindsay Island burials with those from elsewhere along the Murray. Figure 3.12 shows the proportion of burials aligned in different directions in the Lindsay Island cemetery, at non-cemetery sites, and at the cemetery at Roonka, just over 200 km away.

The similarity is striking, with the same dominant westerly orientation and a smaller, but still clear second preference for the north-east.

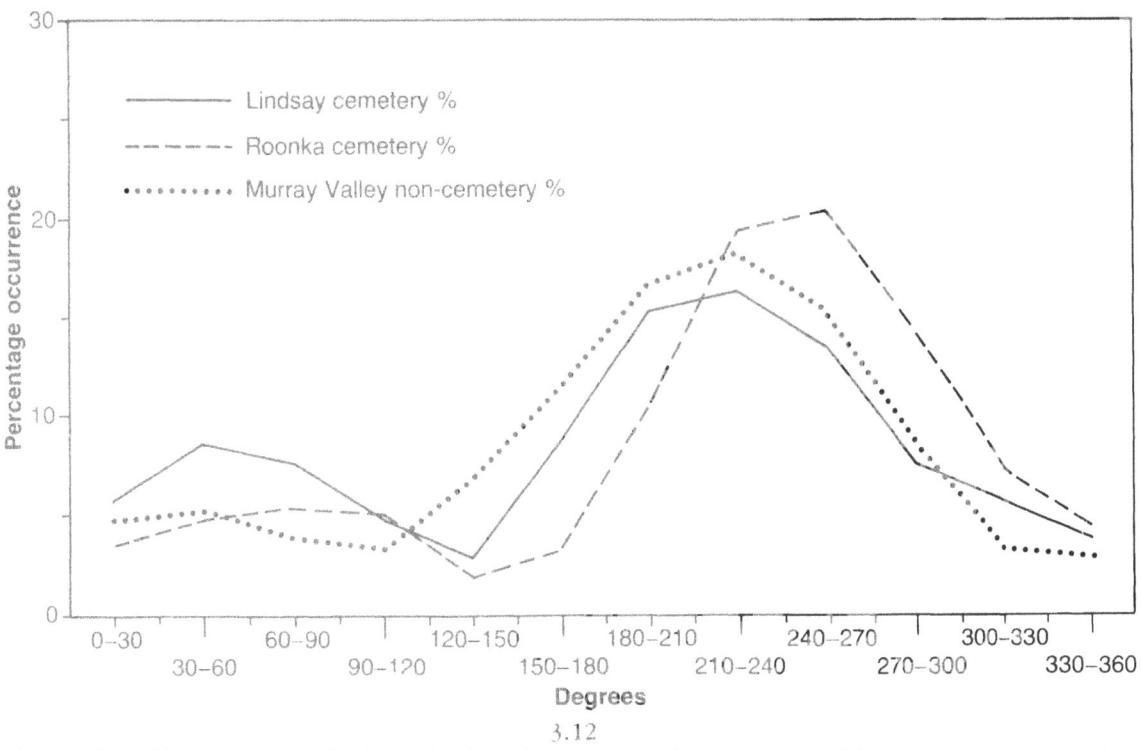

A comparison of burial orientation in the Lindsay Island cemetery with those at Roonka and from non-cemetery contexts along the Murray Valley. The same general pattern is seen in all areas. (After Pardoe 1989, Figure 10)

Non-cemetery burials show less of this second preference.

Pardoe therefore suggests that a common tradition of burial custom unites the widely separated people of Roonka and Lindsay Island.

A MAN FROM COLLARENEBRI

A burial near Collarenebri was turned up by a front-end loader. Before it was reburied Colin Pardoe examined the bones and produced a report for the local Aboriginal community. This illustrates the level of personal information that can be gained from a close study of the skeleton.

The size of the bones, shape of the hips, muscle attachments, fusion of bones, wear on the joints and teeth show that this was a man about 180 cm tall in his late 40s to early 50s.

Two of his front teeth had been knocked out. This is a widespread custom in many Aboriginal societies and indicates that he had been initiated into manhood.

His teeth were worn down to the roots, as a result of a rough diet. The lack of sugar in the diet meant that ancient Aboriginal people did not normally suffer from cavities, but this man had two large and presumably painful abscesses. These would have been caused by the tooth-wear which had exposed the pulp chamber.

When he was younger he broke one collarbone. It healed a little shorter and more bent than the other, so that he later developed severe arthritis of the breastbone and ribs. As he got older other joints also became arthritic, but this would not have caused much discomfort.

There was a large kidney stone about 3 cm across which must have been growing for some time.

He lost the tip of the left thumb. Slight thinning of the bone and the unworn fusion of the remnant to the second joint show that this happened later in life, after the injury to his collarbone. The tip was cleanly cut, perhaps because of an accident with stone tools. Fortunately it did not become infected.

A small lump of bone on the skull shows he received a fairly hard blow on the head a few years before he died. Low on his left side the ribs were swollen. This was the result of a large and serious infection. Colin Pardoe suggests that he may have been wounded in fighting or hunting, and that this may have caused his death.

Finally he was buried lying on his back with one hand on his chest and his head to the north-west. From scatters of stone tools found above the grave it can be suggested that this man from Collarenebri died between 1000 and 2000 years ago.

(Pardoe, C., 1987)

Further discussion

As noted above, Pardoe has previously argued that, unlike most areas of Australia, discrete burial grounds can be identified along the Murray River. Although large numbers of people were also buried elsewhere, both along dunes and occasionally in old oven-mounds, there was a specific and significant use of these cemeteries. These are sometimes close to important resources (stone sources, fish-traps) and so may be related to the use of particular places by larger groups of people or for longer periods of time.

It is also possible to see a social significance in the use of cemeteries. Basing an argument on general analogies and models of social behaviour, Pardoe suggests that the repeated use of a defined burial ground symbolises ownership of territory. Such a symbolic demonstration is not necessary where population is low and resources are dispersed. The presence of cemeteries along the Murray therefore may signal competition for resources brought about by a high population density and, following from this, social structures emphasising group membership and associations with clearly marked territories.

The ideas developed by Webb also suggest a high population density in the Central Murray and possibly also that people were concentrated in particular places. In addition, we may also consider the nature of communication and inter-group relationships. Other analyses of the physical form of people in this region show a cline, or trend, along the length of the river. In each area people were most similar to their neighbours, and gradually more and more different from people further away. This can be seen as showing social links and relationships such as marriage within defined groups and to a lesser extent with their neighbours. In regions such as this with reliable resources, there was little need to establish connections with distant groups to provide access to alternative resources in time of shortage.

Cross-cutting these factors which tend to isolate groups, we have the evidence from Pardoe's analysis of shared burial customs, showing a continuity of tradition in separate areas over very long periods of time. Here we can see how different elements of the archaeological record highlight aspects of a complex overlay of influences, associations and relationships, which will still require much more research before they can be first disentangled, and later reintegrated.

POINTS FOR DISCUSSION

1 Have you ever had an illness serious enough to stop you growing or to affect your teeth? What proportion of people in your class have had such a serious illness?
 Is this different from the proportion among the prehistoric populations studied by Webb? Can you explain any difference?
2 Do you think you would have lived to your present age had you been born in Australia several hundred years ago? Why?

3 Are most present-day burials in Australia oriented in any particular direction?
Do you know why present-day burials take the form that they do?

PICTURING THE PAST

1 Write a biography of the man from Collarenebri.
2 Use the evidence provided by the study of bones to describe and compare the quality of life in different parts of Australia.

A DEBATE: WHO OWNS THE BONES?

Over the last decade there has been a serious debate concerning ownership and control of heritage material generally and human remains in particular. Legislation and regulations in several states now officially recognise Aboriginal rights over this material. Aboriginal communities exercise their rights in different ways. Many see the value in scientific study of ancient skeletons, but still prefer that these remains should be reburied once examined. While many archaeologists support this view, others continue to argue that ancient skeletons provide an irreplaceable scientific resource and should under no circumstances be reburied or destroyed.

> The issue is control. You seek to say that as scientists you have a right to obtain and study information of our culture. You seek to say that because you are Australians you have a right to study and explore our heritage because it is a heritage to be shared by all Australians, white and black. From our point of view we say you have come as invaders, you have tried to destroy our culture, you have built your fortunes upon the lands and bodies of our people and now, having said sorry, want a share in picking out the bones of what you regard as a dead past. We say that it is our past, our culture and heritage, and forms part of our present life. As such it is ours to control and it is ours to share on our terms. That is the Central Issue in this debate. (Langford, R.F., 1983, p. 2)

Any decision taken by Aboriginal communities today that involves destruction of ancient evidence, or bans on studying segments of human existence, suggests gross insecurity. It replaces European cultural dominance by an equally aggressive cultural imperialism. To claim total knowledge of the past and deny the rights of others to question it, challenges the intellectual freedom of all Australians, particularly future generations. (Mulvaney, D.J., 1989, p. 72)

Divide the class into several groups, each adopting a different role: biological anthropologists who study bones for a living; other archaeologists with less personal interest in skeletons; Aborigines; administrators responsible for making decisions on the future of skeletal material; Council for Civil Liberties; general public.

Debate whether or not a collection of ancient skeletons excavated many years ago and now in a museum should be handed over to Aboriginal communities who may wish to rebury them.

References

Frankel, D., 1984, 'Who Owns the Past', *Australian Society*, September 1984, pp. 14–15.

Langford, R., 1983, 'Our Heritage — Your Playground', *Australian Archeology*, Vol. 16, pp. 1–6.

Meehan, B., (ed), 1984, 'Aboriginal Skeletal Remains', *Australian Archaeology*, Vol. 19, pp. 122–147.

Mulvaney, D.J., 1989, 'Reflections on the Murray Black Collection', *Australian Natural History*, Vol. 23, pp. 66–72.

Pardoe, C., 1987, *The Prehistoric Burial at Collarenebri, Northern New South Wales*, Australian Institute of Aboriginal Studies, Canberra.

Pardoe, C., 1988, 'The Cemetery as Symbol. The Distribution of Prehistoric Aboriginal Burial Grounds in Southeastern Australia', *Archaeology in Oceania*, Vol. 23, pp. 1–16.

Pardoe, C., 1989, *Archaeology of the Western Lindsay Island Meander Scroll. A Report to the Victoria Archaeological Survey*.

Pardoe, C., 1989, 'Burial rite and normative behaviour in the archaeological record', Paper presented to the Australian Archaeological Association Conference, Mildura.

Pardoe, C. and Grist, M., 1989, *Traces of the Aboriginal past at Lindsay Island, Northwest Victoria*, Sunraysia and District Aboriginal Co-Operative.

Thorne, A. and Ross, A., 1986, *The Skeleton Manual: A Handbook for the Identification of Aboriginal Skeletal Remains*, National Parks and Wildlife Service, NSW.

Webb, S., 1984, 'Intensification Population and Social Change in South-eastern Australia: the Skeletal Evidence', *Aboriginal History* Vol. 8, pp. 154–172.

Webb, S., 1989, *Prehistoric Stress in Australian Aborigines: A Palaeopathological Study of a Hunter-gatherer Population*, British Archaeological Reports S490.

Coastal shell middens

What are shell middens?

As the name implies, these are the remains of meals of shellfish. The shells which form the main body of middens make them among the most obvious of archaeological sites. In addition to shells, they often contain bones of fish and land animals as well as stone or bone tools.

Shell middens vary considerably. Some midden deposits are found in rockshelters near the coast, but the great majority are in the open air. In some regions of northern Australia, large, high mounds of shell, hundreds of square metres in area and several metres in height may be seen. Many middens in north-western Tasmania have a characteristic doughnut shape indicating that shells were gradually piled up all around circular huts. Although some Victorian middens are of large size, the great majority are smaller, often only thin layers of shells lying in the dunes, surrounded by a characteristic grey charcoal-stained sand.

As coastal dunes are often unstable and subject to erosion by wind and water, many shell middens originally embedded in the dunes are severely disturbed. They appear now as scatters of shells which have lost their original form and structure. Movement of sand can expose, destroy, or cover up parts of middens, so it is not always easy to determine their original size and shape. Many of these deflated middens are small, but some exposures of scattered shell extend over several hectares.

Where middens retain their original integrity, small isolated dumps of shells can sometimes be identified as the remains of single meals or casual short-term 'dinner-time camps'. Larger middens may represent camps where people stayed for weeks at a time, using the site as a central place for exploiting the resources of the surrounding territory. The short-term, smaller sites suggest that shellfish-gathering took place away from the main campsite, which may have been located inland, further from the shore. As with other sites, midden deposits may represent accumulations of material discarded at the same place at intervals over very long periods of time, perhaps hundreds or even thousands of years.

What can we learn from middens?

The great advantage of studying middens is the detail that they can provide on how people made use of the coast and the organisation of this one part of their economy. The obvious questions are to do with diet, but we can also understand the placement and size of camps as part of a complex system of land use and social organisation, while the selection of which shellfish species to collect can be seen as reflecting broader economic decision-making strategies.

In studying middens we can look at three main aspects: location, site structure and site contents. How we use these depends on the questions we are interested in and whether we are looking at broad regional patterns revealed by a general survey or the precise detail afforded by the excavation of one specific site.

SHELLFISH GATHERING IN ARNHEM LAND

Our main source of information on the role of shellfish in an Aboriginal coastal economy is the detailed study of the Gidjingarli people of Arnhem Land carried out in 1972-3 by Betty Meehan. She lived with the Anbarra community for over a year, documenting details of their daily life and, in particular, how they gathered food. In this area shellfish collected from tidal mudflats form an important, although not major, part of the diet. Only during one month of the study period, when other food sources were poor, could shellfish be regarded as crucial. Overall, in terms of the energy intake, shellfish ranged between 6% and 17% of the diet.

But the collection of shellfish, in this area at least, is more significant to the Anbarra than can simply be computed by percentage of the diet.
- Shellfish were regularly collected (on over half the days of the year).
- Shellfish are collected by a wide variety of people, especially older women and those needing to look after young children who cannot go on longer or more strenuous foraging trips.
- Shellfish can be collected efficiently; within about two hours women can collect all the shellfish they need, and so have time for other activities.
- Shellfish are reliable, potentially available at all times of the year, providing a guaranteed source of food, where hunting has greater risk of failure.

The availability of shellfish, the species collected, the strategies for harvesting and

4.1
Ernie Nbrana and Elva Gindjerrkama eating shellfish collected from the tidal mudflats near Maningrida, Arnhem Land. (Meehan-Jones Collection, courtesy AIATSIS)

structure of camps in other parts of Australia were different from tropical coastal Arnhem Land. But it is still possible to use this information as a general analogy for the archaeological evidence found elsewhere. Understanding the low dietary significance of this source of food moderates the otherwise exaggerated view of the importance of shellfish provided by the high visibility of shell middens in the archaeological record.
(Meehan, B., 1982.)

Problems in excavating shell middens

A common practical difficulty in excavating middens is to separate interleaved loose layers of shell. Each layer is itself a mixture of shell, charcoal and soil, and this material can be further mixed as a result of later reuse of the site, when previously discarded shell is dug into, pushed aside, kicked around or scuffed up. Archaeologists therefore often ignore the minor, subtle (even illusory) layering, and excavate sites in arbitrary, artificial 'spits' (commonly 5 cm in depth).

Middens are created by a series of activities in different parts of the site, so that information from one section may give a misleading view. This too justifies a broader scale of excavation or analysis, which might even out minor variation and allow us to see the main underlying pattern.

However, even a small excavation yields thousands upon thousands of shells. It is not only extremely time-consuming to sort and process them, but exceedingly tedious. Often only a small sample of shell (perhaps only that from a 10 × 10 cm column) is analysed in detail, assuming that, at a very general level, it is representative of the site as a whole.

In short, although we can excavate and analyse middens at a fine level we may only be able to interpret our information in very broad terms. If this is so, then is the finest level of excavation really necessary?

4.3
During storms and high tides the platforms are inaccessible.

Case study: Excavations at Moonlight Head

Description

The Moonlight Head midden is in a rather unusual position in a high, shallow overhang at the foot of a cliff on the rugged Otway coast. High tides cover the neighbouring rock-platforms and when it is stormy, waves wash right up to the surviving midden deposit. Wind and rain blow into the site and even in mid-summer it can be cold and uncomfortable. But when the sea is calm the abundance of shellfish on the extensive rock-platforms provide the main attraction for descending the cliffs and using the area.

Largely because of the confined space at the foot of the cliff over 1.5 m of stratified deposit had accumulated. In the sea-eroded face of the site thin layers of shell interspersed with fine sandstone fill were clearly visible, sealed in by massive boulders fallen from the cliff above.

Aims and excavation strategy

Ron Vanderwal and I excavated this midden in 1980 in order to take advantage of this unusually deep and well-stratified deposit to identify change through time.

As the eroded face of the site gave us a preview of the structure of the site, we decided to attempt to remove each fine stratigraphic layer in turn, rather than excavate in arbitrary spits. We also decided to analyse all the shells, rather than smaller samples, to give us as much information on the site as possible.

Several adjacent units were excavated separately. A comparison of all the material from each would show whether we were observing

4.2
Cliffs of the Otway coast at Moonlight Head. The extensive rock platforms abound in shellfish. The excavated midden is at the base of the cliffs.

common, general patterns, or some minor variation within the site.

In the field and laboratory

The decisions to excavate a fairly large area of the midden at a fine level and to process all the shells in the field meant that we spent six weeks, at the site with a large team of assistants. The photographs give an idea of work in progress.

The midden deposits are located towards the back of the overhang. Here one or two people carry out the actual excavation, defining each separate feature or layer and noting its extent, colour, and texture and recording absolute levels before its removal. In the foreground, others, clustered around a sieve, separate out all

4.5
Excavating the midden.

4.4
A general view of excavations in progress at Moonlight Head midden.

4.6
Recording the nature of the excavated deposits.

4.7
The soil from the midden is sieved, and stone artefacts, bones and shells recovered.

4.10
Weighing shellfish

4.8
Shellfish are sorted into species, and counted.

4.11
Ron Vanderwal measuring and recording a stratigraphic section through the deposits.

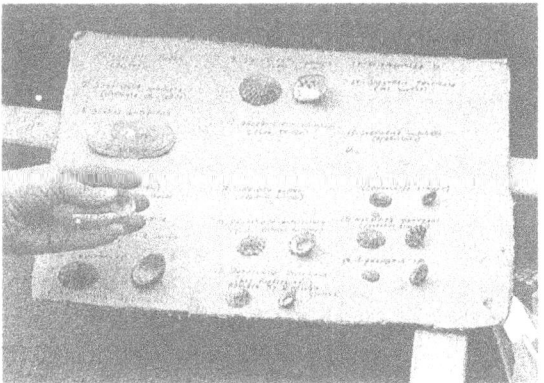

4.9
Identifying shellfish species.

the shell, bone and stone artefacts from the sediments.

While the bones and stones are bagged for later analysis, the shells are sorted into different species, counted and weighed. The history of the site is summarised in the sections exposed through the deposits at different times during the excavation.

The shells from one area of the site were also brought back to the laboratory, to be further processed by, for example, counting the number of specimens in several size classes. The bones were classified into animal species and anatomical part and the form of stone tools was recorded.

Data, and questions

At the conclusion of the excavation and primary processing, we have several sets of data:

1 *The site*
- structure and nature of each defined deposit
- stratigraphic relationships between deposits
- radiocarbon dates from several places in the site

2 *Shellfish*
- number of shells of each species in each excavation unit
- weight of shells of each species in each excavation unit
- number of shells of different sizes in one area of the site

3 *Stone and bone*
- number, weight and form of stone artefacts in each excavation unit
- number of bones identified to species and body part for each excavation unit

Each of these has its own value and meaning, the next step is to provide a framework of appropriate questions and to determine the way to investigate them.

The basic structure is, of course, chronological, so that it is best to start with the stratigraphy and the units of time we can use. Within this temporal framework, we can look at a few specific questions, particularly to do with shellfish gathering and consumption.

Stratigraphy and time-frames

The time-frames we select are crucial, but are still arbitrary and depend on personal decisions and practical constraints. Two different views of our sequence show this clearly, one broader, the other at a finer chronological level.

In the main analysis of material from the site we wanted to compare all the different parts of the site and all the shell, bone and stone. To do this, we had to combine the fine-level excavation units into larger analytical units. At several

4.12
Part of the section through the deposits, showing the fine layers of deposit in the site.

points in our sequence, layers of roof-fall ran across the site, linking the different areas excavated and we felt that these provided appropriate points at which to divide up the deposits. In this way we defined four analytical units (A to D) grouping many finer layers in each. The radiocarbon dates showed that there was a relatively constant rate of sediment accumulation over about 800 years, from about 1000 years ago. As our dividing lines were fairly evenly spaced, this means that each of the four analytical units represents about 200 years of use of the site. They are not individual episodes, or even the result of repeated visits to the site during the course of one person's lifetime, but the combination of many separate events over two centuries and so represent a general pattern, which assumes uni-

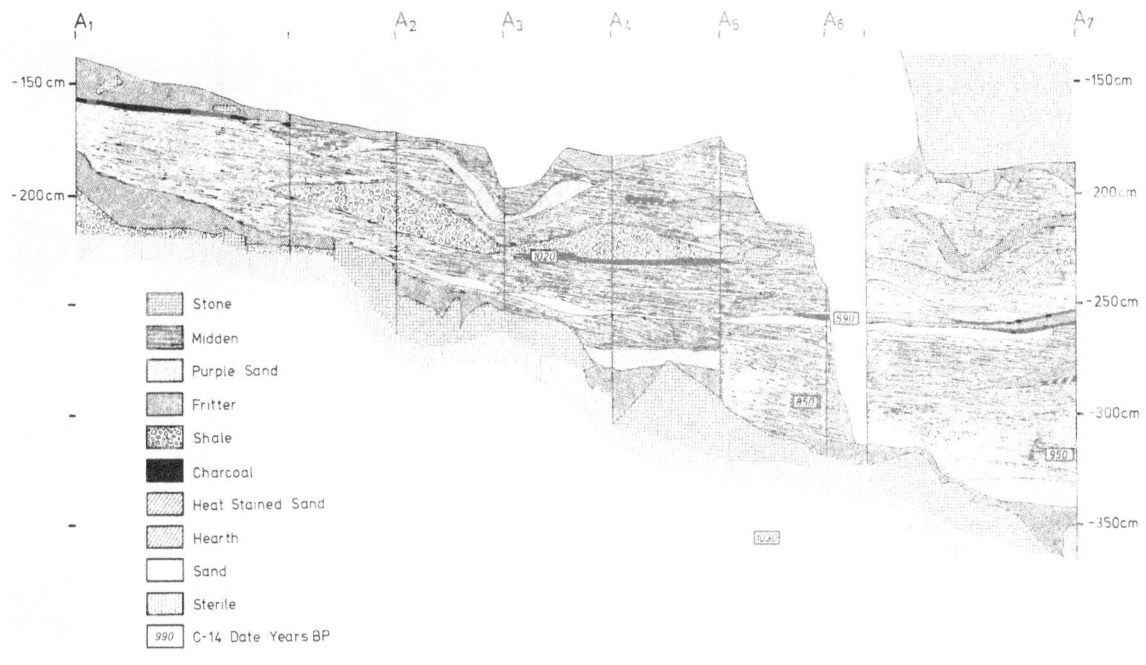

4.13
A drawing of the stratigraphy at Moonlight Head. (Zobel et al 1984, Figure 4)

form behaviour over considerable lengths of time.

A different analysis concentrated on each separate area, avoiding the need to group the material from different parts of the site. The original excavation units were kept separate, not combined with one another. Each represents the finest layering that we could define in the field, probably (but not certainly) individual episodes of activity. There was too little bone and stone to use in this analysis, so here we could only talk about shellfish.

How many animals? How much food?

In any analysis of animal remains in archaeology we need to establish how many animals there are and their relative contribution to the diet. This is most easily seen with shellfish, but the principles apply to land animals as well.

Many shells are broken. We have to decide which shells to count and which to ignore. For some, such as the limpets, we might count only those represented by more than half a shell, or else we can select a specific part (the hard beak of the mussel; the cap or peak of other shells; the hard round opercula or doors of the turbo). A time-saving option is not to count shells, but to weigh them. After determining the average weight of a shell of each species it is easy to calculate relative numbers. Whichever procedure we follow we come up with the Number of Identified Specimens (NISP). If we have large enough samples, the minor variation between counts achieved using different techniques will not be significant.

Not all shellfish have the same number of shells. While many have a single shell, the mussel is a bivalve (two valves or shells) and the chiton has eight plates. Our original counts of identified specimens need to be adjusted accordingly to estimate the Minimum Number of Individuals (MNI) represented.

But not all shellfish are the same size. If we want to consider their relative contribution to the diet we need to compensate for meat weight.

Once again there are several techniques. There is a relatively constant ratio of meat weight to shell weight for most species, so one way is to convert the weight of shell to meat weight contribution. Or else one can determine the average size and weight of animals in each species, and calculate the meat weight contribution from the MNI.

> ## ROCK-PLATFORM SHELLFISH ON THE SOUTH-EAST COAST OF AUSTRALIA
>
> In order to understand shell middens it is necessary to know something about marine molluscs and their ecology. Different species are found in different habitats; some prefer the rough water of exposed, high-energy coasts; others prefer calmer conditions in sheltered areas or bays. Some live on rock-platforms, others in beach sand or in mud-flats.
>
> Table 4.1 summarises information on species found on rock-platforms along the Victorian and South Australian coast. Of particular interest is their location, density, aggregation, and size. All of these species can still be seen along much of the coast, although their numbers are severely depleted where they have been heavily collected for bait and food. Today rock-platform shellfish are protected and it is an offence to collect them.

Sometimes archaeologists attempt to calculate the total quantity of meat represented in a site, when they are interested in estimating the number of people who may have used a site, or how important particular resources were. As we had no idea of the original extent of the site at Moonlight Head, such questions could not be considered. Our focus of attention was the proportions of different species at different times, not the actual quantity of meat.

We applied a general relative meat weight compensation, with abalone counting 60, turbo 2.7, and all others as 1.0. These figures were based on studies of meat weights for different species both at Moonlight Head and by other ar-

4.14
Later classification and analysis of shellfish back in the laboratory.

chaeologists, bearing in mind the sizes of shells represented at our site. These are, obviously, very crude estimates, and any change to them will drastically affect further calculations and analysis.

As should now be clear, as we work through our material we see it is increasingly complex, artificial, and full of problems. We have made personal decisions in the field about what to excavate as a single deposit, which of these excavation units to group together for analysis, which shells to count and how to count them, and how to calculate their relative value. Having done all this, we can now turn toward identifying patterns.

Observations and interpretations

1 *Broad scale analysis*

Figure 4.15 summarises the results of all this work, showing the relative proportions of shell-

Table 4.1 Shellfish species along Victorian and South Australian coast

Species	Location	Aggregation	Size
Turbo *Turbo undulatus*	on platforms, under rocks and ledges, within and below the tidal range	individual, fairly common	medium to large; larger ones found at greater depth
Mussel *Austromytilus rostratus*	on platforms, sheltered from main wave action but with constant trickle of water	in large dense clusters	small to medium
Limpets *Cellana tramoserica* and *Cellana solida*	on platforms within the tidal range. *C. solida* prefers more sheltered locations	individual, common	small to medium
Limpets *Patella peronii* and *Patteloida alticostata*	lower tidal range	individual, not very common	small
Abalone *Haliotis rubra*	crevices in platform below low water mark	individual, fairly common	largest shellfish on rocky coasts
Duckbill *Scutus antipodes*	on platforms and below low tide mark	individual not common	medium
Chiton *Polyplacophera*	various intertidal levels	individual, fairly common	medium
Top shell *Austrocochlea* spp.	all littoral zones	individual, common	small
Dog whelk *Thais orbita*	within tidal range	individual, not common	small to medium

Table 4.2 Number of stone artefacts per cubic metre in each analytical unit

	Flint	Quartz	Other
D	154.1	24.7	25.4
C	90.8	7.1	7.1
B	45.2	11.9	4.8
A	2.9	0	0

fish of each species (by MNI) in each of the four 200-year-long analytical units. Of the ten species represented, only five are really significant and we can look at their changing proportions through time.

In the earliest period (A) between about 1000 and 800 years ago, mussels and limpets were most commonly collected, but with reasonable

Table 4.3 Vertebrate fauna in each analytical unit by MNI

	Fish	Crayfish	Possum	Wallaby	Seal
D	4	6	4	2	–
C	7	1	3	–	1
B	1	1	–	–	–
A	1	2	–	–	1

Table 4.4 Percentage of shellfish species in each analytical unit by MNI.

Species	A	B	C	D
Mussel	32	23	52	49
Limpets	39	36	22	32
Turbo	13	21	11	8
Chiton	12	16	13	10
Top shell	1	3	1	1
Dog whelk	1	1	1	1
Abalone	1	1	1	1
Duckbill	1	1	1	1
TOTAL MNI	10 149	9874	31 874	44 308

quantities of other species. The next 200-year period (B) saw a similar, but slightly more even collection strategy. In analytical unit C (after about 500 or 600 years ago) the pattern changes, with a great concentration on mussels, a pattern which continues, although with some change, in the last 200 years of use of the site.

We have a change, therefore, in the structure of the exploitation system, from a relatively diverse system, with more even numbers of each species, to an uneven, less diverse structure, dominated by one species.

It is possible to calculate measures of evenness or diversity of this kind. Figure 4.16 shows these for the four analytical units at the site, by MNI and by MNI weighted for meat weight. The change is more exaggerated for unweighted than for weighted data, illustrating the effects of this compensation. This is not to say either is wrong, but we should now see that they measure slightly different things. Counts of numbers of shellfish represent collection strategy; estimates of meat weight represent consumption. There may be a significant change in how people collected food, but the impact on the diet may be less important. In both cases, however, the basic pattern is the same, a change from a more even to a less even strategy.

If we consider the nature of the species collected, we see a reduction in those which need to be collected individually and an increase in the smaller mussels which can be gathered in large clusters. There is little evidence of change in size of shellfish gathered. Although the smallest mussels and limpets seem to have been avoided, few large turbo were taken from deeper water, but only those smaller individuals normally found on the rock platform itself. There is no suggestion of an intensive exploitation of larger individuals or species requiring greater expenditure of energy in their collection. The impression we have is of a casual use of easily collected animals, with some change in favour of the most easily gathered.

How are we to understand this change? The evidence from bones and stones gives one possible insight. There is a constant increase in the number of stone artefacts in the site through

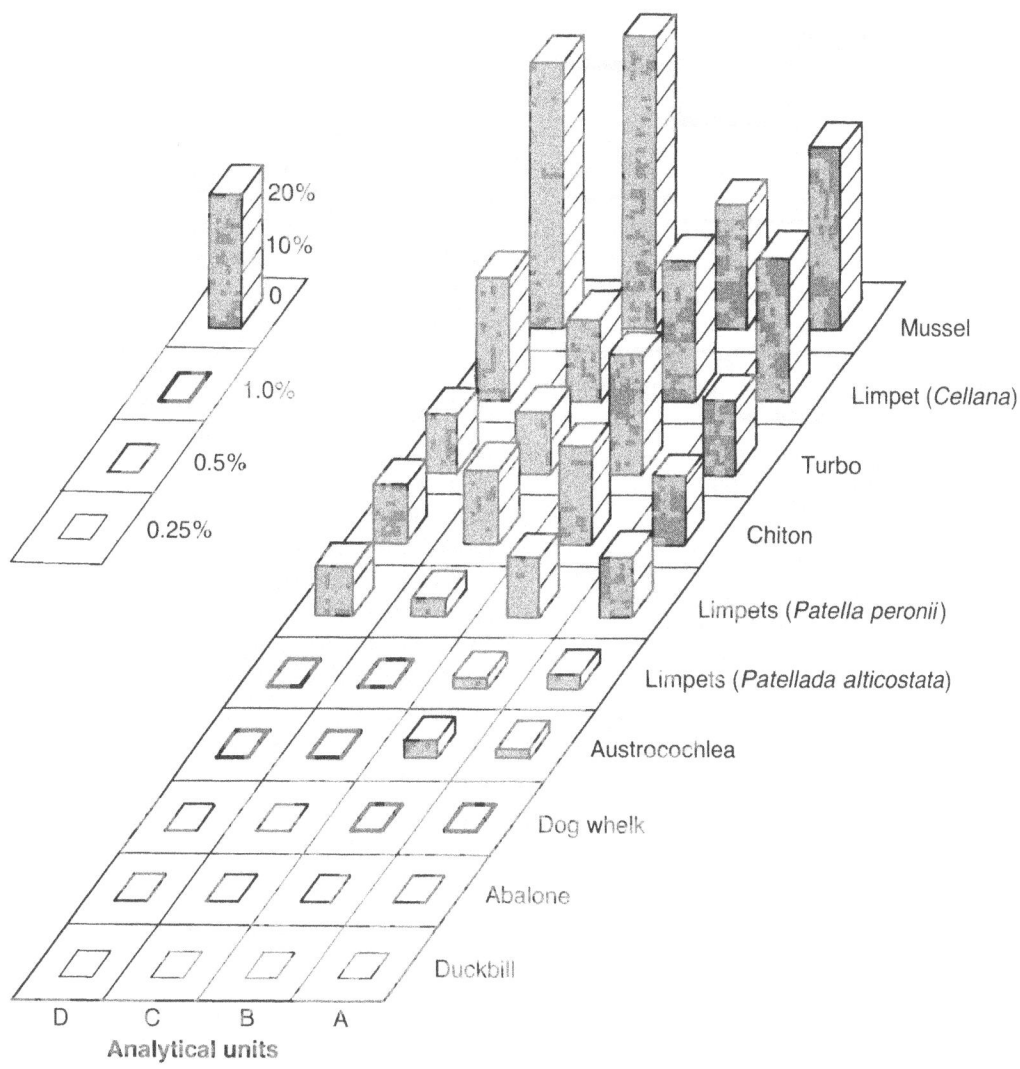

4.15
Proportional distribution of ten species of shellfish in each component at Moonlight Head. (After Zobel et al 1984, Figure 10)

time and, although the numbers are very small, an increase in both fish and land animals such as wallaby and possum.

These may indicate a change in the use of the site in the more recent periods. The earlier use may have been casual, with occasional short visits to the area simply to collect shellfish and, opportunistically, fish or crayfish. In the upper part of the site, where there is more possum and wallaby bone as well as a greater number of stone artefacts, we may see people using the site in a slightly different way, with less casual, more purposeful visits. While shellfish may have provided an important contribution to the diet, less energy was expended collecting them. Although at all times the site cannot represent more than a minor part of people's settlement pattern and economy, in the later periods we can see it as

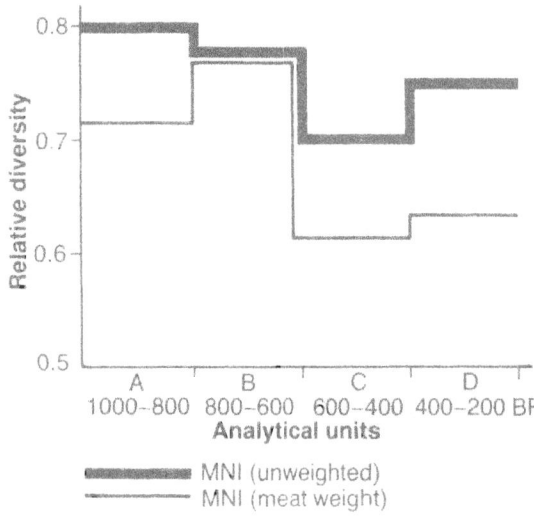

4.16

Relative diversity of shellfish in each 200-year-long Component at Moonlight Head for MNI (reflecting collection strategy) and MNI compensated for meat-weight (reflecting consumption). There are some differences between these measures, but they both show greatest uniformity of shellfish collection and consumption between about 600 and 400 years ago. (After Zobel et al. 1984, Figure 11)

reflecting a shift in local behaviour as it became a camp site involving a wider range of activities and foraging strategies and less of a casual, dinner-time stopover.

Why did this happen? How significant is this change? Is it simply a site-specific shift, reflecting some minor variation in how people were using that particular patch of the coast at intervals over a very long period of time? If we go back to our earlier definition of time-frames and analytical units, perhaps we can pursue this further.

2 *Fine-scale analysis*

If we look at the changes between our original excavation units (short-term events), instead of those between the composite 200-year-long analytical units, what does the pattern look like?

Figure 4.17 shows diversity or evenness measures similar to those used in Figure 4.16 for each thin layer in two adjacent areas in the site. This figure is designed to show up general trends by smoothing out variations in the data. The patterns are basically the same in both areas. Analysed in this way the changes in strategy of

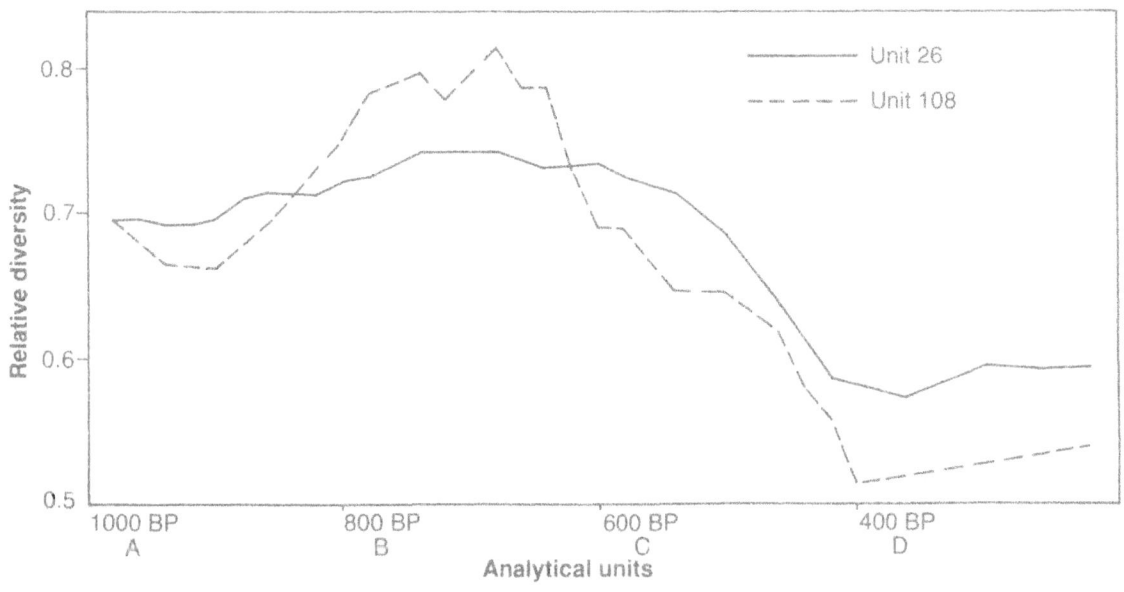

4.17

Relative diversity of shellfish collection at Moonlight Head in each thin layer excavated in two parts of the site. Here the curves have been smoothed to show up the gradual and cumulative nature of change through time.

shellfish collection are seen to be cumulative, with long-term trends.

This presentation suggests that the patterns summarised in the earlier analysis are the result of gradual change in shellfish collection and, presumably, overall use of the site. These changes were probably not planned, deliberate or sudden. Instead they form a series of modifications within a basically uniform economic and settlement pattern, imperceptible at the time and visible only over the long archaeological time-frame.

Conclusions

1 The site was used from about 1000 years ago.
2 Although shellfish prompted use of the site, they were not intensively exploited.
3 There were changes in strategies of shellfish collecting.
4 These changes, and those in other items, reflect a change to a wider range of activities at the site.
5 Use of this part of the coast did not change radically during the last 1000 years.
6 Change was gradual and cumulative, with no obvious external cause.

Other explanations of change in middens

In other regions or sites archaeologists have suggested more specific causal explanations for change observed in middens, relating them to change in population density, environment, or social organisation.

Increasing population

At the broadest level, John Beaton suggested that as few middens are known to be older than about 4000 BP, people hardly used the coast until 2000 years after the sea reached its present level. He argued that this delay in use of marine resources showed an increase in population in the last few thousand years. More people, he suggested, not only created more sites, but also needed to use the relatively unproductive coastal resources which were previously avoided. While other archaeologists have also suggested that the population of parts of Australia increased substantially in the last few thousand years, there are considerable objections to using the evidence from middens to support this idea. One objection is that older middens simply do not survive and where they do they are in so poor a condition that archaeologists seldom spend much time or (more importantly) money to excavate and date them. The sample we have is heavily biased toward recent sites and we should beware of translating more sites into more people.

Reduction of inland resources

Along the south-east coast of South Australia, Roger Luebbers developed a more complex model of changing social organisation, land use and shellfish exploitation, related to climatic change and the evolution of the coast over the last ten thousand years. He carried out extensive surveys, plotted the location of sites, their size and contents and excavated a number of them. From a study of the midden contents, estimates of numbers of middens of different periods and calculations of midden size and dietary contribution (see the section on Richmond River

4.18
Wyrie Swamp, South Australia. The oldest wooden artefacts found in Australia were preserved in these peat deposits. (Photo: Roger Luebbers)

middens, page 55) Luebbers assessed changes in intensity of use of coastal resources.

Before about 6000 years ago people lived beside inland wetlands and swamps, rich in both plant and animal foods. One site of this period, at Wyrie Swamp, provides us with the earliest evidence of wooden tools, boomerangs, digging sticks, and spears, at about 10 000 BP. Later, as the climate changed and the inland swamps dried up, people began to use the coast to an ever-increasing extent. Between about 6000 and 1300 BP sites were generally situated on the back dunes, and species such as the sandy shore pipi (*Plebidonax deltoides*) and the rock platform mussels (*Austromytilus rostratus*) were collected. The sites are small, and suggest only very occasional use of the coast, by small groups of people. After 1300 BP a wider range of species were collected. There are many more sites and they are very much bigger, indicating more and longer visits to the coast by larger groups of people.

Although the bulk of the diet may have come from the wetlands behind the dunes, especially plant foods, the changing patterns of shellfish exploitation and coastal occupation can be used to monitor other changes. Luebbers argues that these reflect changes in social organisation and increased pressure on resources with a growth in population density brought about by environmental change, in particular the reduction in productivity of inland swamps.

New technology and work practices

A different type of explanation for change was developed by Sandra Bowdler. At Bass Point, a midden on the south coast of NSW, she documented a clear change about 400 years ago to a concentration on a more easily collected species of mussel, *Mytilus edulis* (a more drastic change than the subtle variation observed at Moonlight Head). At the same time fish-hooks made of shell appear at this and other sites in NSW. Previously all fishing may have been done using spears, but this new technique, probably learnt from people further north, was now adopted.

Some change in the proportions of species of fish at Bass Point show the effect of this new method of fishing.

From an examination of early historical accounts of Aboriginal people in NSW, Sandra Bowdler observed that while, at least in the eighteenth and nineteenth centuries, only men were allowed to use spears, both men and women could use hook and line for fishing. She therefore suggested that in earlier periods only men fished and that women spent much time collecting the larger species of shellfish. Access to the new method of line fishing about 400 years ago opened up new opportunities for women, who no longer had time to spend collecting the larger, individual shellfish, but instead resorted to those which could be collected more quickly and with less effort. The change in shellfish collection can be seen as part of a general change in women's activities prompted by a new technology.

This social explanation has recently been challenged in a number of ways. It has now been suggested that the change to mussels seen at Bass Point and at other sites on the NSW coast is not the result of choice by Aboriginal people, but is simply because there was a major change in the shellfish populations themselves, as mussels expanded at the expense of other species.

How important were middens?

The evidence provided by Betty Meehan about the significance of shellfish in Arnhem Land suggests that the high visibility of middens exaggerates the role of shellfish in the Aboriginal diet. Two archaeological examples illustrate this further.

In a general survey of sites around Western Port and Phillip Island, Denise Gaughwin recorded 266 sites; 207 middens, 40 surface lithic scatters, and 19 other sites. From this evidence one might be tempted to think that shellfish dominated the diet of the Bunurong people who lived in the area. However, descriptions of their way of life by William Thomas, the Assistant Protector of Aborigines in the middle of last century, clearly indicates that the inland plains and especially the swamps and wetlands, were the favoured areas for camping and hunting and gathering food plants. Why this discrepancy? It is simply that the inland sites are poorly preserved and when the area is well vegetated, sites simply cannot be found. Middens, clearly visible in coastal dunes, therefore dominate the archaeological record and used uncritically give a false impression of their true significance.

In a more complex analysis Geoffrey Bailey attempted to calculate the food-value of an entire midden on the Richmond River in New South Wales. Here a set of three large middens, composed almost entirely of the Sydney rock oyster (*Crassostria commercialis*), built up over 1650 years between 1750 to 100 BP. From excavations and study of early descriptions of the sites their original volume could be estimated at about 33 000 m^3, representing in the order of 23 100 tonne of shell. The average shell weight to meat weight ratio for oysters is 5:1 so that this represents about 4620 tonne of meat, collected over 1650 years; that is about 2.8 tonne of meat per year. Oysters have a calorific value of 50 kcal/100 g of meat, so that this represents 1 400 000 kcal per year. If the average daily requirement is estimated at 2000 kcal per person, we have enough shellfish meat to provide about 2% of the annual requirements of 100 people, or 8% of the requirements of 25 people. Calculations such as these have great potential for error, but even so they give a clear indication that the massive shell dumps represent only a very small part of the overall economy. The midden sites were probably only used for a few weeks of the year, and the bulk of the diet must have come from plant foods, supplemented by fish and land animals.

PICTURING THE PAST

1 Describe a visit to the coast by:
- a group of women and children spending a few hours collecting shellfish to take back to a main campsite further inland
- a group of men looking for nodules of flint (for making stone tools) washed up on the beach beside a rocky headland
- a larger family camping for several weeks in the dunes between the rocky shore and inland swamps

What differences do you think you might see in the archaeological sites produced by these different activities?

EXERCISE

Table 4.4 and Figure 4.15 show the proportions of different types of shellfish collected.
1 Divide these into more easily collected/less easily collected species: is there any significant change over time?
2 Calculate the relative meat weight of each type; does this change your idea of the relative importance of the different shellfish?

References

Bowdler, S., 1976, 'Hook, Line and Dilly Bag: an Interpretation of an Australian Coastal Shell Midden', *Mankind*, Vol. 10, pp. 248–258.

Bowdler, S., 1983, 'Sieving Seashells: Midden Analysis in Australian Archaeology', in *Australian field archaeology: a guide to techniques*, ed. G. Connah, Australian Institute of Aboriginal Studies, Canberra, pp. 135–144.

Coastal Invertebrates of Victoria: An Atlas of Selected Species, 1984, Marine Research Group of Victoria and The Museum of Victoria, Melbourne.

Frankel, D., 1988, 'Characterising Change in Prehistoric Sequences: a View From Australia', *Archaeology in Oceania*, Vol. 23, pp. 41–48.

Meehan, B., 1982, *Shell Bed to Shell Midden*, Australian Institute of Aboriginal Studies, Canberra.

Zobel, D.E., Vanderwal, R.L. and Frankel, D., 1984, 'The Moonlight Head Rockshelter', *Proceedings of the Royal Society of Victoria*, Vol. 96, pp. 1–24.

5

Rockshelters and caves

People use caves and other rocky overhangs for shelter. In limestone areas caves may be deep, while sandstone rockshelters may be more open, but still well protected from the elements. Other shelters may be shallower, below rock ledges or slight overhangs. Some shelters can accommodate large groups of people, others barely two or three. In many parts of Australia rockshelters are rare, but elsewhere (as in the sandstone areas around Sydney) there are hundreds, although not all suitable sites were used.

Most of the sediment which builds up in shelters is blown or washed in, or weathered off the roof. When people living in shelters discard stone, bone, shell and other material it is incorporated into this slow natural accumulation. This contrasts with sites such as shell middens, where almost all of the deposit is brought in by people.

How important were natural shelters?

Despite an archaeological bias toward excavating caves or rockshelters, we are increasingly aware that they were not necessarily very important at all. At all times people probably built shades, shelters, huts or houses. If we do not assume that natural shelters were highly sought after as places to live, then we can begin to ask why they were used, when they were used and how they were used.

In Australia we certainly have archaeological evidence of occupation in rockshelters. Ethnographic or historical accounts of the use of shelters are, on the other hand, very limited. Natural shelters were probably only used when they were in a convenient location, close to food, water, firewood and other resources. They may have been used casually as convenient overnight camps, or for longer periods as a central base from which to exploit surrounding territory.

> **PREHISTORIC CAVE MEN?**
>
> Most of us have a standard concept of 'prehistoric cave men', created and reinforced by innumerable images from films, cartoons and books. The idea that prehistoric men lived in caves started with the earliest excavations in French caves in the middle of last century. These gave people in Europe their first impressions of ancient, ancestral cave dwellers. Until recently archaeologists have continued to concentrate much of their effort on caves and rockshelters, and so have done little to alter this misleading image, now firmly fixed in the popular mind.

5.1
Courtesy Larry Gonick, 'The Cartoon History of the Universe' Volume 2.

They may have been used by the whole band, or by special groups, such as men out on a long hunting expedition. Paintings and engravings in caves may testify to other, sacred significance, as sites visited for ritual rather than mundane purposes.

Why excavate rockshelters?

If caves and rockshelters were of relatively minor importance, why do archaeologists prefer to excavate them?

Caves trap sediments, which can build up over thousands of years. Deep undisturbed deposits seldom accumulate elsewhere. This means that shelters provide:

- relatively undisturbed deposits
- good preservation of organic material, such as bone
- definable assemblages of dateable artefacts and bone
- long chronological sequences
- possibility of showing periods of use and abandonment

These are particularly important in the early stages of research, when we need to establish a basic chronological sequence. In addition, caves and shelters are often easier to find than other sites, especially in regions with dense vegetation. A further advantage is that they provide clearly defined excavated samples useful for comparison within or between sites, in terms of quantity of as well as types of material.

Problems in excavating caves

Problems of sampling

Most excavations are small and deep. Excavations may be limited to one square metre or to only a small part of the site. In order to use our finds we have to assume that these small samples are typical of the site as a whole. For example, one layer may have many more stone tools than another. This may be taken to show that people were using the site more intensively at one time than another. But could it be that stone tools were simply being made, used and discarded in different parts of the site at different times?

Integrity of deposits

Although relatively stable, material within cave sediments can still be disturbed. Even trampling on the slowly accumulating sediment can cause buried artefacts to move underground. Other activities can have more drastic effects, while burrowing animals (especially rabbits) can do enormous damage.

Stratigraphy and time

Some sites have a colourful sequence of different soils, which archaeologists use to separate stratigraphic units in excavation. Many other sites have no visible distinctions, and are excavated in arbitrary spits. Where larger areas are dug, we may need to assume that the rate of sediment build-up was constant across the site or between the specific points in a sequence dated by radiocarbon. In all cases, we seldom deal with individual events or periods of occupation. Normally we have assemblages representing long periods of time, perhaps hundreds or even thousands of years.

Source of material

Birds, bats, and a variety of other animals (including carnivores such as dingoes and Tasmanian Devils) also live in caves. Some of these die there, others bring their prey home and drop the bones in the site. We need to distinguish between this bone and that discarded by people. Of course natural deposits can themselves be of interest. For example, the range of small mammal bones dropped by owls may give us an idea of the environment around the site.

Case Study 1: Devon Downs Shelter, South Australia

Description

As the Murray River flows south through South Australia it cuts deeply into soft limestone, forming high cliffs on either side. Overhangs at

5.2
A view of the Murray River from the top of the cliffs above Devon Downs Rockshelter.

the base of the cliffs provide shelters close to the river bank. Devon Downs is one such shelter, with soft deposits of limestone eroding off the cliff to form the bulk of the deposit.

The limestone walls above and beside the extensive deposits are marked with a series of simple engraved signs.

Excavations

This site has a special place in the history of archaeological research in Australia. In 1929 Norman Tindale and Herbert Hale excavated the site and provided the first well-documented

5.3
Devon Downs rockshelter at the base of the cliff.

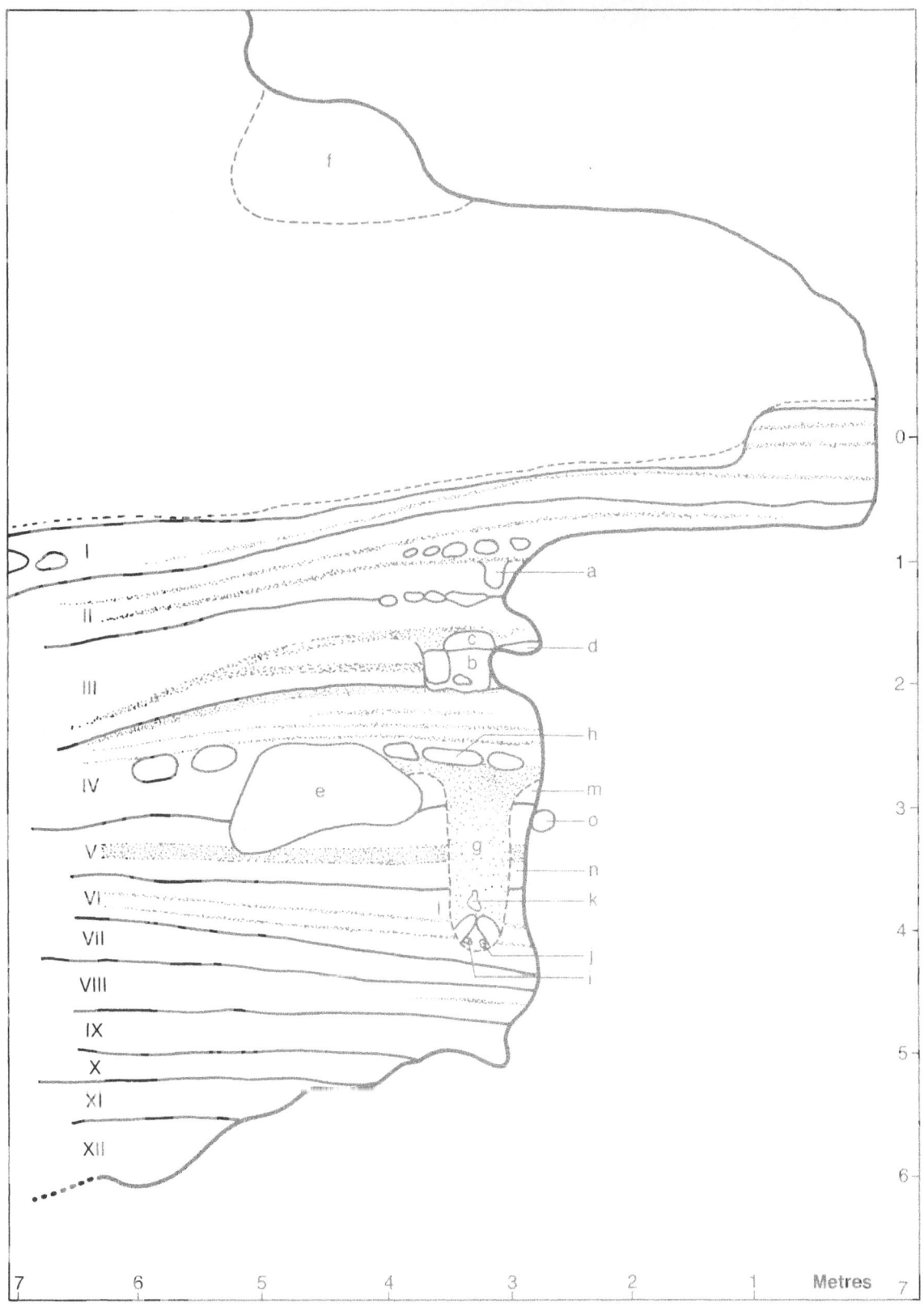

5.4
Section drawing through the deposits at Devon Downs. (After Hale and Tindale 1930)

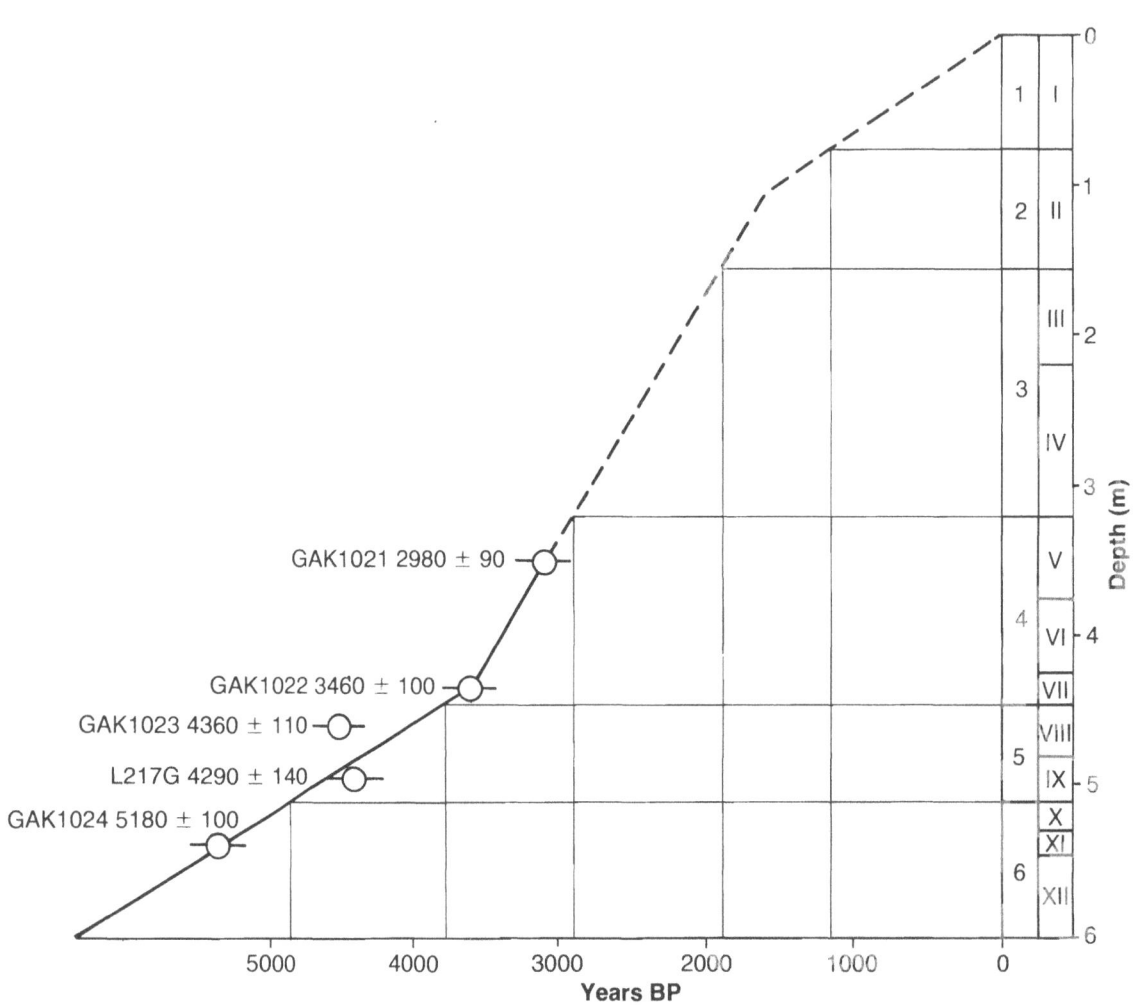

5.5a
Age/depth curves for deposits at Devon Downs. Radiocarbon dates plotted by age and depth give a basis for dividing the site up into equal chronological units. a) Extrapolated curve and division of analytical units according to Smith (1982, Figure 2) b) A different division of the site, assuming a more constant rate of sediment build-up.

stratigraphic sequence of stone tool types, clearly demonstrating prehistoric change.

Several trenches were excavated, the main one to a depth of 6.2 metres, divided into 12 stratigraphic units (I at the top to XII at the bottom).

Analyses

Hale and Tindale used the stone tools in order to define specific types and industries. The need for establishing such a sequence was then of great importance, as before the invention of radiocarbon dating, stone tools provided the only key to the relative age of sites. The industries that they defined are now generally disregarded and different approaches to analysing stone tools have been developed.

Recently the material from these old excavations was reanalysed by Michael Smith, who developed new interpretations of the history and function of the site. His analysis will be discussed here.

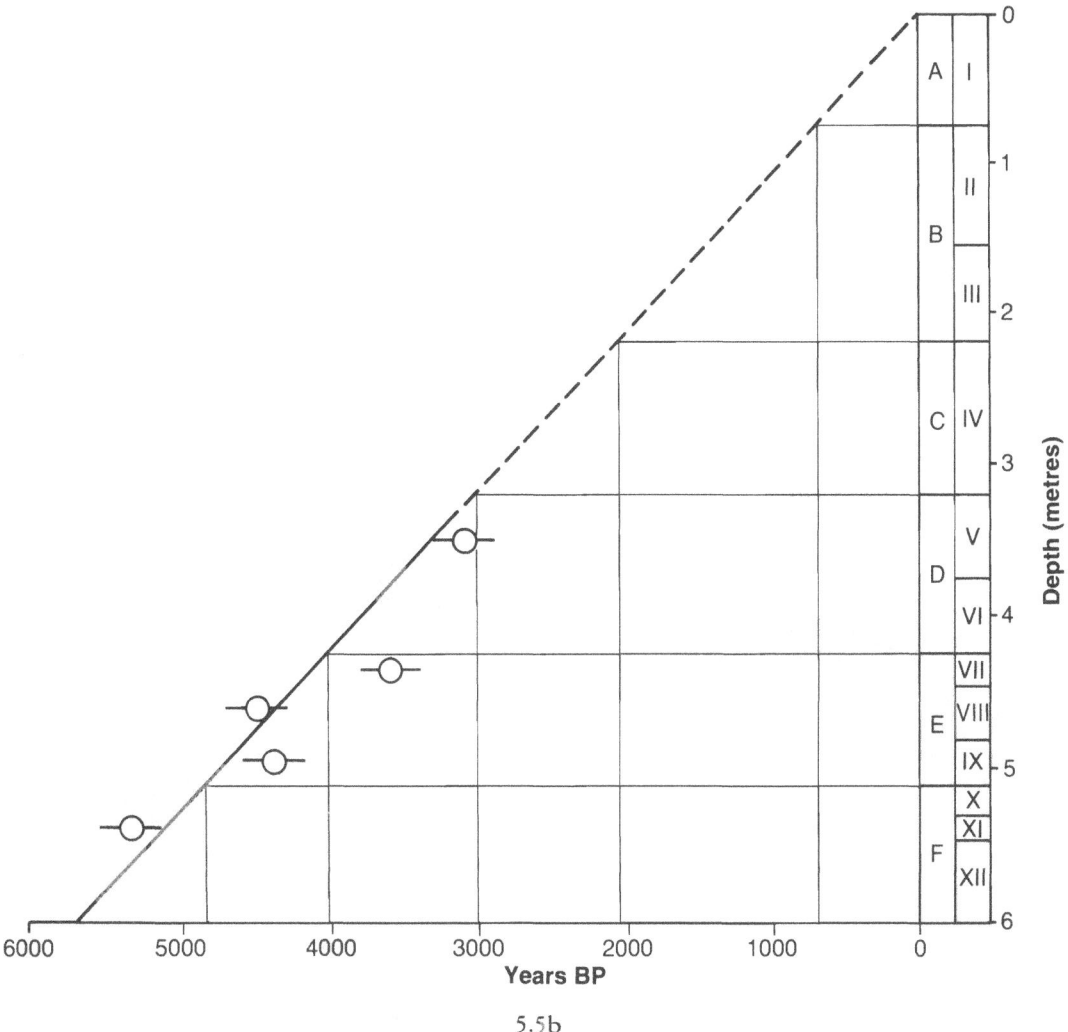

5.5b

Stratigraphy and dating

Five radiocarbon dates from the lower portion of the site show that Devon Downs shelter was occupied from about 6000 years ago, presumably until very recent times (Figures 5.4, 5.5a). Hale and Tindale excavated twelve unequal stratigraphic units. In order to compare relative quantities of material at different times it is necessary to have equal units. Smith decided to create six analytical units, each of about 1000 years duration.

Figure 5.5a shows how he did this. The original excavation units (I to XII) are shown at the appropriate depths on the vertical axis. The horizontal axis represents the age before the present. The five radiocarbon dates have been plotted according to their age and depth. A line through these dates shows the rate at which the site built up. Smith used indirect evidence to argue that the rate of deposition was slower at first, then faster, and finally slower again, and drew his depth/age curve accordingly. Using this he could then read off approximately every 1000 years along the horizontal (age) axis and decide which of Tindale's excavation units fell into each period. The original 12 excavation units (I to XII) were then grouped into six new, more-or-less equal analytical units (1 to 6).

It is possible to divide up the sequence in other ways. If one assumes a constant rate of sediment deposition, then it is possible to draw a straight line correlating depth and age (Figure 5.5b). If we do this, we can group the original excavation units differently to make another set of six new analytical units, which we will label A to F.

We may then have two different sets of analytical units, each including different combinations of the original excavation units in each 1000-year-long block of time, as seen in Table 5.1.

The results of further analyses will depend on which approach we follow. How do we choose which to use? In the absence of further geomorphological evidence on the rate of sedimentation or additional radiocarbon dates, there is no definite answer.

Smith's analysis of the site

Information is available from the site on a range of material: stone, bone, and shell. Smith was interested in comparing the quantity of these in each of his six analytical units, in order to show how the site was used. Tables 5.2, 5.3 and Figures 5.6, 5.7 and 5.8 summarise some of this information.

Stone tools and technology

Units 3 and 4 have many more pieces of stone than the others. Smith suggests that this shows a greater use of the site between 4000 and 2000 years ago.

There is a fairly constant ratio between tools (used pieces of stone) and waste from tool manufacture (unused pieces), but a more detailed look at the proportion of primary flakes that were further modified shows a change. In the lower units, (4, 5, 6) there is a much higher proportion of modified pieces. The earlier flakes are also larger and more uniform, while later ones have less modification and are less uniformly made. Smith therefore argued that there was a technological change between units 3 and 4 (about 3000 years ago).

Stone points (spear barbs) do not occur in the upper two units, suggesting another change in tool types about 2000 years ago.

Bones and economy

The Minimum Numbers (MNI — see Chapter 4) of mammals are also greatest in units 3 and 4, reinforcing the view of a more intensive use of the site between 4000 and 2000 years ago. Emu egg shell is also most common at that time. Crayfish do not occur in the lower units, and it can be suggested that they only began to be exploited after about 3000 years ago. Emus lay eggs in winter or early spring; crayfish are available in autumn. The decline in emu egg shell and increase in crayfish suggests a change in the season of occupation at the site.

Table 5.1 Alternative groupings of Tindale's excavation units into analytical units

Smith's units	Original units	Age, years ago	Original units	New units
1	I	0–1000	I	A
2	II	1000–2000	II+III	B
3	III+IV	2000–3000	IV	C
4	V+VI+VII	3000–4000	V+VI	D
5	VIII+IX	4000–5000	VII+VIII+IX	E
6	X+XI+XII	5000–6000	X+XI+XII	F

Table 5.2 Summary of data from Devon Downs arranged by analytical units defined by Smith

Unit	1	2	3	4	5	6
Age (1000 yr BP)	<1	1–2	2–3	3–4	4–5	5–6
Artefacts						
Total number of pieces of stone	32	47	504	539	255	120
% tools	19	17	14	13	10	15
Number of stone points	0	0	2	2	13	6
Number of bone points	0	1	1	35	20	7
Animal remains						
All mammals MNI	8	13	34	54	18	6
Kangaroo MNI	1	0	2	4	2	2
Fish MNI	4	6	9	9	5	3
Reptiles MNI	7	2	11	17	11	4
Crayfish MNI	61	50	48	2	0	0
Shell weight (g)	1023	390	361	718	782	*
Emu egg shell (g)	0	1	8	15	4	1

Table 5.3 Same data arranged according to an alternative set of analytical units

Unit	A	B	C	D	E	F
Age (1000 yr BP)	<1	1–2	2–3	3–4	4–5	5–6
Artefacts						
Total number of pieces of stone	32	138	413	411	383	120
% tools	19	10	16	11	19	15
Number of stone points	0	0	2	1	14	6
Number of bone points	0	1	0	18	37	8
Animal remains						
All mammals MNI	8	25	22	30	39	6
Kangaroo MNI	1	1	1	3	3	2
Fish MNI	4	12	3	5	9	3
Reptiles MNI	7	7	6	10	25	4
Crayfish MNI	61	73	25	2	0	0
Shell weight (g)	1023	446	205	516	984	*

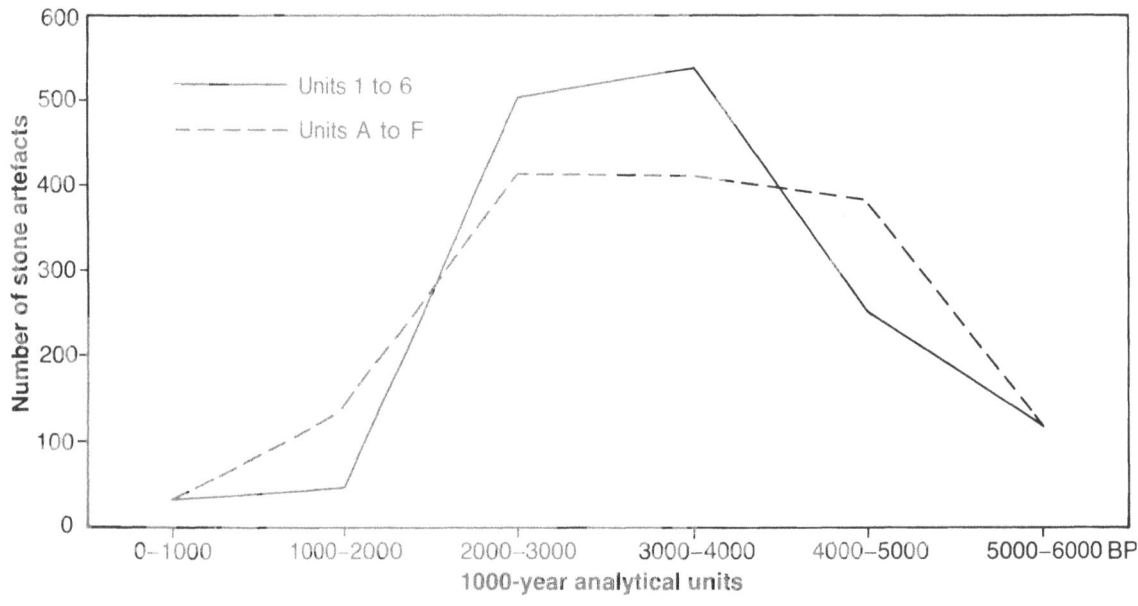

5.6

Number of stone artefacts in each 1000-year-long analytical unit at Devon Downs, using two different rates of sediment accumulation. Units 1–6 according to Smith's division of the site; Units A-F according to an alternative organisation of the material. (Data supplied by M.A. Smith)

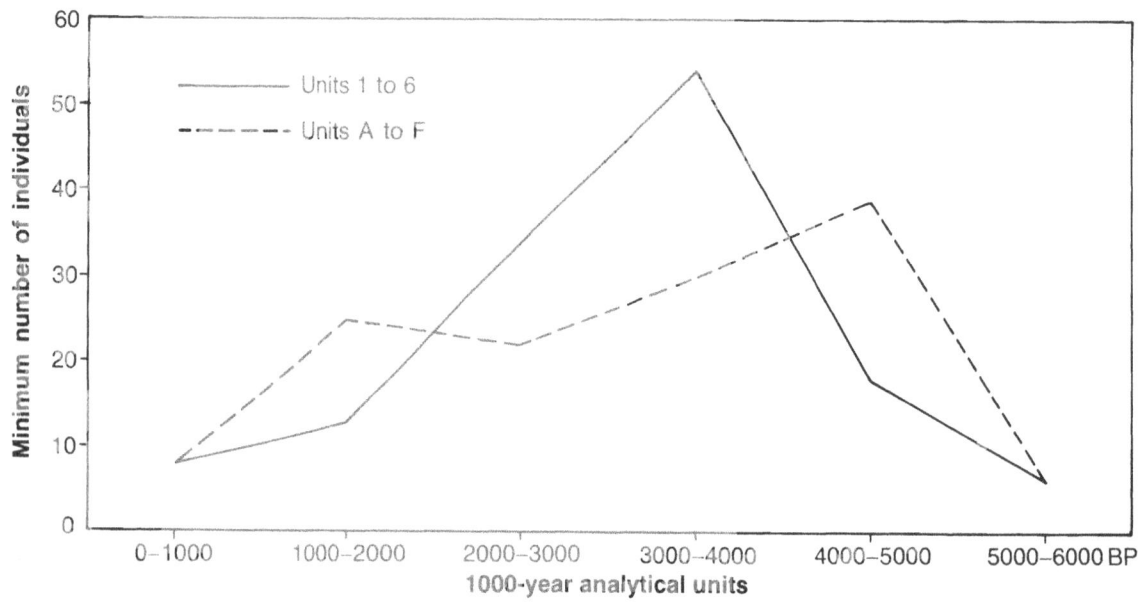

5.7

Minimum number of animals in each 1000-year-long analytical unit at Devon Downs, using two different rates of sediment accumulation. Units 1–6 according to Smith's division of the site; Units A-F according to an alternative organisation of the material. (Data supplied by M.A. Smith)

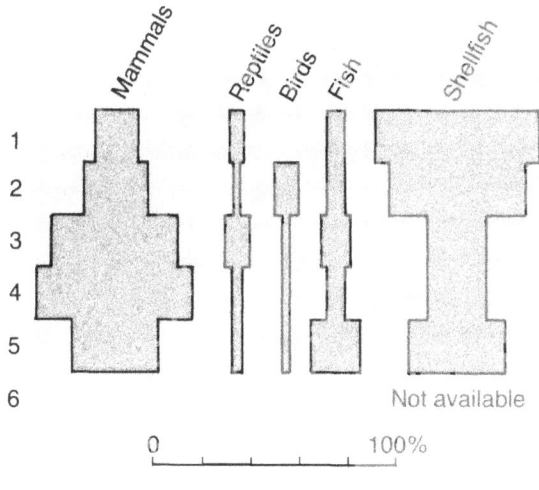

5.8
Relative meat-weight contribution of different resources through the sequence at Devon Downs. Mammals decline in importance while shellfish increase. (After Smith 1982, Figure 3)

If we compensate for meat-weight contribution (see Chapter 4) then we can see changing patterns of exploitation more clearly (Figure 5.8). While fish, reptiles and birds always contribute similar, minor quantities to the diet, the decline in dominance of mammals from unit 4 to unit 1, and the corresponding increase in importance of freshwater shellfish can be clearly seen. There is therefore a change in the way the site was used, especially after about 2000 years ago.

The drop in mammal consumption is largely a measure of the reduction in the number of large kangaroos in the upper units. This correlates with the dropping of stone points, indicating a change in emphasis in large-game hunting.

Analysis using alternative analytical units

The data prepared by Smith is reorganised in Table 5.3b and Figure 5.7 according to the set of analytical units defined using a uniform rate of sedimentation. Some basic structures are the same, but there are some interesting differences.

A high number of stone artefacts and mammal bone is now seen in three units (C, D, E) suggesting a constant intensity of site use for 3000 years, rather than the shorter, more intensive period of use. This makes the high number of points in the second-lowest unit (E) easier to understand. It is also possible that the sudden drop in numbers of stone points between units E and F indicates that this tool-type dropped out of use about 4000 years ago. The few later examples may be old items, moved or redeposited by later activity at the site.

Conclusions

Hale and Tindale originally viewed the site as a succession of different stone tool industries representing a series of new groups of people coming into the area. This can now be replaced by a more complex view of change.

Smith's main conclusions may be summarised as follows, with alternative suggestions based on the different view of sedimentary history.

1. A marked increase in intensity of site use between 4000 and 2000 years ago. Alternatively, a more constant intensity of site use between 5000 and 2000 years ago.
2. A basic change in stone technology about 3000 years ago (alternatively, 4000 years ago).
3. A change in seasonal use about 3000 years ago, from winter or spring to autumn.
4. Greater use of shellfish around 2000 years ago, with a slow reduction in the proportion of mammals in the diet. Smith suggests that this reflects local changes in the river channel.

Whichever form of the data one uses, it is clear that there were a number of changes in how people used the site, when they used it and what foods they ate. These changes did not all come at once and we have a series of different shifts in behaviour. Some, such as the increasing use of shellfish, may be responses to very local changes in the environment. Others, such as the season of use of the site, must reflect changes in how people scheduled their activities through the year. Changes to simpler tools may be part of general trends across much of south-east Australia, while the dropping of stone spear-barbs may reflect a change in hunting strategy or techniques.

Case Study 2: Koongine Cave, South Australia

Description

Koongine Cave is set in a limestone ridge, about 4 km from the sea. One can look south from the site across low swampy wetlands to the 'beach ridge' of the present coastline.

The accessible area of the cave is about 11 m wide and 25 m deep. The present floor is about 1.5 m below the roof near the entrance, but drops down about one third of the way in as there are no accumulated sediments toward the back of the cave.

Nodules and veins of flint, suitable for making stone tools, protrude from the walls and roof of the cave, and may also be traced along the ridge outside.

On one wall is an extensive panel of long sets of parallel lines scratched into the soft surface. Although there is a suggestion that these are animal markings, they may have been made by people, and are part of a widespread tradition of similar marks found in limestone caves from Perth to eastern Victoria. Those deep underground in Koonalda Cave in the Nullarbor Plain are 20 000 years old.

5.9
Excavations in progress outside the entrance to Koongine Cave in the lower south-east of South Australia.

5.10
Ken Mulvaney excavating the initial test-pit at Koongine Cave in 1985.

Aims and excavation strategy

I used two different styles of excavation at Koongine Cave; a small test-excavation and an extensive open-area approach.

Test excavations in 1985

The aim was simple; to see if there were any undisturbed deposits in the cave, and to obtain a first impression of their depth, age and contents. A 1 m × 1 m area was excavated to a depth of about 2 m, separating each definable layer. As the sediments in this site are clearly distinct in colour and texture they could easily be separated. Rabbit burrows were a nuisance but, as they could easily be identified, they did not confuse the stratigraphy.

Open area excavations in 1986-7

The aim in this later season was more unusual, complex and open-ended. The clear stratigraphy in the site made it possible to consider tracing different deposits, over large areas, in order to

5.11
In 1987 excavations removed single layers across wide areas of the site.

5.12
Stratigraphic layers in the test-pit at Koongine Cave in 1985.

investigate spatial patterning within the cave and how people made use of this enclosed space.

To do this I used a different style of excavation, taking off thin layers over a large space rather than digging deeply in a small area. Each thin layer (2 to 3 cm) of different sediment was removed in turn over its entire extent, and the bones and stones recorded within small cells, 25 cm × 25 cm. Excavation on this scale is very time-consuming and we were only able to excavate the upper deposits on one side of the cave.

Stratigraphy and dating

The 1985 test excavation provides a basic view of the history of use of this cave. The sequence of deposits is seen in Figure 5.13. From the radiocarbon dates we see that most of the sediment accumulated in the site over about 1500 years, from some time after 10 000 to nearly 8000 years ago. The cave was then no longer used, and for over 7000 years no sediments built up in it. Within the last few hundred years people once again made use of the site.

This history of use and abandonment of the cave contrasts with Devon Downs, where there was apparently continuous sedimentation, and no break in occupation.

The later excavations in the eastern half of the cave show how some of the upper, very recent

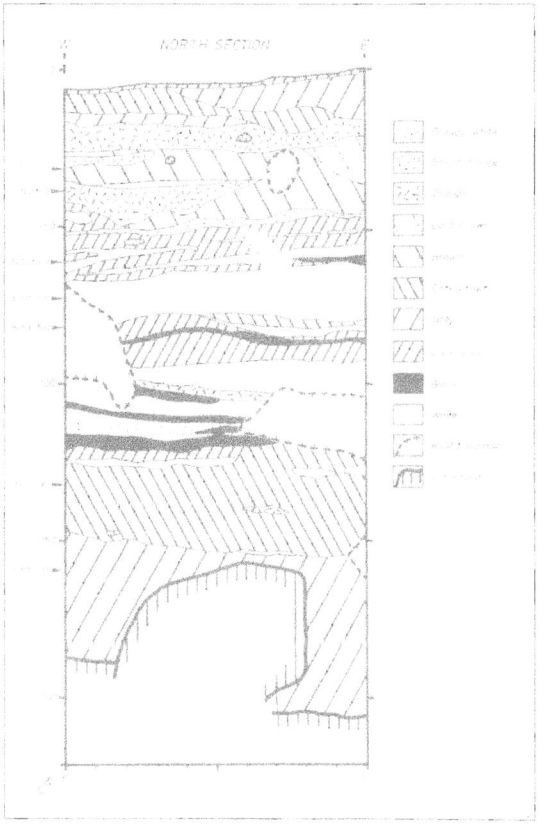

5.13
Section drawing through deposits at Koongine Cave, showing depth of seven radiocarbon dates.

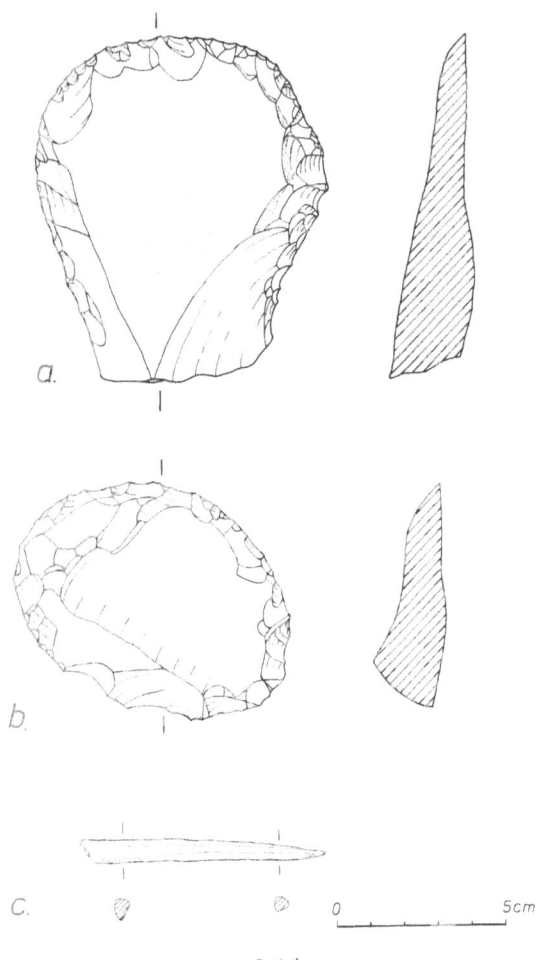

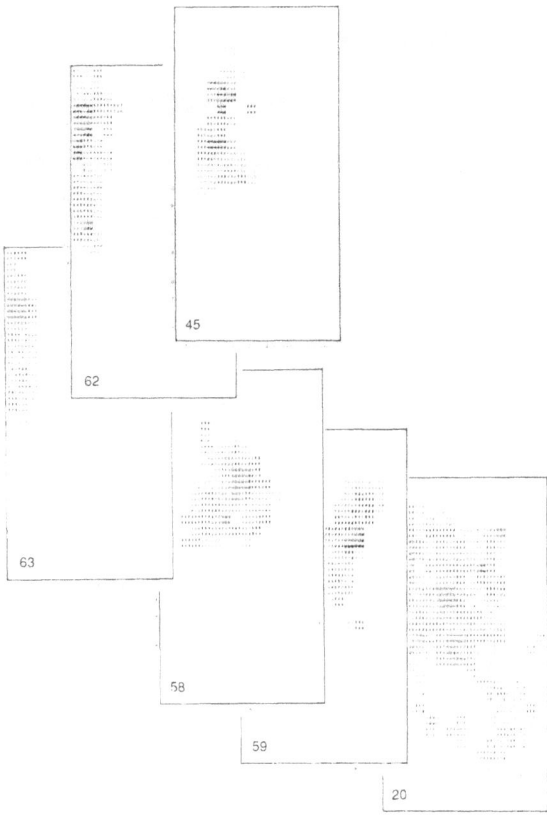

5.15
Distribution of archaeological deposits in space. Different soil colour and texture are used to define and separate layers. Each is a different size and shape. The rectangle around each is the same, but has been offset so that the position of each of the six superimposed layers can be seen. The density of shading indicates the relative quantity of flint fragments in each part of the site.

5.14
Figures a and b are large flint tools of the 'Gambieran Industry' from the lower part of Koongine Cave. Figure c is a bone point from the site.

sediments were deposited, as small patches, partly overlapping in an uneven mosaic. This demonstrates the complexity of site formation and sediment accumulation.

Spatial patterning in the site

Figure 5.19 shows the distribution of stone and bone fragments in one thin (2 to 3 cm) stratigraphic layer over an area of about 12 m² in part of the site. The blank square is where the earlier test excavation was carried out. It is immediately apparent that the distribution of material was far from even; some areas have far more pieces than others, and bone and stone differ from one another. There are similar patchy distributions of a range of other categories, such as the proportion of burnt stone and bone, size of pieces of stone and so on.

What are the implications of this?

Although nearly half of the floor area was investigated in this way, this is still not enough to allow us to discuss how people made use of space in the cave. Nevertheless some things can already be seen. For example, stones and bones were not tossed or swept aside to the edges of the cave as one might have expected. The variability in density across space reminds us of the

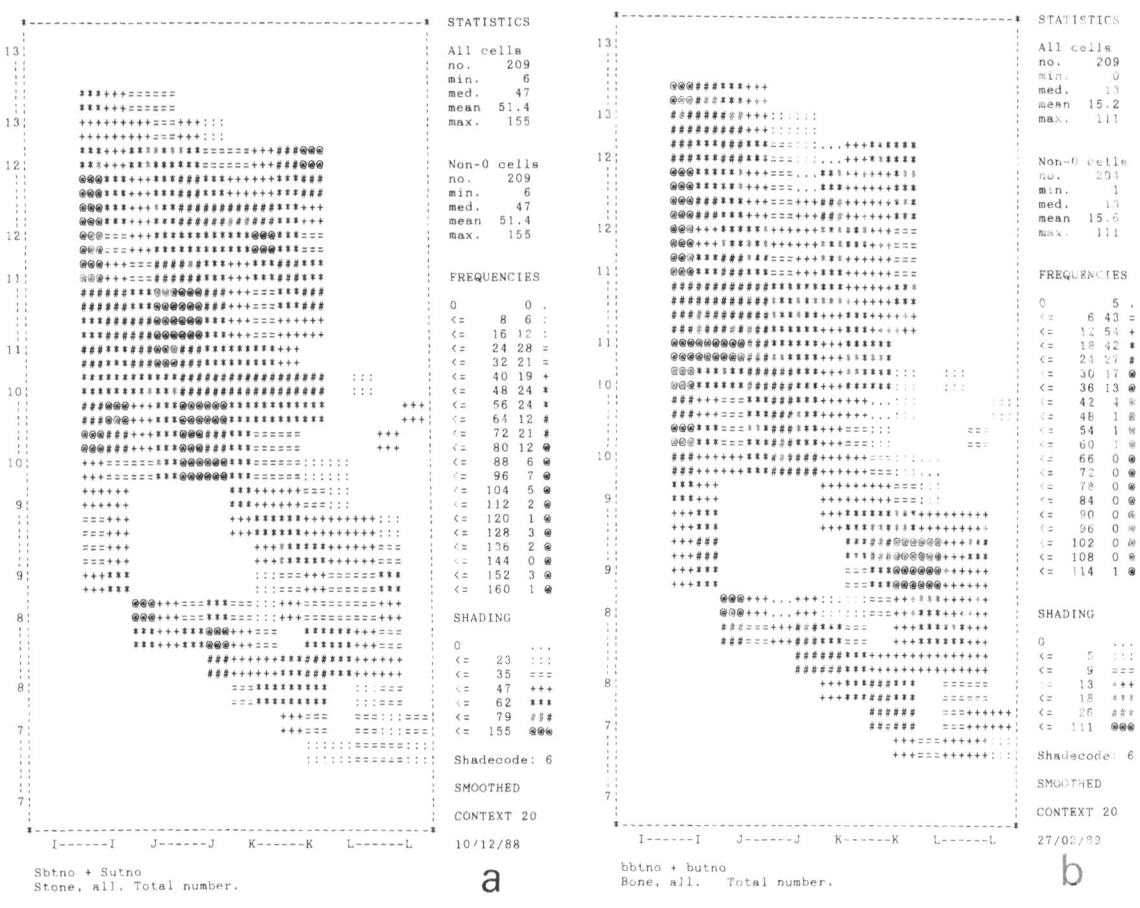

5.16
Distribution of material in one thin layer at Koongine Cave. a) Number of pieces of stone. b) Number of pieces of bone. The 1 m × 1 m blank square marks the location of the previously excavated test-pit.

dangers of using evidence from small excavations to suggest changing intensity or nature of site use.

Site history

The early period, before 8000 years ago, contains large stone tools typical of the 'Gambieran Industry' characteristic of the local area at that time. Hundreds of these tools have been collected from open sites nearby, but the only other site with similar tools in a dated context is at Wyrie Swamp, about 40 km to the north-west. The Wyrie Swamp tools are associated with a unique collection of 10 000-year-old wooden artefacts, preserved in the peat. The boomerangs, single-piece spears and digging-sticks show what was made using some of these stone tools and reminds us of what is missing from all other archaeological sites.

As noted in the section on middens, Roger Luebbers regards the Wyrie Swamp site as typical of wetland occupation common in the region between about 10 000 and 6000 years ago. He argues that later climatic changes reduced the extent and productivity of the wetlands and people began to make more use of the coast.

Similar environmental changes, together with the effects of rising sea-levels, may account for the abandonment of Koongine Cave. Here it is important to recognise that although fixed in space, a cave (or any other site) can change its place in the landscape. Sites do not always have the same relationship to resources.

People make choices about which resources they will use and how they use them. Settlement patterns reflect these choices. It is obviously better to camp near fixed food resources (such as plants) rather than mobile ones (such as kangaroos) but is it better to be closer to water, shade, protection from the wind or firewood? When is it better to be based near the sea with easy access to shellfish or inland nearer to useful plants? In general, people will organise themselves to live at the most convenient locations—those which give the most efficient access to the most resources.

One hypothesis to explain the abandonment of Koongine is based on a general model of a separation between inland and coastal exploitation. We can suggest that in some seasons people based themselves behind the beach dunes, with easy access to seafood in one direction, and plants and animals of the wetlands in the other. At other times inland resources of the open woodland were preferred and camps were placed to give efficient access to these areas as well as the coastal wetlands. Camps would be situated so that the territories exploited from each did not substantially overlap.

Figure 5.17 applies this model to Koongine at two different times, as it changed its place in the landscape.

At the time of main occupation, between 10 000 and 8000 years ago, sea levels were lower and the coast would have been 15 or 20 km from the site. A wide area of low-lying wetland probably stretched between the beach dunes and limestone ridge in which the cave is set. The coastal dunes and the inland ridge would each have been used as the focus for one half of our hypothetical two-part pattern of settlement. Koongine Cave was at this time in an appropriate place in relation to woodland to the north and coastal swamp to the south, so that people took advantage of the natural shelter it provided.

Later, as the sea rose, the place of the limestone ridge and the cave changed. The coastal dunes were now only four or five kilometres away from the limestone ridge. People camped near the beach could have access to all the wetlands. Inland camps would be placed further north, away from the territory exploited from the coastal sites. While centrally located in relation to woodland resources, they could still include the wetlands at one extreme of their territory. The cave was no longer an efficient place from which to forage, and so dropped out of use.

Further discussion

At the eastern end of Discovery Bay in Victoria, about 150 km east of Koongine Cave, another important limestone cave, Bridgewater Cave South was excavated by Harry Lourandos. In general terms the location and history of occupation of this site is similar to that at Koongine, with a roughly contemporary early period of occupation followed by an equally long abandonment and recent reuse in the last few hundred years.

Lourandos argues that the two periods of use are very different, and that the recent phase shows a far more intensive use of the site than the earlier one. He builds this into a general history of prehistoric developments in western Victoria. In essence he argues that over the last 4000 years there was a marked increase in social and economic activity, possibly linked to a growth in population. There are therefore more sites, and a more intensive use of sites.

In other words he sees the history of occupation at sites such as Bridgewater Cave representing a broad regional process of change. This contrasts with the environmental explanation suggested above for the history of occupation at Koongine. At Devon Downs, too, much change was seen as response to local factors, rather than symptomatic of cultural evolution.

Which approach is the better? When is it appropriate to explain individual sites in local terms, and when as representing regional developments? Which aspects of change are part of general trends, and which are not? These are fundamental questions, for which we still have no clear answers. Later chapters concentrate again on individual sites, but we must also attempt to combine the evidence from all these separate

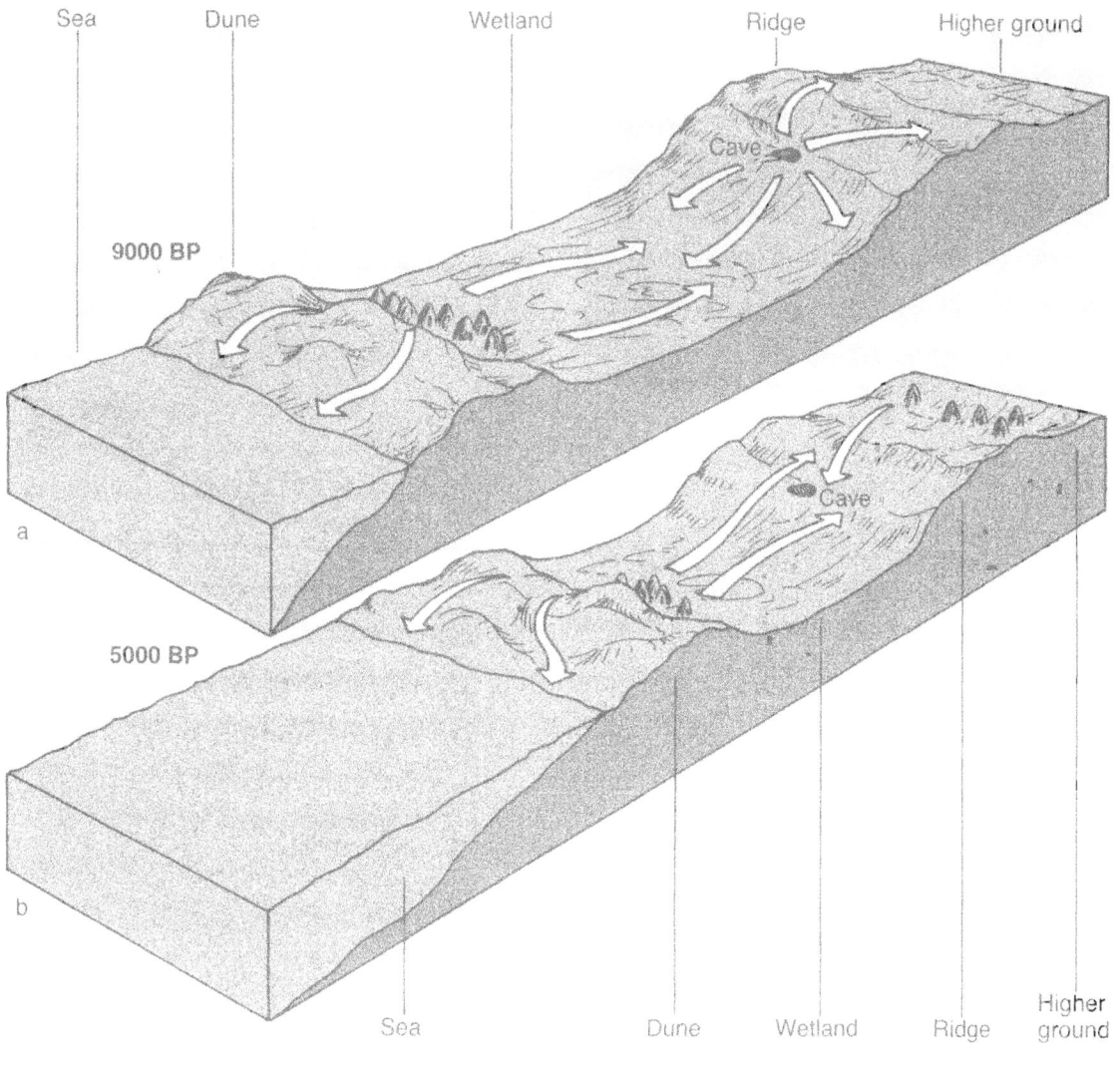

5.17
Hypothetical model of settlement pattern and exploitation strategy for two periods. a) About 10 000 to 8000 years ago, when Koongine Cave was most frequently used. At this time the sea was much further south. We may imagine occupation sites behind the dunes from which marine and swamp resources could be exploited. The cave was conveniently located and served as a base for exploiting drier woodland to the north and swamps to the south. b) After sea-level rose, the cave was no longer in a favourable position, and the focus of inland exploitation moved further north.

studies to understand how and why societies in Australia developed the way that they did.

POINTS FOR DISCUSSION

1 The analyses at Devon Downs grouped material into 1000-year analytical units or 'periods'.

How many generations of people may have lived during 1000 years?
What do we really mean by 1000 years of occupation at a site?

2 To what extent can material from older excavations be reanalysed; what limits are placed on it by the nature of the original excavation?

5.18
Bridgewater Caves at the eastern end of Discovery Bay, Victoria.

3 Should the Devon Downs site be re-excavated?
4 What was the impact of rising sea levels on the people who sometimes used Koongine Cave?

PICTURING THE PAST

Describe the activities carried out by people using the Devon Downs shelter:

- between 4000 and 3000 years ago
- after 3000 years ago

When did people use the site? What food did they collect and eat? What else did they do there?

DEBATE: TIME OR SPACE

A suggested debate in Chapter 1 contrasted the relative merits of surveys and excavations. Similarly, small, deep excavations give stratigraphy and chronology, but little idea of the way sites were used. Broad-scale excavations may give details of short episodes, but little idea of change and development. Debate the advantages and disadvantages of these two approaches.

EXERCISE: SITE LOCATION

Fig. 5.19 shows the distribution of various resources: where would you choose as the most convenient place to camp?

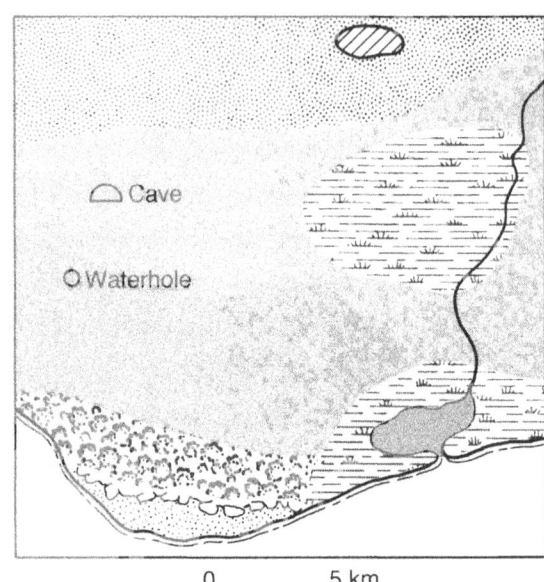

Estuary (fish, waterfowl)
Wetlands (plant food)
Coastal scrub (wallaby, plants)
Rock platform (shellfish)
Grassy plains (emu, kangaroo, grass seed)
Hilly open woodland (possum, wallaby)
Stone quarry

5.19

EXERCISE: DEPTH AND AGE AT DEVON DOWNS

Some analyses of Devon Downs depend on how you assess the rate at which sediment built up. Two slightly different diagrams are discussed in the text. These use conventional radiocarbon dates.

An added complication in using radiocarbon dates is that radiocarbon years are not the same as calendar years. As we go further back in time, radiocarbon dates are increasingly younger than the 'real' age. Various techniques are now available for calibrating radiocarbon dates to provide ages in calendar years.

Table 5.4 gives the radiocarbon dates (Age

Table 5.4 Radiocarbon dates from Devon Downs

Layer	Aprx. depth in cm	Lab Code	Age BP	Age range CALBP
5	350	GaK-1021	2980 ± 90	3004–3338
7	425	GaK-1022	3460 ± 100	3629–3859
8	475	GaK-1023	4360 ± 110	4849–5214
9	500	L 271 G	4290 ± 140	4648–5040
11	550	GaK-1024	5180 ± 100	5729–6165

BP) and the range of their equivalent calibrated dates in calendar years (CALBP) for Devon Downs. Use this information to draw your own depth/age curve for the site. What difference does this make?

♦How would you group the original excavation units to create thousand-year-long analytical units?

References

Frankel, D., 1986, 'Excavations in the Lower South-East of South Austalia, November 1985', *Australian Archaeology*, Vol. 22, pp. 75–87.

Frankel, D., 1988, 'Characterising Change in Prehistoric Sequences: a View From Australia', *Archaeology in Oceania*, Vol. 23, pp. 41–48.

Frankel, D., 1989, 'Koongine Cave Excavations 1986-7: Investigating Spatial Patterning', *Australian Archaeology*, Vol. 28, pp. 3–13.

Hale, H.M. and Tindale, N.B., 1930, 'Notes on Some Human Remains in the Lower Murray Valley, South Australia', *Records of the South Australian Museum*, Vol. 4, pp. 145–218.

Lourandos, H., 1983, 'Intensification: a Late Pleistocene-Holocene Archaeological Sequence from Southwestern Victoria', *Archaeology in Oceania*, Vol. 18, pp. 81–97.

Smith, M.A., 1982, 'Devon Down Reconsidered: Changes in Site Use at a Lower Murray Valley Rockshelter', *Archaeology in Oceania*, Vol. 17, pp. 109–116.

6

Mounds

Mounds, as an archaeologically defined site-type, are open inland sites artificially raised above their surroundings. Although the term conjures up images of large, high structures, the majority are small and low, and are now often barely visible.

Mounds have a limited distribution. They are only found in parts of the tropical north and certain sections of south-eastern Australia. In the low-lying floodplains and wetlands of Arnhem Land, Aboriginal people build raised dry foundations out of old termite mounds for their seasonal camps. Mounds in the south-east take a variety of forms, and in this chapter we will concentrate on those of the Murray River valley and western Victoria.

Historical accounts of Aboriginal mounds

We have numerous accounts of Aboriginal mounds written last century by European explorers, officials, and settlers. Some even conducted excavations to test their ideas about mound construction and function. Some also report personal observations of Aboriginal people occupying mound sites. Most describe abandoned mounds and discuss their form and possible function with varying degrees of reliability.

Murray River mounds, although also used as camping places, are generally recorded as 'oven-mounds' formed by heaping up the rake-out from earth ovens. In this area plants and perhaps also animals were cooked in earth ovens. Fires were set in shallow pits and lumps of clay heated in them. When the clay balls were hot they were removed, and the pit lined with damp grass on which the food was placed and covered with another layer of damp grass. The hot clay balls were then put on top and the pit covered over. When cooking was complete the pit was re-opened, the clay heat-retainers and ash and other debris raked aside, and the food eaten. Rake-out from repeated cooking gradually accumulated to form a mound.

Similar functions are ascribed to 'myrnong-mounds' of western Victoria, but these are more commonly described as occupation sites and hut foundations.

HISTORICAL DESCRIPTIONS OF MOUNDS

George Augustus Robinson, Chief Protector of Aborigines for Victoria (1839–1849) saw numerous mounds on his travels through western Victoria in 1841:

> ... a large mound of at least 4 feet high and 10 feet long and 5 wide [1.2 × 3 × 1.6 m].

6.1
Sketch by William Thomas of a group of huts in western Victoria. Similar huts may have been built on mounds. (MS 8781 R.Brough Smyth Papers, State Library of Victoria)

My native companions said it was a black man's house, a large one like a white man's house. There were pieces of sticks among the earth, about 3 inches [7.5 cm] diameter, and it appeared that the whole had been burnt down. A short distance from this, was the remains of another hut of a similar description. (Presland, G. 1977, p. 48)

Two years later he travelled through the area again, and noted more:

[Crossing] from Faries to Muston's passed several large mounds or ash hills. 3 were together and others at a short distance. 1 was 8 feet high by 40 feet wide, 50 long [2.4 × 12 × 15 m]. Others I saw at a distance. It is not possible to look on them and say that the N[atives] were not a human race. (Clark, I.D. 1988, p. 18)

In 1868, J. Francis, the superintendent of the Condah Mission Station wrote in a letter that Aboriginal people at the Mission explained that:

The mounds are the remains of old mia-mias and the accumulations of ashes. We lived in them. (this is the testimony of several old people

— J.F.) ... we used to cook the old kangaroos ... in ovens as they are termed — a hole made in the ground or ashes, which was made but with live embers, and sometimes hot stones ... (Williams, E., 1988, p. 11)

James Dawson, writing in 1881 about Aboriginal life as he observed it earlier in the nineteenth century, argued that:

> Native mounds, so common all over the country ... were the sites of large, permanent habitations, which formed houses for many generations. The great size of some of them, and the vast accumulation of burnt earth, charcoal and ashes which is found in and around them, is accounted for by the long continuance of the domestic hearth, the decomposition of building materials, and the debris resulting from their frequent destruction by bush fires. They were never ovens, or original places of interment, as is generally supposed ... The popular notion of their having been ovens is refuted, not only by the unanimous testimony of all the old aborigines, but also by careful examination of the structure and stratification of the mounds. (Dawson, J., 1881, p. 103)

P. Beveridge published several accounts of observations of Aboriginal life in the Murray.

> Black fellows' ovens are not by any means misnomers, as to all intents and purposes they are essentially genuine cooking places, or cooking places and kitchen middens combined, and following is the manner of their formation: A family, or perhaps several families, as the case may be, select a site for their camp, where abundance of game and other sources of food obtain and are procurable with the least expenditure of time and labour ....
>
> ... several of the *lyors* (women) go off with their yam sticks; when they reach the spot selected for the purpose, they begin with a will to excavate a hole about 3 feet (90 cm) in diameter and nearly 2 feet (60 cm) deep; during the digging of this hole any pieces of clay which they chip out, in size similar to ordinary road metal, are placed carefully on one side with a view to their future use.
>
> When the hole has been dug sufficiently deep, it is swept or brushed out with some boughs or a bunch of grass; it is then filled to the top or a little above with firewood, which the *lyors* have previously selected for that purpose. On top of the firewood the selected pieces of clay are then carefully placed, the wood then ignited, and by the time it is all burned the clay nodules have become baked until they are exactly similar to irregular sections of well burnt brick; of course they are red hot. When this result has been properly achieved, the hot clay is removed from the hole; for this purpose they use two pieces of stick about 8 inches [20 cm] long .... {food and hot clay balls are placed in the hole and covered.}
>
> When cooking has been completed, the covering is scraped off, and the debris, consisting of calcined clay and burnt earth, becomes the nucleus of a black fellow's oven, such as are to be seen at the present day. This process being repeated at short intervals, over a series of years, perhaps centuries results in the mounds which are in reality black's ovens ....
>
> As a general rule the Aborigines do not erect the *loondthals* (huts) on these cooking mounds; an exception to this exists, however on the extensive reedy plains of the lower rivers, which are annually inundated, remaining so for at least five months of the year. (Beveridge, P., 1883, pp. 37–39)

Questions about mounds

The historical and archaeological evidence that we have at present opens up several closely related questions:

- Are all mounds the same?
- When did mounds develop, and why?
- What were mounds used for?
- In which regions are mounds found?
- How were mounds positioned on the landscape?
- Are groups of mounds long-term, large villages?

Problems in investigating mounds

One of the main problems in studying mounds is that they are frequently poorly preserved. As

6.2
A very large mound (DP/1) near Swan Hill, during excavations by Peter Coutts of the Victoria Archaeological Survey. (Photo: Victoria Archaeological Survey)

6.3
A mound rises above flood waters near Swan Hill. (Photo: Victoria Archaeological Survey)

mounds are generally softer and looser than surrounding soil, they attract rabbits, whose burrows disturb or destroy the archaeological deposits. This destruction has been taken further by farmers and rabbiters in their attempts to eradicate rabbits. Mounds have also often been ploughed away, especially in the richer agricultural areas of western Victoria. Similarly flood controls and agricultural development in the Murray River system destroys these sites. In that area, silt deposited by floodwater may gradually cover mounds, so that only the most recent can be seen.

As always we are limited in our ability to determine the age and length of occupation of sites, or to show that any two mounds were used at the same time. This makes it difficult to argue that groups of mounds were part of the same settlement system, or represent single villages.

Case study 1: Barham, NSW

Geographical setting

Before controlling barrages were built, the water level in the Murray River and its branches and channels fluctuated regularly through the seasons. Water would gradually rise in the autumn, reaching a peak in winter, between May and July. By November flood levels were beginning to fall, and the water level would be low over the summer, especially between February and March.

At all times there would have been a wide and reliable variety of food resources in the area, which was one of the richest in all of Australia. There were fish, shellfish and yabbies in the rivers as well as plant foods, water fowl and a variety of land animals.

The Wakool River is a major side-branch of the Murray, meandering through the flat lands of the central Murray Valley. Each year as the water rose it would flow up shallow side-branches, filling in depressions. Eventually, at the height of the flood it would overflow and wash across the flat open woodland. In spring and summer the water retreated, leaving isolated billabongs which gradually dried out until water remained only in the main channel.

In 1983 Annette Berryman was working on a postgraduate research project on Murray Valley mounds. A 250 ha section beside the Wakool River provided a suitable location for detailed study, and she and I spent two field seasons surveying and excavating in the area.

Aims and approaches

Archaeological survey. Our initial fieldwork was a complete survey of the 250 ha block. Our interest here was in the spatial patterning of mounds, to see where sites were located in relation to one another and to different water channels and other landscape features.

Excavation of selected mounds. By excavating small areas of several mounds we hoped to demonstrate their form, history of construction and age.

Off-mound activity. Much activity probably took place beside, rather than on top of, mounds. We hoped to find some evidence of this by testing the area around mounds.

Archaeological survey

Thirteen of us spent four days surveying the area.

In order to ensure that we looked over the whole area completely and to help us locate the position of each site, we set out fixed markers at intervals across the block, and marked out a series of 100 m wide transects running back from the main channel. Teams of three or four people than walked up and down these lanes, identifying mounds, plotting their location as accurately as they could on air-photos, measuring their size and recording their appearance. We were fortunate that at that time a two-year drought had broken and new grass was just beginning to grow in the most favourable locations — the softer, richer soils of mounds. This made initial identification of the smaller examples much easier.

Later we went back to each mound, checked its description and took a series of levels over the whole block, as well as beside and on top of every mound. We then had information on the relative height of the ground surface and of each mound, which we could relate to changing flood levels.

In this way we recorded 95 mounds as well as 11 trees bearing the scars where bark had been

6.5
Mound F3, one of the larger mounds beside the Wakool River.

6.4
Roger Hall plotting the location of a mound on an aerial photograph of the Wakool study area.

6.6
Surveying mound F3.

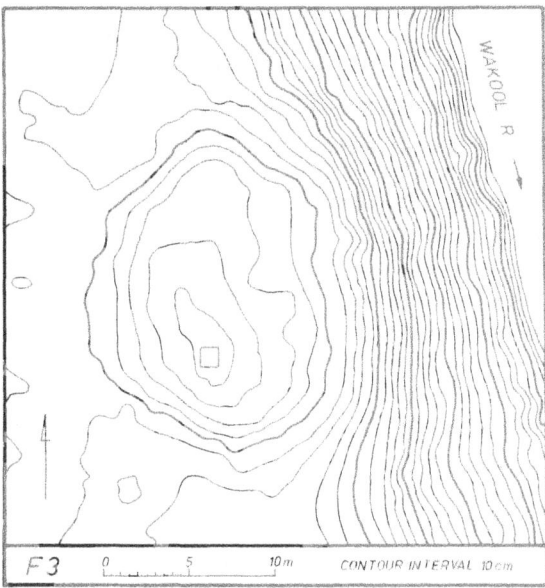

6.7
A contour plan of Mound F3. (Berryman and Frankel 1984, Figure 4)

6.8
Recording one of the smaller mounds further from the main water-channels.

6.9
A tree beside the river bears a scar showing where bark was removed, perhaps to make a small canoe.

removed to make canoes. The location of the mounds is shown in Figure 6.10.

The mounds vary in diameter from 8 m to 48 m, but most are between 10 m and 22 m. Most are less than 40 cm high, but some rise as much as 1.5 m above the surrounding soil.

The biggest mounds are only found along the main river channel and billabongs and appear to be fairly evenly spaced along them; medium-sized mounds are more widely spread.

Excavation of selected mounds

A much larger team worked for two weeks in May 1983 when we carried out limited excavations at three mounds, one of each size. Although somewhat disturbed by rabbit burrows, the way in which the mounds were formed was clear, with numerous lumps of baked clay in a very hard, thick clay matrix.

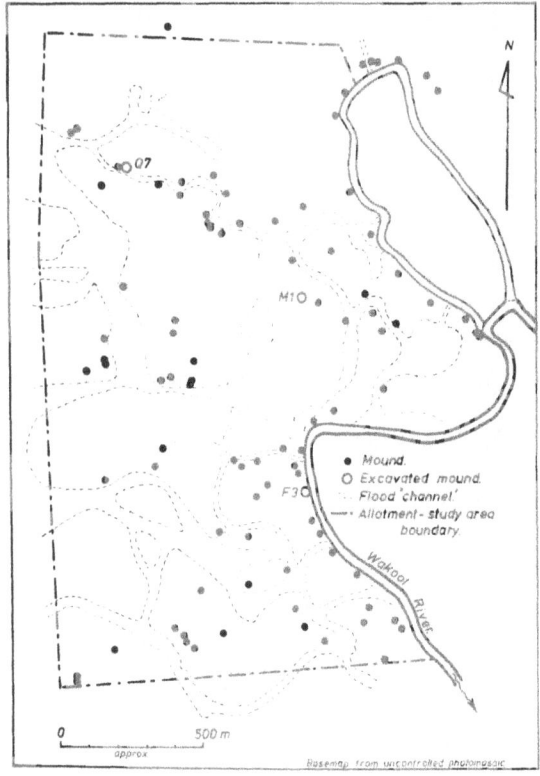

6.10
Map of the Wakool study area beside the Wakool River near Barham, showing the location of mounds and water courses. (Berryman and Frankel 1984, Figure 3)

6.11
Excavations reveal a pile of baked clay heat-retainers, still in the same position as they were when raked out of an earth oven 4000 years ago.

The smallest mound gave the best impression of the scatter of clay balls, still in position as discarded after the final activity at this site. The larger mounds have a greater quantity of soil matrix. Some of this may derive from later camps on the site, but some is a natural build-up of sediment deposited by floodwaters. The disturbed soils and richer organic material of mounds stimulate vegetation growth, which in turn serves to trap silts. Larger mounds therefore develop naturally as well as culturally.

Radiocarbon dates from these three mounds show that they began to be used between about 4000 and 2000 years ago. Unfortunately no artefacts or any animal bones, shellfish or other food remains were preserved in these sites.

We also excavated a series of small test pits away from the mounds, in the hope of locating fireplaces or other signs of activities which took place around or beside the mounds. Unfortunately we found no evidence of this sort.

Results and discussion

Age

The date of 4160 ± 300 from one of the sites is the oldest so far for any mound. The few other mounds in the Murray Valley that have been excavated and dated provide us with dates between about 2000 years ago and the present.

Function

The smallest of the three excavated mounds shows the initial stage of mound formation, with a scatter of clay balls raked out of a fire-pit. The largest mound, with more soil matrix, may have been used as a campsite as well as an oven. This fits with other ideas of mound-types, with some seen as simply oven-mounds, while others were subsequently also used as campsites, perhaps allowing occupation of the area to continue longer into the flood season. Mounds were also occasionally used for burials.

Mounds and flood levels

There is a general correlation between size of mounds and their location. Figure 6.12 compares the available land area with the proportions

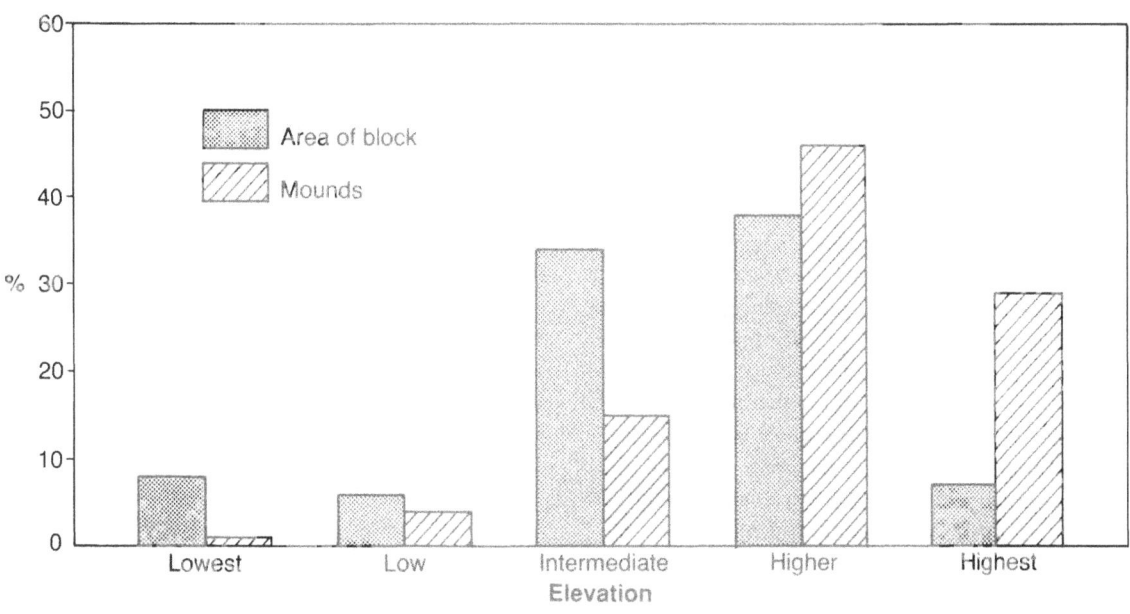

6.12
Proportion of mounds compared with the available land area at different elevations. There is clearly a preference for placing mounds on higher ground. (Data supplied by A.J. Berryman)

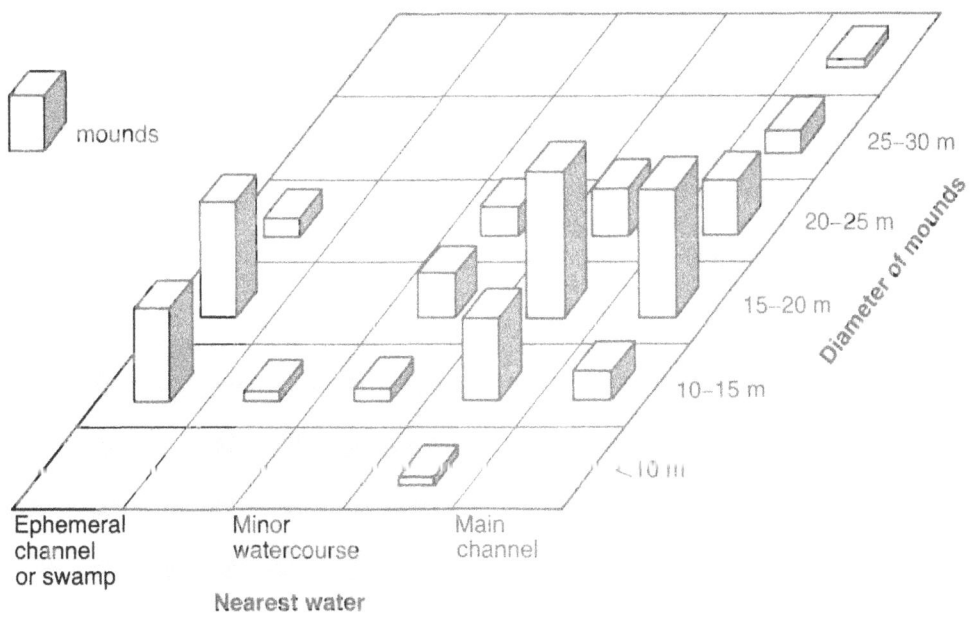

6.13
The relationship of mounds of different sizes to the nearest water course. Medium sized mounds are found near to both minor and major waterways, but the largest mounds are only near the main channel of the Wakool River. (Data supplied by A.J. Berryman)

of mounds at five different heights. There is an obvious preference for higher ground. Figure 6.13 shows that the largest mounds are only found near the main channel, while others are found near smaller water courses or shallow areas of ponding and swamps. We can argue that when flood waters were at their height, people camped at any point around the edges of the water. Later, as the waters retreated, people moved back closer to the river channels, camping for longer periods or in greater numbers beside the larger billabongs and channels, finally concentrating along the main river itself. Mound placement therefore reflects water levels and presumably access to other resources such as fish, shellfish and yabbies in the river and waterholes and plant foods in the surrounding areas.

During the height of the flood the small islands formed by mounds could still be reached by bark canoes, providing a base for exploiting the area even when the main campsites had moved to the edge of the floodwater.

Mounds and mounds

Although this is harder to demonstrate, mounds appear to be evenly spaced from one another. If sites were occupied simultaneously, then we could argue that this reflects a social spacing, people placing themselves as far from one another as possible. It is unlikely however that many of these sites would have been occupied at any one time. Why then are they so evenly spaced? Did people deliberately distance themselves from older mounds? Did they identify mounds as significant features on the landscape, marking previous occupation of the area? If so, can we suggest that some mounds became signals of particular individual or group ownership of territory and resources? Certainly some of the historical accounts suggest that rights to particularly rich areas along the rivers were 'owned' in some way, or at least controlled by particular people.

Changes in cooking technology

Whether or not mounds have this type of social significance, they do show the introduction of a new cooking technique in the last few thousand years. A little to the north, around the dry Willandra Lakes, there is also evidence of a change in the type of hearths and fireplaces used. When rock or similar material is heated, the magnetic particles align themselves with the earth's magnetic field and become fixed in place as the material cools. By measuring the direction of magnetism in heat-retainers (like the clay balls in the Murray mounds) it is possible to determine whether or not they were moved after cooking was completed. In the Willandra area earlier cooks used calcrete nodules as heat-retainers in cooking-pits, raked them aside after use and used the same rocks on many occasions. Later, after about 4500 years ago, termite nests began to be used. These heat retainers were not disturbed after heating. Instead food seems to have been placed on top of the hot lumps of the hearth, which would be used only once.

Case study 2: Caramut, Victoria

Description

The central Western District of Victoria is a fairly flat, well-watered plain. Swamps and wetlands abound, and the rivers and creeks are

6.14
A mound in the western District of Victoria, badly damaged by rabbit burrows.

6.15
Victoria Archaeological Survey excavations at a mound near Chatsworth in western Victoria.

subject to flooding at times of high rainfall in the winter months.

Numerous mounds have been recorded in the region, especially on slightly higher ground beside rivers and swamps. One cluster of mounds near McArthur Creek was investigated in detail by Elizabeth Williams. Here two larger and five smaller mounds lie close to one another, within an area of about 100 m by 60 m.

Historical documents describe an Aboriginal 'village' of between 20 and 30 huts somewhere in this area. These were solidly made dome-shaped structures of wood and bark sealed with mud, about 3 m in diameter and 2 m high.

Aims and approach

In excavating these sites, Elizabeth Williams' main aims were:

1 to see if the mounds were occupation sites
2 to document the form of any structures
3 to see if these sites could represent a 'village' as described in the documents

The local Aboriginal community did not want the larger mounds excavated, as they felt that these might contain burials. Excavation was restricted to two adjacent smaller mounds — Mounds 5 and 6.

A large area of the upper 10 cm of each mound was stripped off in order to expose any structural evidence and the distribution of any material within each. The lower deposits were excavated on a more limited scale. A narrow trench between the two mounds was excavated in order to trace any relationship between them.

Analysis of the texture and structure of the sediments was as important as the location of artefacts and structural features, as it could show if and how the site was built up. The intensive use of a site, leaving organic material from fires, cooking and other refuse, can result in higher concentrations of chemicals such as nitrogen and phosphorus. The chemical composition of the soils was therefore plotted as well as the distribution of stone and bone within the sites.

Results

Stratigraphy and site formation

The uppermost 10 cm of deposit on both mounds showed the final phase of Aboriginal occupation of the mounds. Mound 5 provides the clearest evidence of the last structure on the site, with patches of charcoal and wood which Williams takes to indicate the position of the wooden uprights which would have supported the roof of a circular hut.

The soil immediately below this was also seen to be artificially built up, with dumping and resurfacing of the area using the local gravelly volcanic soils. Lower deposits, although contain-

6.16
McArthur Creek Mound 5 at the completion of excavations. (Photo: E. Williams)

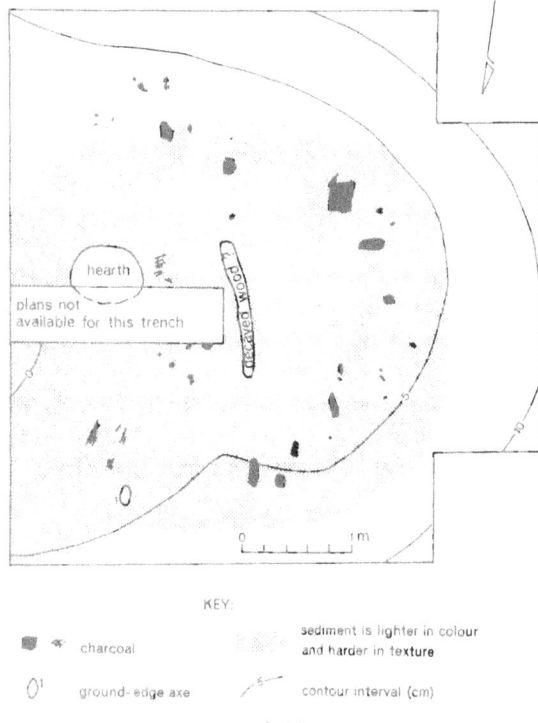

6.17
Plan of McArthur Creek Mound 5 after removal of the top 10 cm of deposit. (Drawing courtesy E. Williams).

ing artefacts, gave no sign of artificial mound construction or resurfacing, although natural rises may have formed the base for mound construction.

In the lower layers between the mounds were six small pits and concentrations of burnt basalt rocks. These are probably hearths or ovens.

Dating

Radiocarbon dates from different points in the sequence in both mounds show that the area of Mound 6 was first used nearly 2000 years ago and Mound 5 about 1000 years later. These initial periods of occupation preceded the development of the mounds, or the resurfacing of the area with clean fill. Dates of 440 ± 70 and 760 ± 100 BP show that Mound 5 continued to be used at intervals until the most recent occupation, dated both on Mound 5 and in the oven pits to 'modern' in radiocarbon terms — that is, within the last few hundred years. There is no indication that the two mounds were ever occupied at the same time.

Finds

The small amount of bone found was very broken up so that animal species could not be determined. The greatest concentration of bone was outside the hut on Mound 5.

Higher concentrations of nitrogen and phosphorus mark the hearths and cooking pits, as well as the area behind the hut wall where food refuse, such as animal bones, was discarded.

Most of the stone tools were made of quartz, with smaller quantities of other raw materials. All the stone was brought in to the site from distant sources. Most came from within 30 km of the site, but some types, such as flint found on the coast, from at least 50 km away. Two greenstone hatchet heads were found. Unlike the other tools, these were probably not manufactured on the site. Implements such as these were often highly prized and the stone distributed over long distances from well-known quarries (see Chapter 10). The stone for these two axes came from local quarries. Why were these axes abandoned at the site? Could they have been in the hut, or stored on the roof, when it accidently burnt down?

The range of tool types suggests that a variety of activities was carried out in and beside the huts, including woodworking and butchery. The distribution of artefacts varies, and the concentrations of quartz and flint shatter from tool-manufacture on both mounds shows that tools were made within the huts.

Further discussion

This excavation gives a good view of the activities associated with Western District mounds. From both these Caramut sites and other mounds investigated in the Western District by the Victoria Archaeological Survey it is clear that they were probably occupation sites, unlike the oven-mounds typical of the Murray Valley.

None of the ten mounds so far excavated in the Western District are more than 2500 years old. What does the recent development of this new site type mean? Although hundreds of mounds have been recorded in the Western District of Victoria, there are also large numbers of scatters of stone tools in the area. These are also the remains of campsites. Why were some houses built on mounds, and others not? Are they a significantly different type of site, or merely a particular variety?

The answers to these questions depend partly on how we understand the formation of the sites. As mounds are often associated with rivers, it is often suggested that their main function was to provide dry foundations. On the basis of his work in the area, Peter Coutts argued that these mounds were deliberately constructed with soil brought in to form raised dry platforms on which to build houses. This idea is followed by Elizabeth Williams and could also fit with the evidence from Caramut described here.

Despite the problems of establishing contemporaneity, she and others have suggested, on the basis of some nineteenth century accounts, that some large clusters of mounds represent permanent 'villages'. Their appearance after 2500 years ago is thought to signal a change in population density and structure, with more people more densely packed in the area, exploiting resources more intensively.

Other explanations are possible. Perhaps these sites were created simply by the repeated use of particular camping places, and the same spot for building, or rebuilding huts. Perhaps much of the earth fill of some mounds derives from the mud-plaster used to seal in bark huts. The collapse of huts would leave raised areas of earth, which could be smoothed off, leaving raised areas favoured as foundations for later building. This might also fit with the Caramut evidence, which shows that the site was used before the mound was formed.

We can then suggest that people simply took advantage of the accidental initial formation of mounds which they could use as dry platforms for houses. This would be most important during the wetter winter months. Perhaps, then, mounds were a seasonal site type. In the winter, when travel was more difficult, and resources more readily available, people may have stayed in one place for longer periods of time and may have built more substantial housing. These two factors, added to the utility of higher, drier foundations and the accidental accumulation of occupation debris and collapsed turf and mud-lining, might explain the function and formation of mounds.

We still need to explain why this type of site only developed after 2500 years ago. Studies of lake levels show a series of changes in climate and water-availability. After 6000 years ago conditions were fairly dry, but became wetter after about 2500 years ago. Perhaps the development of mounds is a local response to this change in climate with a slight shift in seasonal settlement pattern and house-form, rather then a reflection of a significant change in social organisation.

POINTS FOR DISCUSSION

1 Is it possible for archaeologists to identify a 'village'? What are the problems associated with doing this?
2 What are the differences between mounds along the Murray and in south-western Victoria?
Why did mounds develop in these two areas?

PICTURING THE PAST

Use the evidence provided by burials (Chapter 3) together with that on mounds to describe what life was like along the Murray River.

References

Berryman, A. and Frankel, D., 1984. 'Archaeological Investigations of Mounds on the Wakool River, near Barham, New South Wales', *Australian Archaeology*, Vol. 19, pp. 21–30.

Beveridge, P., 1883, 'On the Aborigines Inhabiting the Great Lacustrine and Riverine Depression of the Lower Murray, Lower Murrumbidgee, Lower Lachlan and Lower Darling', *Journal and Proceedings of the Royal*

Society of New South Wales, Vol. 17, pp. 19–74.

Coutts, P.J.F., Witter, D., McIlwraith, M. and Frank, R., 1976, 'The Mound People of Western Victoria: a Preliminary Statement', *Records of the Victorian Archaeological Survey*, Vol. 1.

Coutts, P.J.F., Henderson, P. and Fullagar, R.L.K., 1979, 'A Preliminary Investigation of Aboriginal Mounds in Northwestern Victoria', *Records of the Victorian Archaeological Survey*, Vol. 9.

Clark, I.D., (ed), 1988, *The Port Phillip Journals of George Augustus Robinson*, Monash Publications in Geography, No. 24, Melbourne.

Dawson, J., 1881, repr. 1981, *Australian Aborigines*, George Robertson, Melbourne.

Presland, G., (ed), 1977, *Journals of George Augustus Robinson: March–May 1841*, Records of the Victorian Archaeological Survey, Vol. 6, Melbourne.

Williams, E., 1984, 'Documentation and Archaeological Investigation of an Aboriginal 'Village' Site in Southwestern Victoria', *Aboriginal History*, Vol. 8, pp. 173–188.

Williams, E., 1987, 'Complex Hunter-gatherers: a View from Australia', *Antiquity*, Vol. 61, pp. 310–321.

Williams, E., 1988, *Complex Hunter Gatherers*, British Archaeological Reports S423, London.

7

Stone structures

People often express surprise when they learn that Aboriginal people built stone structures. Why should this be so? It probably stems from two related misconceptions. One is the idea that 'stone houses' show architectural sophistication and permanent settlement. The other is an equally mistaken view that Aboriginal people did not build or create anything substantial.

Aboriginal people in many parts of Australia built stone structures of different types. In Chapter 8 stone fish-traps are described. Stone arrangements were set up at many ceremonial sites, where some are still in use. There are stone hunting-hides, behind which men would wait to intercept passing game. In addition stone was occasionally used in housing. This is best documented in parts of western Victoria.

HISTORICAL ACCOUNTS OF STONE HOUSES

George Augustus Robinson travelled to western Victoria in April 1842 to investigate claims of attacks on European settlers by Aborigines. Near Lake Condah he

> ... crossed a swamp to some stony rises, and succeeded in conferring with the blacks; they had a sort of village, and some of their habitations were of stone. I passed several stone and wooded weirs for taking fish, also places for snaring birds; their dwellings are among rocky fragments and loose crags, thickly wooded and bounded by swamps. This country extends to the coast a distance of at least 30 miles. To remove the natives from these fastnesses by means of horsemen would be impossible, and footmen would find it difficult to travel. (House of Commons Sessional Papers 1844. Papers relative to the Aborigines, Australian Colonies, Vol 34, p. 209.)

P. Manifold, who had lived in the Western District of Victoria for thirty years, reported in the 1870s that:

> The natives formed these wind-breaks of stone, placed on edge in a circular form, some of them very perfect, leaving the entrance generally toward the east, the prevailing winds coming from the north-west and south-west. These circles are common on the plains or eastern parts of this property, where the branches of trees could not be procured for giving shelter. When we first occupied this country it was quite common for the natives to use these circles as camping places, always having the fires in the centre. The fires were very small, as they had frequently to carry the wood long distances. The circles were generally formed of large stones on their edges, and bedded in the ground close together, without any other stones on the top, thus forming good protection from the wind as they lay around the fire. The stones are of the

> common basalt, there being no other in the district. The situation selected was generally where water was convenient, or in some favourable place for game. The circles were about the size of ordinary mia-mys, that is from ten to twenty feet [3 m to 6 m] in diameter. (Smyth, R.B., 1878; Vol II, p. 235)

Case study: Allambie, Victoria

Lava from recent volcanic eruptions in western Victoria flowed over large areas. The fractured and broken blocks of basalt form long narrow regions of rugged, rocky 'stony rises'. In many places the original vegetation of tall woodland of manna gum and blackwood still survives.

Around Lake Condah (itself created by the lava flows from Mount Eccles, as described in Chapter 8, page 101) numerous stone structures, mostly small circles, have been found in this rocky terrain. Sometimes these are in small groups, but elsewhere dozens occur in close proximity to one another. One of the largest sets is on 'Allambie' a property 2 km east of Lake Condah.

In 1981 Jane Wesson undertook fieldwork on the 'PAL complex' at Allambie as part of a general project of the Victoria Archaeological Survey, under the overall supervision of Peter Coutts.

Aims and approach

Previous excavations of other stone houses by the Victoria Archaeological Survey had left considerable doubt as to whether they were prehistoric or not. The primary aim of research at Allambie was therefore to determine their age and ethnicity as well as their function.

Within this broad objective, more specific detail was sought on a range of aspects, such as the size of the structures, the techniques of building and possible rebuilding, their relationship to one another, and the activities that took place in them.

Fieldwork in the PAL complex at Allambie had three components:

1 the identification and mapping of all the stone structures
2 detailed stone-by-stone recording of one tight cluster of structures
3 the partial excavation of one structure (PAL 20) in this cluster

The excavation included half of the structure, and a larger area in front and beside it. A total of 18 m² was excavated, in two spits, each approximately 5 cm in depth. Material was excavated and recorded within 1 m × 1 m squares, except the hearth or fireplace features, which were excavated separately. In order to examine the sequence and techniques of

7.1
A stone structure at Allambie.

7.2
A camera mounted on the end of this hydraulic mast is used for taking vertical photographs of stone structures.

7.3
Stone structure PAL 20 at Allambie during the course of excavations by the Victoria Archaeological Survey. (Photo: Victoria Archaeological Survey)

7.4
Stone house PAL 20 at Allambie, after the completion of excavations. (Photo: Victoria Archaeological Survey).

7.5
Photograph looking directly down at a circular stone structure near Lake Condah. (Photo: R. Frank)

construction, the location and height of all large pieces of basalt was recorded.

Results of fieldwork

Excavations in PAL 20

Sediments and features. Between 10 and 30 cm of deposit had accumulated within and beside the structure, but no distinct layering could be observed within it, so that all the material comes from one archaeological horizon. Four features could be interpreted as hearths. Three were in front of the structure, and one within. All appear to have been used throughout the life of the building. The stratigraphic evidence suggests that there was little or no sediment in the area before the structure was built. Upper sediments filling in around fallen blocks have comparatively few artefacts in them, which suggests that sediment continued to be trapped in the site after it was abandoned, and that it was not rebuilt or reused.

Dating. Three radiocarbon dates were obtained for deposits in PAL 20. They all gave results indistinguishable from modern samples. This house must therefore have been used within the last 200 years or so. The absence of any European

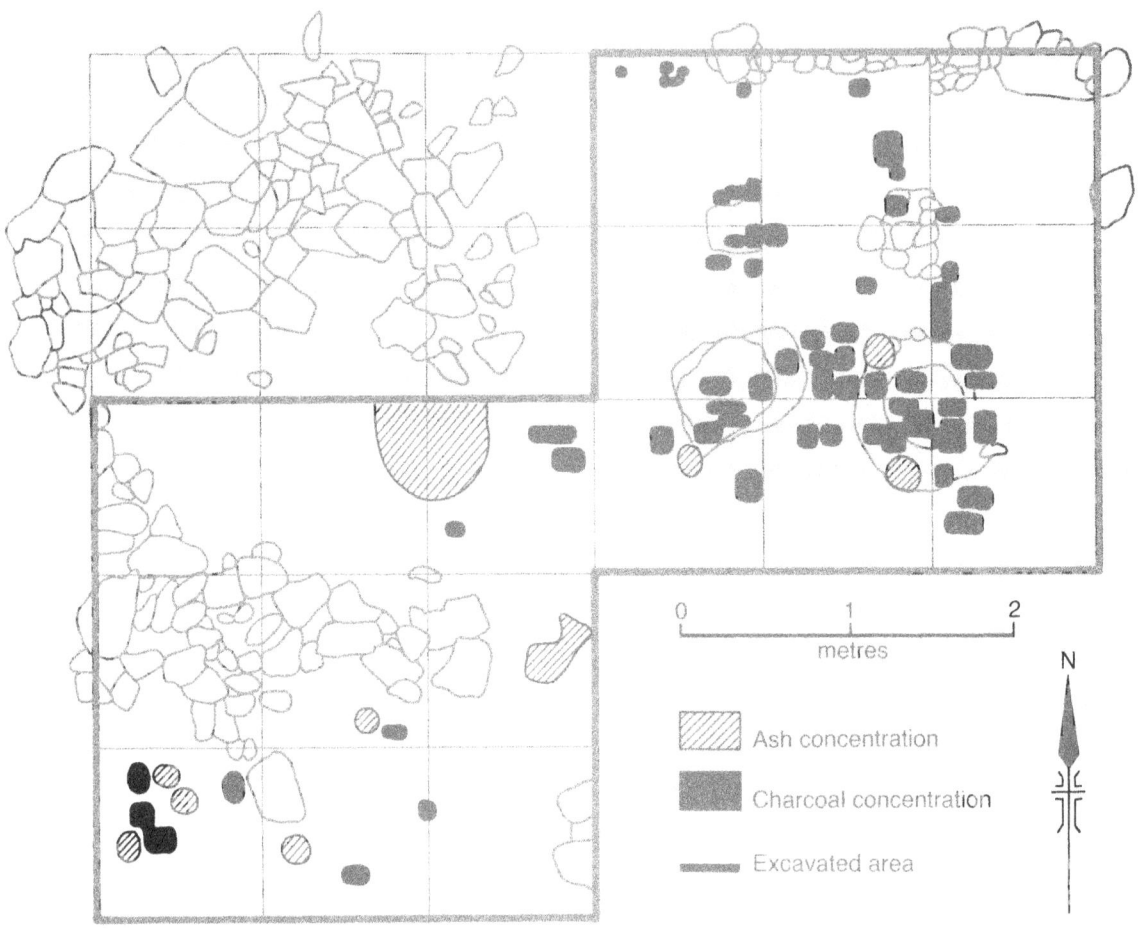

7.6
Plan of the excavated stone structure at Allambie (PAL 20) showing the layout of the excavations and position of concentrations of charcoal and ash. (After Wesson 1981, Figure 15)

material may be taken to suggest that the site was probably used before, or only shortly after, first European settlement in the area (1842).

Stone artefacts. 1750 pieces of chipped stone were found. Wesson looked at these in a variety of ways.
- Raw material. Over 94% of the pieces are coastal flint, collected from the beaches 40 km to the south. It is therefore probable that the people using the Condah area moved between it and the coast.
- Tool types. 38 of the pieces were identified as 'tools'. The remainder are waste material, the by-product of stone tool manufacture and use. 15 of the tools are informal irregular flakes showing signs of deliberate retouch or use-damage. The others are backed blades; that is, small blades blunted along one edge. These are usually regarded as barbs, set in spears, but some of the PAL examples have other damage, and so may have been used for other purposes as well.
- Breakage and burning. A very high proportion (40%) of the waste material was broken and 35% showed signs of having been burnt. Waste from tools was therefore left lying around areas of general use where they were

broken by trampling and tossed into the fireplaces.

Bone and shell. 680 pieces of bone were recovered, all of them less than 2 cm long, and most of them burnt. Only two pieces were whole, only eighteen could be identified to anatomical part and no species could be identified. They all appear to be from marsupials, both very small and large. None of the identifiable bone came from fish or birds.

Little can be learnt from this, other than that animals were brought into the site, cooked and eaten beside and within the structure. As only small fragments were found this might also suggest that larger bones were disposed of away from the living area, perhaps by dingoes.

Thirteen tiny pieces of shell may be from freshwater mussels.

Activities at the site. Jane Wesson documented two areas of concentration of stone and bone, one inside the structure, the other to the south. She suggested that these represent a pattern of eating inside the structure and cleaning up outside, but the evidence for this distinction is not really adequate and no clear division of activity areas can be made. Nevertheless the finds do show that stone tools were made, and food was prepared and eaten both within and outside this structure. It is possible to see this site, therefore, as a general living area, rather than any special purpose camp.

The complex as a whole

Extent. A basic problem was to distinguish artificial arrangements of stone from natural features among the continuous scatters and piles of rock. The Victoria Archaeological Survey team identified 128 sites within an area of 10 ha. 116 were semi-circular arrangements of stones, which they classified as 'house-sites'. Two of the others have straight walls, and the remainder are less regular.

There is, of course, no information available on the relationship between most of the structures and no way of showing how old they are or if any were built or occupied simultaneously. They may well be the result of separate visits to the area by small groups of people over a long period of time. We should also remember that Aboriginal camps often spread over a large area, with separate camps for different groups of people such as the boys and younger men.

Seasonality. In an attempt to determine the most probable season of occupation, Jane Wesson plotted which direction the structures faced. It is most likely that openings faced away from the wind. Figure 7.7 shows that most openings were to the east and north-east. Prevailing winds are from the west and south-west for most of the year, but the pattern fits best with wind directions in November and December. It is possible that these houses were more likely to have been built at that time of the year than in the winter.

Form of stone houses. Most of the stone houses in the PAL complex at Allambie are circular, with the entrances to the east and north-east.

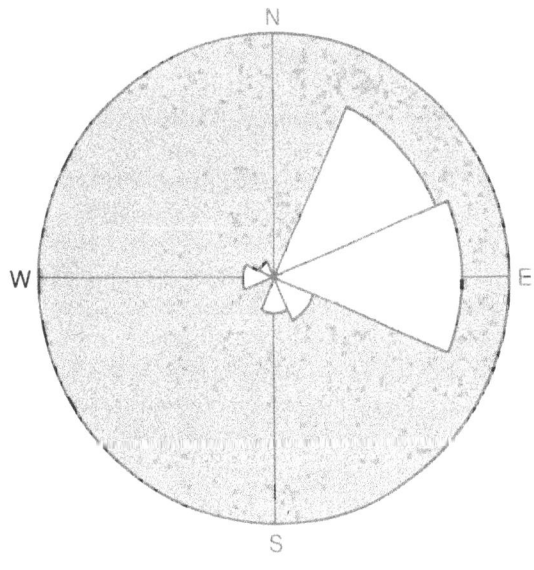

7.7

Orientations of stone structures at Allambie, as recorded by the Victoria Archaeological Survey in 1977. Most have their entrances to the east or north-east, facing away from the prevailing winds. (After Wesson 1981, Figure 27)

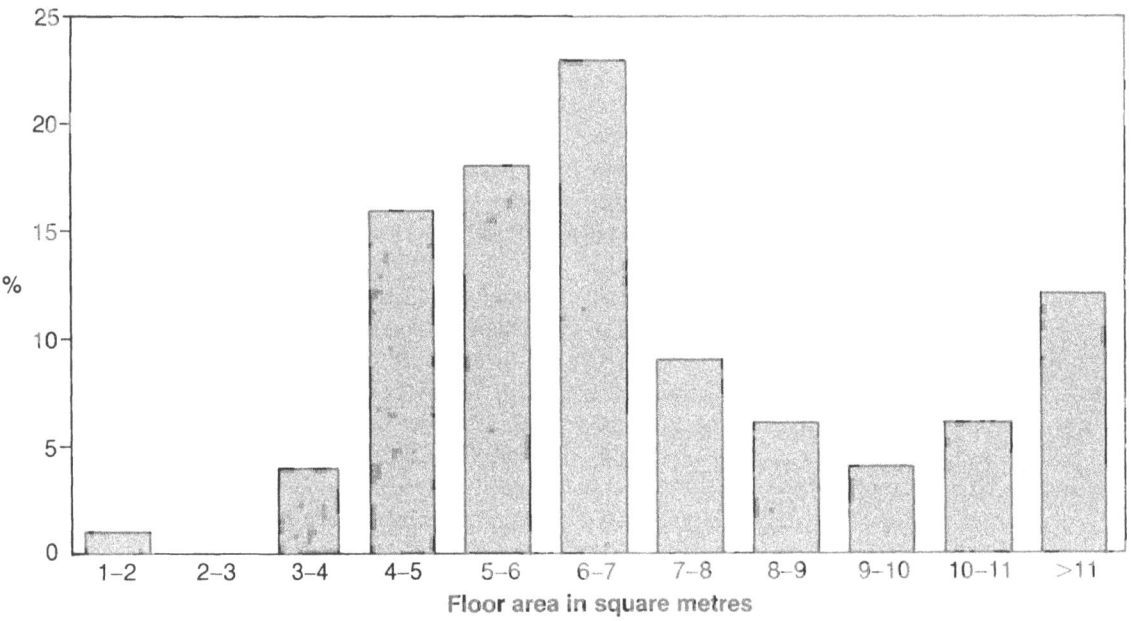

7.8
The floor area of stone structures at Allambie, as recorded by the Victoria Archaeological Survey in 1977. Most enclose an area of between 3 and 7 metres. (Data from Wesson 1981, Appendix 3)

The majority have a floor area of between 4 and 7 m^2.

The Victoria Archaeological Survey attempted to reconstruct the height of a wall of one structure at another site, using blocks beside and apparently fallen from the remains. Even if the wall was only one stone wide, the maximum height would have been about one metre. Most walls would certainly have been much lower than this. They were really low footings rather than walls. These were, according to an Aboriginal informant from the Lake Condah mission in 1898, 'roofed over with boughs and bark like an ordinary hut'. That is, they were probably dome-shaped structures, with stone footings of blocks cleared aside and placed in position in such a way as to hold the uprights forming the roof in position. There is no need to see these houses as anything other than the obvious way of setting up shelters in rough stony regions.

Further discussion

Too little has been excavated at this site, or at any others, to allow us to ask some of the more interesting questions concerning the size and use of groups of structures in the stony rises of western Victoria.

A further problem has recently arisen from a re-examination of the Allambie complex undertaken for the Victoria Archaeological Survey by Anne Clarke. She casts doubt on the original identification of many features, regarding them as natural arrangements of rocks rather than built structures. Our view of the density of structures here, and elsewhere, may need to be considerably revised.

We have still no idea about how long people have been using the stony rises. Another stone house excavated by The Victoria Archaeological Survey had both Aboriginal and European

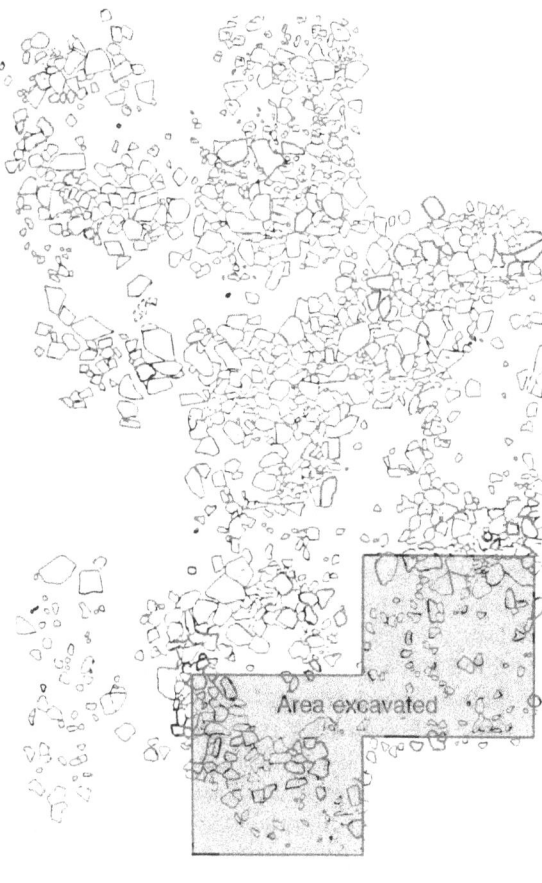

7.9
Stone-by-stone drawing of part of the Allambie complex. It is particularly difficult to determine which basalt blocks are in their original position as part of structures, which have fallen from structures, and which were never part of structures. (After Wesson 1981, Figure 10).

artefacts in it, while one investigated by Elizabeth Williams is also very recent, if not post-European (one radiocarbon date of 'modern' and another of 380 ± 150 BP). The presence of these sites in different areas, and the lack of European artefacts in PAL 20, suggests that some pre-date European settlement. The stony rises were unattractive to European settlers as they were unsuitable for agriculture. It is possible that many of the stone houses were nineteenth century refuge areas for Aboriginal people displaced from richer areas nearby. These refugees may not all have been powerless victims. It has recently been suggested that the stony rises may have served as a base for parties of Aborigines who actively resisted the invasion by engaging in a form of guerilla warfare, making systematic raids on European settlements.

POINTS FOR DISCUSSION

1 Are most of the houses where you live oriented in any particular direction? What are the reasons for any regular orientation?
2 Should the structures described in this chapter be called 'stone houses'?
3 In what way could you demonstrate that the stone structures in the stony rises represent Aboriginal refuges in the period following, and in response to, European settlement in the area?

PICTURING THE PAST

Describe your impression of what a camp in the stony rises would have looked like.

References

Clark, I.D., 1988, *The Port Phillip Journals of George Augustus Robinson*, Monash Publications in Geography, No. 24, Melbourne.

Coutts, P.J.F., Witter, D.C. and Parsons, D.M., 1977, 'Impact of European Settlement on Aboriginal Society in Western Victoria,' *Records of the Victorian Archaeological Survey*, Vol. 4, pp. 17–58.

Kenyon, A.S., 1930, 'Stone Structures of the Australian Aboriginal', *Victorian Naturalist*, Vol. 47, pp. 71–75.

Smyth, R.B., 1878, *The Aborigines of Victoria*, Government Printer, Melbourne.

Wesson, J., 1981, 'Excavations of Stone Structures in the Condah Area, Western Victoria', unpublished MA(Preliminary) thesis, La Trobe University, Melbourne.

8

Fish-traps

Hunter-gatherers can manage resources in several ways. One way is by scheduling activities and moving from one region to another, congregating in richer areas during periods of abundance and dispersing at other times. These need have little long-term impact on the environment. Other strategies can involve a greater degree of interference with natural systems. Although Australian Aboriginal people never developed farming, in some places they deliberately enhanced resource availability, reliability and productivity.

Fish-traps are one of the more obvious techniques of improving productivity. These were used in many parts of the continent. Along coastal areas tidal fish-traps were built, sometimes taking advantage of natural reefs and rock-pools. At high tide fish would swim into enclosures, and were then trapped as the water level fell a few hours later. On some rivers stone or wicker pens were used. These might operate automatically, as with tidal systems, but otherwise people would herd fish into small enclosures where they could easily be speared or simply collected by hand. In other cases barriers across waterways would channel fish through narrow openings, so that they could be efficiently harvested.

8.1
*Sandy Paddy collecting fish at the Mulagan trap.
(Photo: Western Australian Museum, Anthropology Dept. Acc. No. B82. 6.12)*

EFFICIENCY OF TIDAL FISH-TRAPS IN NORTH-WEST WESTERN AUSTRALIA

In 1982 Sandy and Esther Paddy, the traditional owners, demonstrated to Moya Smith the techniques of building and operating a stone wall fish-trap in the tidal sand flats near Swan Point. This area experiences substantial tidal fluctuations, with a range of about 10 m. At high tide the area of the trap is under 6 or 7 m of water, at low tide the water retreats 300 m seaward. The trap is sufficiently exposed for work or collection about 5 hours every day.

The *Mulagun* trap had been disused for over twenty-five years, but the foundations were still in place. Rebuilding, using the stones from the older trap, took about 6 person-hours. About 7500 stones were used to form a wall 25 m long and about 1.3 m high linking natural outcrops into a trap 43 m in total length. After several days, the trap was deliberately destroyed, so that no further fish would be caught in it. Another trap at *Lalanan*, One Arm Point, is kept in repair, and visited daily by people from the nearby settlement. The yield from this trap is higher, and a better reflection of the efficiency of the technique.

Traps are the most efficient and reliable method of catching fish in the area. Spears, poisons and fishing boomerangs are also used, but a trap '. . is the only one where you don't have to stand around or herd the fish . . . you don't need a wire [metal rod used as a spear] just pick them up'.

The One Arm Point trap can provide a regular source of food all year round. Fish-traps operate most efficiently between January and March during the wet season when king tides bring more fish inshore. These and other seasonal resources (such as turtle eggs) provide the subsistence base for large-scale gatherings and ceremonies held at that time of the year. (Smith, M, 1983.)

8.2
The Mulagun trap at low tide. (Photo: Western Australian Museum Anthropology Dept. Acc. No. B82. 3.11)

Questions about fish-traps

- Where are fish-traps found?
- How old are these techniques?
- How much energy was required to build traps?
- How efficient were they?
- What is the relationship between traps and social organisation?
- What other effects did traps have on local environments?

Table 8.1

Day	No. of people	Minutes worked by each person	gm fish per person	% daily protein requirement	% daily energy requirement
Mulagun trap					
1	6	90	121	43	6.3
2	6	25	488	142	26.6
3	6	28	23	65	12
One Arm Point Trap					
1	6	33	1600	450	77

8.3
The Brewarrina fish-trap. (Photo: Henry King; courtesy of the Trustees, Museum of Applied Arts and Sciences, Sydney)

FISH-TRAPS AT BREWARRINA, NSW

The well-known fish-traps at Brewarrina in northern New South Wales are typical of large riverine systems.

Here extensive stone pens were constructed in the Darling River using river boulders to form a complex maze of weirs and pens of varying size and shape stretching along 500 m of the river.

The stone walls were kept in good repair, especially before the spawning season in the spring, when vast numbers of fish would travel upstream. As soon as enough fish had entered a trap, men and women would block up the openings. The fish were then herded into the smaller enclosures, where they could be speared, clubbed, or caught more easily by hand.

Pens at different heights came into operation in sequence, as the water-level in the river rose or fell.

Problems in analysing fish-traps

Preservation. Wood or reed fish-traps rarely survive. Even stone systems are vulnerable to destruction, especially as they are located in rivers or the sea, and therefore subject to strong tides and currents.

Identification. Distinguishing between natural features and artificial ones is often difficult.

Dating. Fish-traps are not the sort of site where datable deposits of material accumulate. They are therefore difficult, if not impossible, to date.

Case study 1: Toolondo, Victoria

Flat open woodland stretches west of the sandstone ranges of the Grampians. The area is poorly drained, and water fills any slight depression, forming chains of small lakes and swampy wetlands.

The remains of shallow ditches or drains could be seen linking Clear Swamp and Budgeongutte Swamp near Toolondo. Aldo Massola published a brief account of them in 1962, suggesting that they were part of an Aboriginal system of fish or eel traps.

Eels abound in the rivers and swamps of southern Victoria. In late summer or early autumn adult eels congregate in large numbers before beginning their journey to the sea to spawn. Young eels eventually make their way into estuaries and move up the rivers further inland. The swarms of migrating eels provided a major seasonal food resource for Aboriginal people.

8.4
One of the channels at Toolondo.

Research aims and strategy

In 1976 and 1977 Harry Lourandos undertook a detailed investigation of the Toolondo complex as part of a larger study of south-west Victorian prehistory. He defined several specific aims:

1 to trace and document the extent of the system
2 to investigate how the ditches were formed
3 to date the system
4 to show if the ditches were natural or artificial
5 if they were artificial, to see if they were Aboriginal or European
6 to identify the purpose of the system

A field survey defined the extent of visible or surviving traces of the system. This, together with details of the level of the ground surface and swamps, documented the physical setting and scope of the system.

Ten trenches were excavated across the ditches at different points, to investigate how they were formed and later filled in.

As in other circumstances, historical records play an important part in identifying the function of these sites. Apart from other sources and local informants, Lourandos discovered important evidence in the unpublished diaries of George Augustus Robinson, in which Robinson described Aboriginal eeling and an impressive complex of canals and ditches near Mount William on the other side of the Grampians.

Results of fieldwork

Extent of the system

Budgeongutte Swamp and Clear Swamp are about three kilometres apart, separated by a slightly higher area where a series of natural hollows form a marsh in the wet season. About 3.75 km of channel could be traced between the two, as well as a further ditch running south. For most of this distance only a single ditch survived, but in one area there is evidence of a more complex set of parallel channels and subsidiary drains.

The ditches do not form a neat, straight line, but link up a series of hollows in the soft soils between the two swamps.

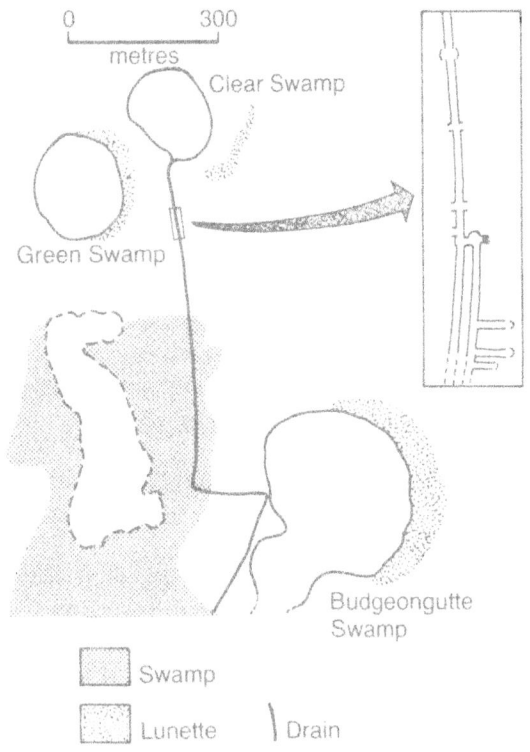

8.5
Plan of the channel linking Clear Swamp and Budgeongutte Swamp near Toolondo, with a detail of part of the system. (After Lourandos 1980, Figures 3, 4)

Form of the ditches

From his excavations Harry Lourandos showed that the deeper sections the main ditch was cut into the clay subsoil in a V-shape, about 40 to 50 cm wide and 40 cm deep along most of its length. It is larger closer to the two swamps — up to 2.5 m wide and 1 m deep. Some of the subsidiary ditches are smaller and shallower.

In one trench round holes in the clay subsoil can be interpreted as post-holes, which may have held basketry weirs or traps in position.

Stratigraphy and history of use

In some sections evidence of recutting of the system could be seen, where one channel cut through some of the fill of an earlier one, and where two depressions ran side-by-side. Otherwise a common pattern is shown by geomorphological analysis of the ditch fill. After the ditches were dug there was an initial period when water ran fairly swiftly, with the deposition of coloured layers of coarser-grained sands. Later fill is different, and represents the gradual silting up of the ditches.

There is, therefore, evidence of two main periods. Earlier on the channel was dug and recut, and there was a steady flow of water through it. Later, when the system was no longer used, it gradually filled in.

One radiocarbon date (210 ± 120 BP) is from the lower silts, and Lourandos argues that it is from the final period when the drain operated actively. This could have been several hundred years ago or as recently as the late nineteenth century. Perhaps the latter is the more likely, signalling the abandonment of this system when the local Aboriginal community was displaced.

Origin of the system

The V-shaped ditches, parallel and complex subsidiary drains, recutting and evidence of a single channel running over a rise all show that this was not a natural water-course.

Could the channels have been a European drainage-ditch rather than an Aboriginal system? Three lines of evidence point toward it as an

Aboriginal construction. The congruence with historical descriptions is good. Aboriginal but not European artefacts were found in the lower ditch-fill. Finally, the original family of European settlers at Mount Talbot Station always recognised the system as Aboriginal and claimed not to have undertaken any work in the area.

Labour costs

Lourandos calculated how much labour would be needed to dig the system as it now appears: a volume of 7644 m^3 of soil. on the basis of analogies to the efficiency of ditch-digging using wooden tools recorded in Papua New Guinea (0.6 m^3 per person per hour) this represents 12 700 person hours. At four hours a day that would occupy 100 people for a month.

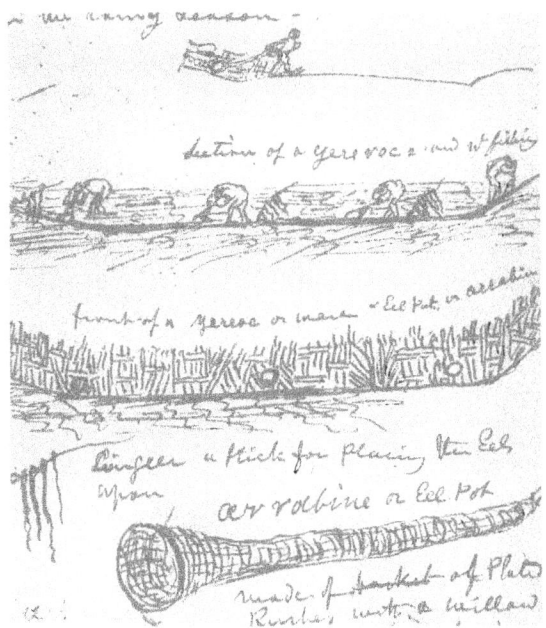

8.6
Sketches by George Augustus Robinson showing Aboriginal people collecting eels at basketry weirs in western Victoria in 1841. (Mitchell Library, Sydney)

ABORIGINAL EELING IN 1841

In the autumn and winter of 1841 George Augustus Robinson (Chief Protector of Aborigines, 1839–1849) toured the Western District of Victoria. In April he was near Lake Keilambete, north of Warrnambool:

> From conversations I had with the natives it appears that this was a favourite spot. It was the home of several families. [name illegible] took me to several spots where he had resided and had *worns* or huts. He also took me to a fine and very large weir and went through, with several other of the natives, the process of taking eels and the particular spot where he himself stood and took them. I measured this weir with a tape, 200 ft [60 m] 5 ft high [1.5 m]. It was turned back at each end and two or three holes in the middle was left for placing the eel pots as also one at each end. The eel pots are placed over the holes and the fisher stands behind the *yere.roc* or weir and lays hold of the small end of the *arrabine* or eel pot. And when the eel makes its appearance he bites it on the head and puts it on the lingeer or small stick with a knob on the end, thus. . . . or if near the bank, he throws them out. The fishing is carried on in the rainy season. . . . . *Arabine* or eel pot made of bark or plaited rushes with a willow round

> mouth and having a small end to prevent the eel from rapidly getting away.
>
> There *yere.roc* or weirs are built with some attention to the principle of mechanics. Those erected on a rocky bottom have the sticks indented in a groove made by removing the small stones so as to form a groove. The weir is kept in a straightline. The small stones are laid against the bottom of the sticks. The upright sticks are supported by transverse sticks, verging or forked sticks as shown above. These sticks are 3, 4 or 5 inches [7 to 13 cm] in diameter some of the weirs are in the form of a segment of a circle. (Presland G. (ed), 1977, pp. 61-65)

Near Mount William, east of the Grampians, he saw a far larger complex of ditches and canals:

> At the confluence of this creek with the marsh observed an immense piece of ground trenched and banked, resembling the work of civilized man but which on inspection I found to be the

8.7
Sketch by George Augustus Robinson showing a section of the complex of channels near Mount William in western Victoria, which he saw in 1841. (Mitchell Library, Sydney)

commit it to paper in the way I could have wished. All its varied form and curious curvilinear windings and angles of every size and shape and parallels, etc; at intervals small apertures left and where they placed their *arabines* or eel pots. These gaps were supported by pieces of the bark of trees and sticks. In single measurement there must have been thousands of yards of this trenching and banking. The whole of the water from the mountain rivulet is made to pass through this trenching ere it reaches the marsh; it is hardly possible for a single fish to escape. I observed at short distance higher up, minor trenching was done through which part of the water ran its course to the more extensive works. some of the banks were 2 feet [60 cm] in height, the most of them a foot [30 cm] and the hollow a foot deep by 10 or 11 inches wide. The main branches were wider. (Presland, G., (ed), 1980, pp. 91–92)

work of the Aboriginal natives, and constructed for the purpose of catching eels. A specimen of art I had not before seen of the same extent and therefore required some time to inspect it, and which the absence of transport enabled me to do. These trenches are hundreds of yards in length. I measured at one place in one continuous triple line for the distance of 500 yards [450 m]. These triple water courses led to other ramified and extensive trenches of a most tortuous form. An area of at least 15 acres [6 ha] was thus turned over. . . . These works must have been executed at great cost of labour to those rude people the only means of artificial power being the lever the application and incentive of which force being necessary. This lever is a stick chisel, sharpened at one end and by which force they threw up clods of earth and thus formed the trenches, smoothing the water channel with their hands. The soil displaced went to form the embankment. . . . .

The plan or design of these ramifications was extremely perplexing and I found it difficult to

Further implications and discussion

The function of the channels as eel-traps is clear, but Lourandos takes the argument further and suggests that it had a significant effect on the local water-systems and the range and productivity of eels. The water-system created by a maze of channels such as Robinson describes for Mount William, and which may have had its equivalent at Toolondo, may well have encouraged eels into the area, and undoubtedly increased the efficiency of their capture, but it is by no means certain that these systems had any other substantial impact on the environment, or that they were intended to have any such effects.

Historical accounts record the speedy and efficient capture of enormous quantities of eels at times of seasonal migration. These provided a rich, reliable and efficient source of food. Large-scale systems such as that at Mount William and presumably that at Toolondo, could have supported large numbers of people; Lourandos suggests that these facilities allowed people to gather in very large numbers for ceremonies and other activities. Although no specific gatherings are known to have taken place at Toolondo, Lourandos notes that it was ideally located for this purpose, at the border of the territories of three adjacent clans.

Following this line further, he argues that the creation of these resource management facilities shows large-scale organisation of labour, investment of energy for future return and the development of new and complex social integration.

A major problem with this view of the creation of eeling systems is that we have no idea of their antiquity, or over how long a period they developed. If we do not accept that the Toolondo channels form a single, planned system of swamp management we may regard it, and the system Robinson saw at Mount William, as the product of generations — perhaps thousands of years — of activity. Questions about the organisation of labour to build then become irrelevant.

Instead we may suggest a slow development, in which, over very long periods of time, smaller dykes and trenches at the edges of swamps were gradually enlarged, redug and extended.

Case study 2: Lake Condah, Victoria

120 km south of Toolondo is another well-documented system of fish-traps, on the margins of Lake Condah. Unlike the Toolondo or Mount William system, this system consists of a series of stone weirs, channels and races, taking advantage of local conditions.

Lake Condah was created about 27 000 years ago when basalt flows from the eruption of the Mount Eccles volcano blocked Darlot Creek. The margins of the lake are a rugged tumble of fractured and fragmented basalt blocks. Before drainage canals were dug from the 1880s onward, the lake basin would have filled and flooded periodically, particularly in the winter. At these times water would slowly rise, filling in one rocky hollow after another. As flood-water subsided pools would progressively empty as the lake reverted to swampy marsh.

8.8
Cleared stones form a channel among the rugged basalt outcrops beside Lake Condah.

8.9
A V-shaped weir at Lake Condah.

8.10
Water flowing along a narrow race or channel into a shallow pond which acts as a fish-trap. (Photo: Victoria Archaeological Survey)

Research aims and techniques

Initial research by the Victoria Archaeological Survey under the direction of Peter Coutts had the basic aims of documenting the form and extent of the fish-traps and of working out how they operated. This was primarily an exercise in surveying. First they had to map the complex rocky topography of the lake margin, surveying the area both on foot and using aerial photography. Next all the artificial lines or structures of stones had to be identified. Finally they were mapped and recorded with stone-by-stone drawings of the main features.

More recently Lesley Head has undertaken a different type of research in the area, looking at its environmental history and attempting to date the fish-traps. Her work involves examination of pollen extracted from cores drilled out of the sediments deposited on the floor of the lake.

Form and function

The Victoria Archaeological Survey defined several different types of stone structure:

- Stone races or channels, up to 1 m wide. These were built of parallel rows of basalt blocks, and some are over 50 m in length.
- Canals made by removing loose rock, to form channels in the bedrock, some of which are over 300 m long.
- Traps or weirs built across the stone races, canals or natural water-courses. Gaps in the weirs mark where nets or baskets would have been set.
- Stone walls enclosing embayments in the rocky lake margin.

All these took advantage of natural features, directing water and blocking its flow in such a way as to channel eels and other fish into basketry traps or to isolate them in rocky pools. Parts of the complex are at different heights, so that as water-levels in the lake rose or fell each would begin to operate in turn.

As with the Toolondo system, this can either be viewed as a major engineering project built at one time, with a great investment of organised labour, or else as a complex system which developed slowly over hundreds or thousands of years.

Environmental history

Lesley Head looked at the history of the lake itself by studying the sediments accumulated in it and the adjacent Condah Swamp. Her particular speciality is the analysis of pollen incorporated in sediments. Figure 8.11 shows the relative proportions of different plants through an 8000 year sequence. These provide the basis for assessing changing vegetation and ecology.

The basic sequence of sediments in Lake Condah shows earlier deposits of lake muds and clays, with the development of peat about 4000–3000 years ago. That is, there is a change to marshy boggy conditions at about that time.

Dryland vegetation changes little through time: a mixture of *Casuarina* (she-oaks) and Eucalypt woodland together with flowering plants (*Asteraceae*) and grasses (*Poaceae*). The higher proportion of *Asteraceae* in the oldest, lowest levels indicates a more open vegetation structure, seen also in other parts of Victoria about 10 000 years ago.

The most significant of the wetland plants are several species of the aquatic herbs *Myriophyllum*. Their presence can show changes in habitat, and suggest that the site was at its driest between 8000 and 4000 years ago and wetter after that time. This is also seen in the replacement of high quantities of saltbush (*Chenopod*) by water-ribbons (*Triglochin*) later in the sequence.

Age of the system

At the time the Victoria Archaeological Survey undertook their main research in the area it was thought that the Mount Eccles eruption was very recent, perhaps 6000 or 7000 years ago. On this basis Peter Coutts therefore argued that the Condah systems were younger than that; there was no other evidence of their age.

The recent research on the sediments in the floor of the basin by Lesley Head and others show that the basalt flows must be much older, probably dating to 27 000 years ago. What does this mean for the history of the fish-traps?

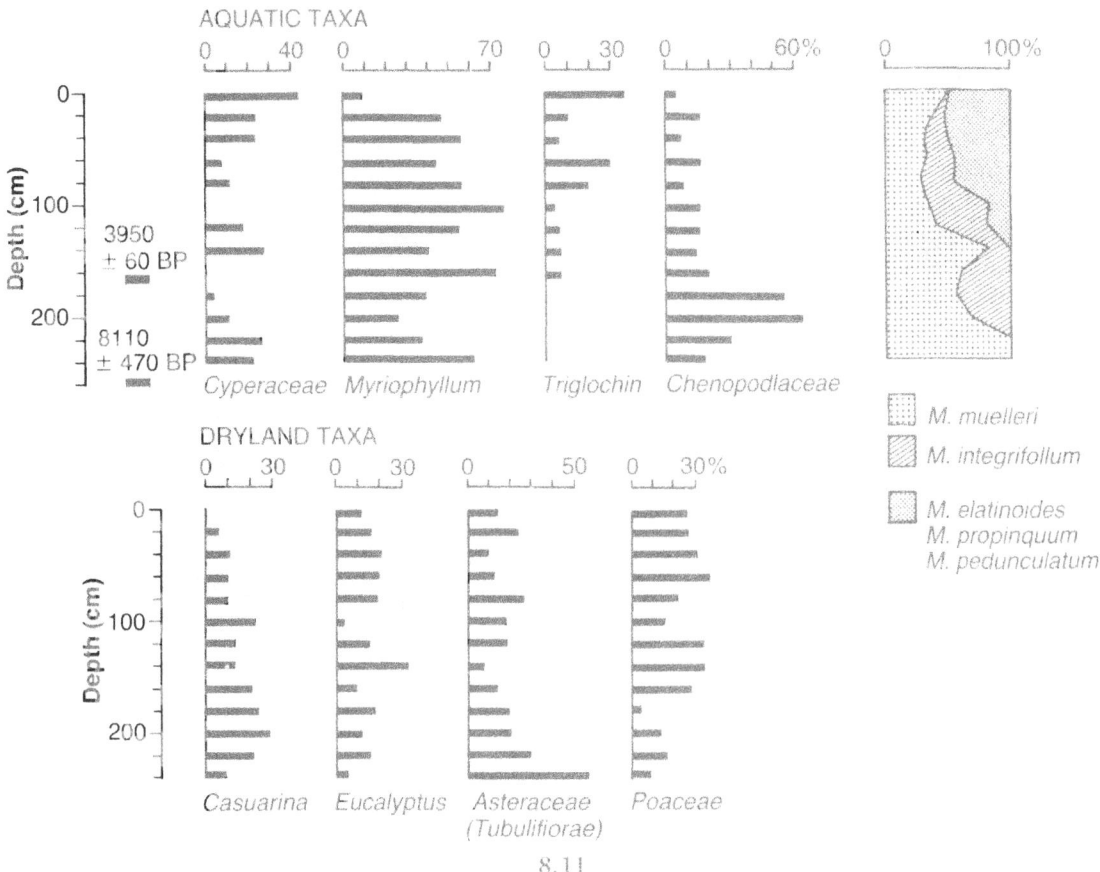

8.11
Changing proportions of pollen from different plants in the sediments at Lake Condah. The higher proportion of Asteraceae in the lowest levels indicates that there was a more open vegetation structure in the area at that time. The changing proportions of species of Myriophyllum reflects a trend from drier to wetter conditions. (After Head 1989, Figure 4)

On the basis of sediments and pollen it can be argued that there was always much the same depth of water in the lake. As sediments accumulated so the general water level rose. Most of the stone fish-traps that we can now see would have been high above water level before 4000 years ago, and could only have functioned as traps during rare, abnormal floods. After 4000 years ago the present system would have operated more frequently at times of seasonal flooding. In other words, the particular structures that we see today are unlikely to be older than 4000 years. As any older ones would be now covered by sediment accumulation, we are still not able to determine when stone fish-traps began to be built beside Lake Condah.

Other environmental manipulation

Fish-traps and similar facilities show local manipulation or enhancement of resources. Other techniques also were used. Of these, fire had the greatest impact. Many argue that Aboriginal burning of vegetation created the Australian ecosystems that we now regard as 'natural'. Certainly in many areas today, Aboriginal people regularly burn off dry vegetation, 'cleaning up the country' and allowing new growth. Such a deliberate practice of burning has even been termed 'fire-stick farming'. Large areas are also burnt for other purposes; for example, as 'fire-drives' to catch animals.

While recognising the local effects of Aboriginal burning, other researchers argue that Aboriginal burning should not be seen as having had any significant impact on the Australian ecosystem. This question is of more than academic importance, as some currently fashionable fire control or management regimes, based on the assumption that Aboriginal strategies of regular burning off are the most appropriate, may in fact turn out to be extremely damaging. It is therefore important to establish the extent and antiquity of the practice of burning.

POINTS FOR DISCUSSION

1 Is it important to know whether the fish-traps at Condah or Toolondo were developed over 10, 100 or 1000 years? How can we tell?
2 To what extent did Aboriginal people alter the environment?

PICTURING THE PAST

Write a description of a time at either Toolondo or Lake Condah when people were harvesting a major run of eels.

A DEBATE: PRESERVING THE TOOLONDO COMPLEX

Parts of the canal system had already been destroyed when Harry Lourandos investigated the eel-traps at Toolondo. More may have been destroyed since then. In April 1986 I received this letter from a landowner in response to a request to visit the site:

> Owing to a run of very dry years, and the 1982–3 drought there is practically nothing to be seen of the so called fish trap area.

> The gully had to be filled in for the following reasons
> (1) We are plagued by trespassers, especially spotlight shooters, and under the new trespass laws I would be liable for any injury incurred as a result of an accident within the erosion gully.
> If someone was killed whilst spotlighting even if trespassing it could possibly cost me the farm.
> (2) It was causing serious erosion, with rabbit infestation making it worse. It was also preventing the proper use of the paddock.
>   Yours sincerely

Debate whether or not the landowner is justified in his actions.

What steps could have been taken to prevent this destruction?

What incentives could we give landowners to compensate them for the loss of use of land on which sites occur?

How much would *you* be prepared to pay to preserve sites such as this?

References

Coutts, P.J.F., Frank, R.K. and Hughes, P., 1978, 'Aboriginal Engineers of the Western District, Victoria', *Records of the Victorian Archaeological Survey*, Vol. 7.

Dargin, P., 1976, 'Aboriginal Fisheries of the Darling-Barwon Rivers', *Brewarrina Historical Society*.

Godwin, L., 1988, 'Around the Traps: a Reappraisal of Stone Fishing Weirs in Northern New South Wales', *Archaeology in Oceania*, Vol. 23, pp. 49–59.

Head, L., 1989, 'Using Palaeoecology to Date Aboriginal Fish-traps at Lake Condah, Victoria', *Archaeology in Oceania*, Vol. 24, pp. 110–115.

Horton, D., 1980, 'The Burning Question: Aborigines, Fire and Australian Ecosystems', *Mankind*, Vol. 13, pp. 237–251.

Lourandos, H., 1980, 'Change or Stability?: Hydraulics, Hunter-gatherers and Population in Temperate Australia', *World Archaeology*, Vol. 11, pp. 245–264.

Lourandos, H., 1980, 'Forces of Change: Aboriginal Technology and Population in South-Western Victoria', Unpublished PhD Thesis, Sydney University.

Massola, A., 1962, 'The Native Fish-traps at Toolondo, in the Wimmera', *Victorian Naturalist*, Vol. 97, p. 162.

Presland, G., 1977, 'Journals of George Augustus Robinson, March–May 1841', *Records of the Victorian Archeological Survey*, Vol. 6.

Presland G., 1980, 'Journals of George Augustus Robinson, May–August 1841', *Records of the Victorian Archeological Survey*, Vol. 11.

Smith, M., 1983, 'Joules from Pools: Social and Economic Aspects of Bandi Stone Fish Traps', in *Archaeology at ANZAAS 1983*, ed. M. Smith, Western Australian Museum, Perth, pp. 29–45.

9

Ceremonial sites

Ceremonies are important in Aboriginal society. Esoteric knowledge and performance of appropriate rituals are fundamental to traditional Aboriginal life. Where Aboriginal communities have been able to maintain these activities, they can not only identify places of significance, but control them. Our concern here is more with situations where communities have been dispossessed from land and traditional lore and practices have been suppressed. The archaeological identification of ceremonial sites in these cases may be of more value to Aboriginal people than to academic archaeologists.

Ceremonial and sacred sites can take different forms. Natural features may be the embodiment of creation figures or their actions. So too with rock paintings and stone arrangements. Although painted or built by living people, they may still embody the continuous event of the Dreaming. Ceremonies need not be confined to sacred sites, but are often held at places specially set up for the event, with no lasting significance.

Many Aboriginal ceremonies draw large numbers of people together, and must therefore be timed to coincide with the availability of sufficient resources to feed hundreds or even thousands of participants for several days or weeks. Such large-scale gatherings also serve as meeting places for more mundane activities, opportunities to exchange goods and information, to arrange marriages and to settle disputes. An immediate archaeological question is the antiquity of these ceremonial systems.

In this chapter we examine two attempts to identify a sacred and a ceremonial site, and then consider some more general discussions involving ceremonies in the past.

Case study 1: Sunbury, Victoria

Description

Three shallow circular hollows, several hundred metres apart, are set in the upper slopes of a hillside overlooking a river. Each consists of a low earth bank, better preserved on the uphill side, forming a ring around the shallow interior. The largest, with a diameter of about 25 m has two concentric rings. The other two are about 15 m in diameter, and one has a pile of stone in the centre.

The problem and approach

When first archaeologically recorded in 1978 these were the only sites of this kind known to exist in Victoria. Although similar earth rings ('bora grounds') are well known in NSW and south-east Queensland as Aboriginal ceremonial grounds, the lack of comparative information in Victoria posed two basic questions. Firstly, were they Aboriginal sites?, Secondly, if they were, what was their function?

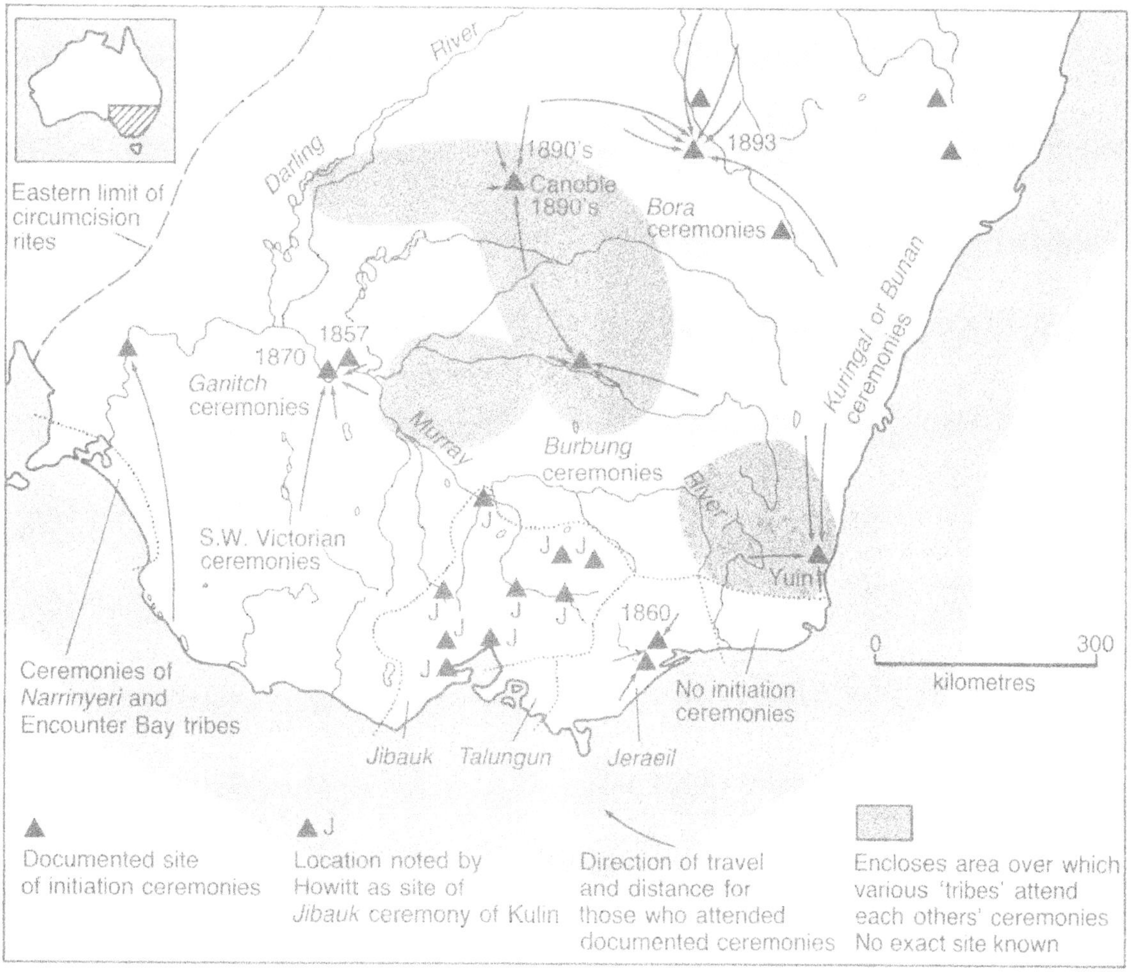

CEREMONIAL SITES   107

9.1

Documentary evidence for major ceremonies in south-eastern Australia. (After McBryde 1984: Figure 8)

9.2

A stone arrangement at Carisbrook, Victoria.

Two complementary lines of investigation were undertaken, archaeological and historical.

By excavating one of the rings I hoped to show whether or not they were associated with Aboriginal activities (for example, by finding stone tools), and to provide details on the method of construction which might clarify their function.

An examination of historical and ethnographic accounts of Aboriginal ceremonies and ceremonial grounds in Victoria and elsewhere in south-eastern Australia could provide supporting evidence and help to identify the function of the sites.

9.3
An aerial view of the largest earth circles near Sunbury. The two concentric rings can be clearly seen.

Archaeological research

Recording

As the rings are so shallow and the banks poorly preserved, it is difficult to define their exact size and shape, especially as the ground itself slopes. They are also difficult to photograph. In order to document and illustrate them we made use of modern technology, with computer-aided mapping. We laid out a north-south grid of 1 m squares over each ring, and measured the height of the ground at every metre interval. Using this data a computer generated contour plans as well as projections of the ground surface. These give an accurate record of the shape and a clear image of the appearance of each ring.

Excavating

We only excavated the central ring. A large area (54 m²) was opened up, to increase the likelihood of recovering artefacts, but the main aim was to dig through the bank to see how the ring was formed, and to expose the loose pile of stones visible on the surface in the centre of the circle. A subsidiary trench was cut through the bank at the lowest point of the ring where a smaller pile of stones could be seen.

9.4
Computer-drawn contour plan and three-dimensional projection of the surface of a ring at Sunbury. The slopes of the surface in the three-dimensional drawings have been exaggerated, to show up the shape of the rings more clearly. (After Frankel 1982, Figure 2)

As the shallow soil deposit in the ring was affected by vegetation, by worms and by hooves of sheep and cattle, no significant stratigraphic features could be defined, and there was no possibility of obtaining radiocarbon dates. The only stratigraphic evidence is for the construction of the banks and the stone cairns.

The sections through the banks illustrate how the ring was constructed. Higher up the slope deeper clay deposits were cut down and the spoil thrown back to form a bank at least 1 m wide

9.5
Excavations in progress on one of the earth banks forming the ring at Sunbury.

9.8
The cairn fully exposed, with loose rocks removed.

9.6
The central stone cairn before excavation.

9.9
A trench through the bank, with a small cairn just outside the circle.

9.7
The cairn partially excavated.

and over 40 cm high. In the southern, downhill area, material from both inside and outside the ring was scraped together to form the bank. The centre of the circle was scraped clear of loose gravel and stone to expose the rock surface and the cairns of stone were then neatly built on it.

164 stone artefacts were found in the site. Twelve were cores, the pieces of stone from which almost all the other small flakes and blades were stuck. The pattern of distribution of the artefacts in the site is shown in Figure 9.11. From the concentration of flakes and cores near the centre of the circle it is clear that this was a focus of some special activity.

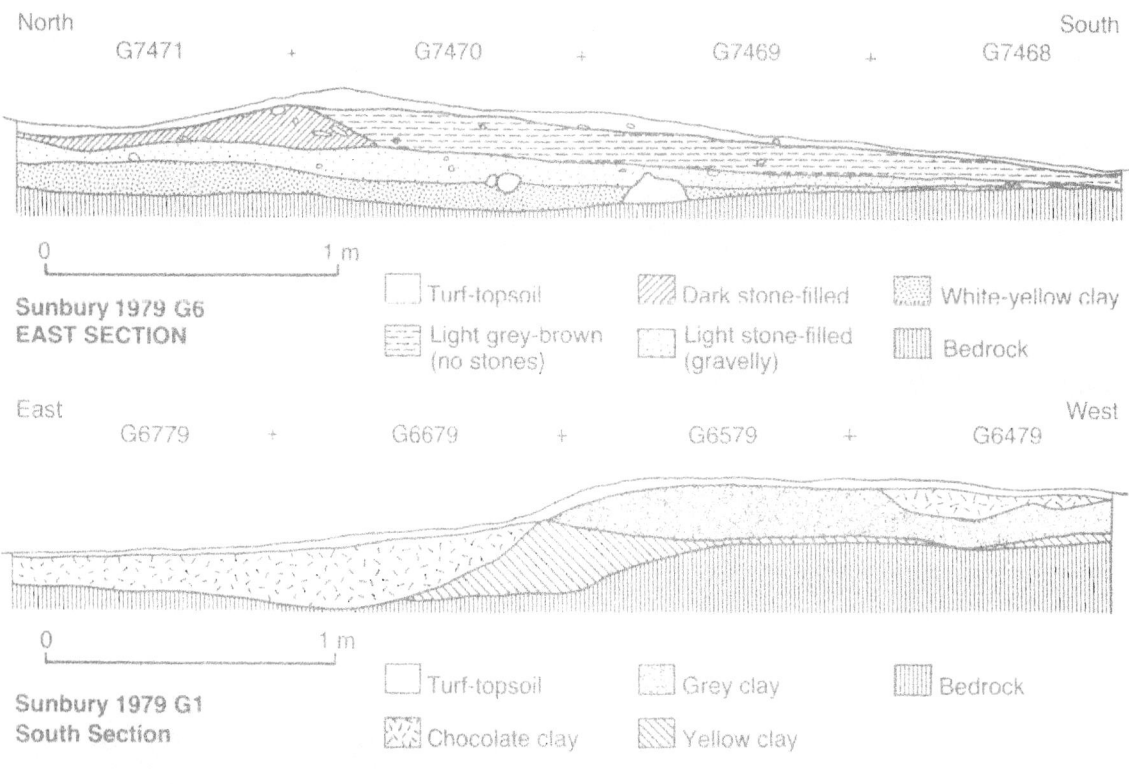

9.10 *Stratigraphic sections through the surround bank of the earth ring. The differences between them show how in the one case (upper figure) soil was heaped up to form the bank, while in the other (lower figure) earth was cut away as well as heaped up. (After Frankel 1982, Figures 6 and 7)*

Four small pieces of European pottery were also found, three of them from the same plate. There is so little of this material compared with the much larger number of stone flakes, that these sherds cannot be regarded as related to construction or use of the ring.

Historical research

What Aboriginal activities might the rings represent?

Many Aboriginal rings and other earth structures are known from New South Wales and Queensland, where a number of European observers recorded details of Aboriginal life in the nineteenth century. As there are few accounts available for central Victoria, we have to argue that the structures and associated activities known from these other areas had parallels here. This is one example of a common problem in archaeology — explaining artefacts, sites, or general patterns of behaviour by using analogies from other areas. In doing this we need to bear two questions in mind. Are we limiting our options by assuming that what we find must have some ethnographically known parallel; and over what distance in space and time are we justified in using this information?

Descriptions of the general shape and appearance, as well as the method of making rings by scraping back and heaping up soil to create a clear area match the way that the Sunbury rings were made. There is a wide range of variation in other individual features so that it is possible to

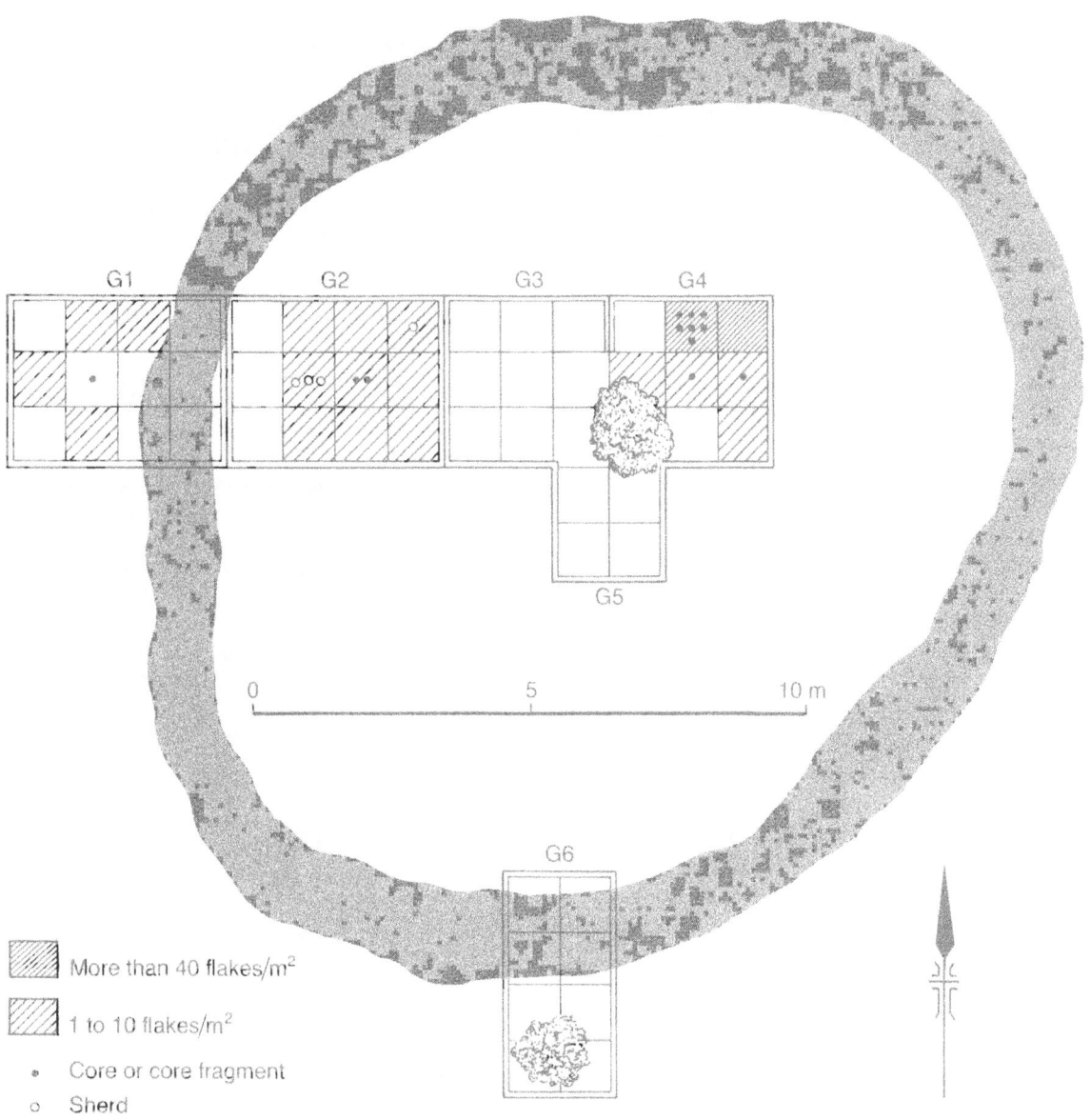

9.11
Plan of the excavations at Sunbury, showing the distribution of stone artefacts. (After Frankel 1982, Figure 5)

match each attribute of the Sunbury rings at some other site, although none are identical in all respects.

Although single, isolated rings may have been used for more secular meetings and activities, most historical accounts of rings connect them to initiation ceremonies. The initiation of young men was always of great significance, involving a series of ceremonies, sometimes lasting several weeks. Much of this activity was secret, attended only by men. Elaborate earth sculptures were often created on these occasions, while circular grounds provided a focus of activity.

Was this the purpose of the Sunbury rings? The cairns in the centre of the excavated ring may fit better with ceremonial rather than secular use of the site. The placement of the three rings out of sight of one another fits the emphasis on isolation and secrecy often associated with these ceremonies. The manufacture of small stone flakes may be explained (or explained away!) by arguing that their sharp edges were required for ritual hair-cutting, blood-letting, scarification or some similar activity which may have formed a part of initiation ceremonies here as in other areas.

One early account of the Sunbury area describes Aboriginal people harvesting exceptionally large quantities of *murnong*, the tuber which formed a staple part of the Victorian Aboriginal diet. Such rich resources could have provided the supplies necessary for large-scale gatherings in the area.

Although the archaeological evidence pointed toward an Aboriginal use of the site, there was still a possibility that they were European constructions, such as dams, buildings, animal pens or the circular paths of horse-powered machinery. They do not fit with the specific features or location expected for any of these better-known structures. More problematic are less predicable activities, such as those which might have been associated with military manoeuvres known to have been held in the vicinity in the middle of last century; the general lack of European material argues against this possibility.

CEREMONIAL GROUNDS IN THE NINETEENTH CENTURY

Bora initiation ceremony of northern NSW and southern Queensland:

> Two circles were formed on the ground, very much resembling the rings at a circus, only larger; these circles were cleared of all timber and grass, and carefully swept; the surface of the ground within them levelled, and slightly hollowed, so as to obtain sufficient loose earth to form the surrounding walls, which were about a foot high. The largest of these circles which was the one nearest the general encampment was about 70 feet [22 m] in diameter, most regular in shape, and in the centre stood a pole about 10 feet [3 m] high with a bunch of emu's feathers tied on top; in the western wall of this enclosure an opening about 5 feet [1.5 m] in extent was left as an entrance . . . . From the opening referred to, an ordinary uncleared bush track runs for about 23 chains [450 m] connecting it with another and smaller circle about 45 feet [14 m] in diameter. The scrub around the latter circle was denser than at the other one, and it was, besides, further from the camp and more secluded. This circle was not so perfect in shape as the other and the walls were roughly made; there was, moreover, no opening left for the purpose of ingress or egress, as in the larger circle, but any one wishing to enter it had to step over the wall of loose earth. Near the centre of this circle were two saplings that had been taken out of the ground by the roots; the branches were then cut level across, after which they were fixed in the ground with their roots upward. These inverted saplings were for use as seats by the old men when inspecting their novices. Although the surrounding country was quite level, one circle was not visible from the other, owing to the dense intervening scrub. (Mathews, R.H., 1895, p. 414)

Burbung initiation ceremony of northern NSW:

> In close proximity to the camp is the *burbung* or public ring, bounded by a low earthern embankment, with a narrow sunken *maro*, leading about four or five hundred yards into the forest to another circular space, formed in the same manner, known as the *eeteemat*, in the floor of which the butts of two saplings are firmly inserted, having the rooty ends upward . . . . Within the *eeteemat* there are also sometimes two, and sometimes four, heaps of earth, about a foot and a half or two feet high. (Mathews, R.H., 1898, p. 56)

JERAEIL CEREMONY IN GIPPSLAND, 1884

In 1884 A.W. Howitt organised the first major initiation ceremony to be held in Victoria for about thirty years. Despite the complaints of missionaries and impediments imposed by officials, many senior Aboriginal men took advantage of this opportunity to perform these important ceremonies for the last time.

Conclusions

1 The sites are Aboriginal.
2 They were probably used for ceremonies, most probably the initiation of young men.
3 The use of earth rings in ceremonies in Victoria is confirmed, extending their known distribution, with implications for cultural links.
4 As rare examples of this type of site, the Sunbury rings are of great heritage value.

Further considerations

More recently another ring, near Ballarat, has become known to archaeologists. In this case the European landowners have a family tradition dating from the middle of last century recognising the ring as an Aboriginal ceremonial ground. In fact it owes its survival to this tradition, as the farmers have therefore refrained from ploughing the area.

This raises another issue; preservation and identification. Rings such as these are hard to identify unless one is aware of the possibility that they might be found. They are also very easily destroyed; one pass of a plough might eliminate

9.12
Men preparing for the initiation ceremony in Gippsland in 1884. (Photo: State Library of Victoria)

all trace. How many other rings may have been unwittingly destroyed? How many are still awaiting identification?

The Sunbury rings themselves are not totally safe. Suburban development in the area makes land more valuable, so that we have a conflict here, as in so many other areas, between development and preservation. How valuable are these sites? How much would you spend to preserve them?

Case study 2: Mumbulla Mountain, NSW

This example raises social rather than technical issues concerning the validity of different types of data or sources of information, and considers Aboriginal sites that are natural, rather than artificial.

In 1978 Aboriginal people of Wallaga Lake raised objections to logging of a particular forest on the south coast of New South Wales. They claimed that logging would adversely affect a sacred site on the southern slopes of Mumbulla Mountain. Foresters and others rejected the Aboriginal claim, arguing that there was no record or knowledge of their associations with the area and that their 'oral traditions' were fabricated for political purposes. Aboriginal protests were, however, strong enough to halt logging temporarily while an archaeologist, Brian Egloff, investigated the traditions and the sites, and assessed the validity of the Aboriginal claim.

Three lines of evidence were pursued, archaeological, oral and historical documentary.

Archaeological

The granite boulders and the creek valley of the sacred area are natural features. Unlike the case at Sunbury there are no specific elements which could serve to identify the sites. Scatters of tools in the vicinity testify to Aboriginal use of the area, but not this special use.

Oral evidence

Some oral testimony provided by local Aboriginal people (such as that of Guboo Ted Thomas, a leader of the community) were not specific, but part of a general tradition of the significance of the area. Another older member of the community, Percy Davis, was able to testify to his initiation by elders on the mountain early this century.

Historical

Among the unpublished papers of A.W. Howitt, Brian Egloff located a description and map of an initiation ceremony which took place

9.13
Mumbulla Mountain from the air. (Photo B. Egloff)

9.14
Guboo Ted Thomas and archaeologists at work near Mumbulla Mountain. (Photo. B. Egloff)

in 1883 at a location which closely resembled Mumbulla Mountain.

Assessment

The historical evidence was taken to confirm the Aboriginal beliefs, and eventually 7508 ha of the forest was declared an Aboriginal Place (The Biamanga Aboriginal Place). A core area of 1100 ha containing the sacred sites was totally protected from logging.

The assumption that Aboriginal people 'invented the sacred site' as soon as logging approached the area is a common response by developers and characterises much conflict over sacred sites and mining elsewhere in Australia. A fundamental problem is that for many Aboriginal people such places are not only powerful or dangerous but also secret, the true significance being revealed only to fully initiated men. Only the imminent threat of destruction forces them to disclose their knowledge. A closed, secret register of sites provides one possible solution, where information can be lodged before crises develop and so avoid the charge of 'invention' of sites. Otherwise some external arbitration and validation may be called for. In the Mumbulla Mountain case, century-old European documentation provided crucial support for the Aboriginal claim.

The validation of this claim provides an important precedent for accepting other claims by Aboriginal groups who are perceived to have lost their traditional way of life and all knowledge of past practices.

Ceremonies in archaeological perspective

Beyond these specific problems of site identification, much archaeological interest is directed toward the significance and history of ceremonies and large-scale gatherings, and the long-distance social interaction and exchange systems that accompany them. An important consideration here is the connection between gatherings and seasonal abundance of food required to feed large numbers of people.

The importance of ceremonial activities in providing a framework for social interaction cannot be denied. Not only is this clearly seen in the historical accounts, but also from the numerous 'bora' rings known in south-east Queensland. Leonn Satterthwaite and Andrew Heather documented sixty-two of these earth circles in the Moreton Bay region. On general ethnographic evidence, they consider them to be ceremonial sites. Most occur toward the coast, where Aboriginal population density was greatest. As far as can be seen from the present surviving evidence, these rings were fairly evenly spaced across the landscape, normally within a short distance of water.

Satterthwaite and Heather argue that the large number of sites and their even placement reflects a system of periodic large-scale gatherings of people, which placed excessive demands on local sources of food. Ceremonies were therefore held at different sites in turn. The overall pattern seen in the ceremonial grounds is therefore one of a closely integrated network of relationships within the region. How this and other similar systems of social interaction developed is clearly an important area for further research.

One discussion of this question by John Beaton is certainly provocative. In his excavations in the Carnarvon Range in Queensland, Beaton noted remains of cycad (*Macrozamia moorei*) meals dated at about 4300 years ago. The seeds of these palms are highly toxic. We know from ethnographic studies that Aboriginal people were well able to remove the poisons, principally by leaching, fermentation or roasting, so that cycads could be eaten. Beaton argued that the time-consuming nature of these techniques meant that cycad preparation would not have been an everyday occurrence, but would have been reserved for special occasions. He therefore suggested that cycad use 4300 years ago should be seen as indicating a new development of large-scale gatherings of people, made possible by the introduction of leaching technology at that time. A further suggestion was that there was deliberate 'fire-stick farming' to enhance and regulate the productivity of cycads.

This scenario of a development of cycad processing and major ceremonial gatherings in the last 4000 or 5000 years is obviously speculative. Two pieces of evidence run counter to it. One is the subsequent discovery of cycad seeds at Cheetup Cave in south-west Western Australia dated to 13 000 BP. The other is the demonstration that knowledgeable people can select old, naturally leached seeds, and so deliberate processing of cycads is not always necessary.

Michael Morwood, working in south-east Queensland, is among a number of other archaeologists who have also argued for a growth in social interaction and large-scale ceremonies in the last few thousand years. In his study-area he suggested that a greater number of recent sites reflects a growth in population, while an increase in social interaction is demonstrated by the spread and development of art — symbols of identity and relationships. He sees changes in types of artefacts (particularly the abandonment of small stone spear-barbs in the last 1000 years) as showing a change from individual pursuit of larger animals to communal hunting and fishing, using nets and traps, as described in nineteenth century accounts of Aboriginal people in the area.

According to Morwood, a crucial factor in these developments was a change in the availability and structure of resources. Once the sea reached its present level about 6000 years ago winter runs of fish attracted people to the coast, while in the summer, seasonal availability of Bunya Pine nuts provided the abundance of food necessary for large numbers of people to gather together.

Once again counter arguments can be developed. Numbers of sites may be a poor indicator of population, as older sites (especially coastal sites) may not have survived. The changes in artefacts are not definite indicators of a major change in hunting patterns. It is difficult to demonstrate the absence of complex social interactions, exchange systems and ceremonial gatherings in earlier periods. All these arguments require more evidence and further justification. Some further consideration is given to related ideas of social developments in the last chapter.

POINTS FOR DISCUSSION

1 What important ceremonies have you attended?
   Describe and explain all about the ceremony (purpose, activities, location, participants) to someone who has not seen it. If they later write out a description, how accurate a picture does it give of the event?
2 How much reliance would you place on claims for a sacred site based on:
   * archaeological evidence
   * a nineteenth century account
   * present-day Aboriginal opinion
3 Besides ceremonies, what activities took place during large-scale gatherings?

PICTURING THE PAST

Describe the process of selecting and preparing a site for a ceremony.

A DEBATE: PRESERVING THE RINGS

In this chapter I argued that the archaeological evidence, taken together with analogies from other parts of Australia was sufficient to say that the sites at Sunbury were associated with Aboriginal initiation ceremonies. Not all archaeologists necessarily agree.

A hypothetical scenario: suburban development near Sunbury puts pressure on land and facilities. Developments are planned which will destroy the rings. When the developers' plans are blocked by the Victoria Archaeological Survey, they take their case to the Planning Appeals Tribunal, claiming that these are not Aboriginal sites, and anyway, even if they were, they are of little value. Barristers are employed to argue the case, and call on expert witnesses. Divide the class into several groups:

- expert witnesses including archaeologists who believe in preserving the rings and other archaeologists employed by the developers
- representatives of the Victoria Archaeological Survey, Aboriginal community groups, the Australian Conservation Foundation; members of the parliamentary opposition
- the developers
- residents of Sunbury
- members of the Appeals Tribunal who judge the case

Debate whether or not development should proceed if it involves:

1. a housing estate
2. a casino
3. a hospital
4. a factory

References

Beaton, J.M., 1982, 'Fire and Water: Aspects of Aboriginal Management of Cycads', *Archaeology in Oceania*, Vol. 17, pp. 51–58.

Byrne, D., 1984, *The Mountains Call Me Back: a History of the Aborigines and the Forests of the Far South Coast of NSW*, NSW Ministry of Aboriginal Affairs, Occasional Paper 5.

Egloff, B., 1979, *Mumbulla Mountain: An Anthropological and Archaeological Investigation*, National Parks and Wildlife Service, Occasional Paper 4.

Frankel, D., 1982, 'Earth Rings at Sunbury, Victoria', *Archaeology in Oceania*, Vol. 17, pp. 89–97.

Mathews, R.H., 1895, 'The Bora or Initiation Ceremonies of the Kamilaroi Tribe', *Journal of the Royal Anthropological Institute*, Vol. 24, pp. 411–427.

Mathews, R.H., 1898, 'Initiation Ceremonies of Australia Tribes', *Proceedings of the American Philosophical Society*, Vol. 37, pp. 54–73.

Morwood, M.J., 1987, 'The Archaeology of Social Complexity in Southeast Queensland', *Proceedings of the Prehistoric Society*, Vol. 53, pp. 337–350.

Mulvaney, D.J., 1989, 'The Anthropologist as Tribal Elder', *Mankind*, Vol. 7, pp. 205–217.

Mulvaney, D.J., 1989, *Encounters in Place: Outsiders and Aboriginal Australians 1606–1985*, University of Queensland Press.

Satterthwaite, L. and Heather, A., 1987, 'Determinants of Earth Circle Site Location in the Moreton Region, Southeast Queensland', *Queensland Archaeological Research*, Vol. 4, pp. 5–53.

10

Quarries

Many types of stone were used by Aborigines. Fine-grained highly silicious stone (such as quartz, flint or silcrete) is best for making chipped stone tools with sharp edges or points. Harder, denser rocks were preferred for hatchet heads with longer-lasting cutting edges for heavy use. Sandstone was used for grindstones, and soft orange or red ochre was used in ritual and painting.

Some types of stone are common. Others have a more limited distribution. In Victoria, for example, most chipped stone tools are made of quartz, silcrete or flint. Quartz, can be found almost everywhere, silcretes are also widespread, but flint can only be collected on the coast where it is washed up from offshore reefs. Other stone, such as the tough, shock-resistant greenstone much sought after for hatchet heads, could only be quarried at particular places.

The differing availability of stone allows us to view this raw material in economic and social as well as mechanical or functional terms. Stone may be obtained in three ways: *immediately* from close to a camp, *directly* when individuals obtain exotic stone for themselves, perhaps by going on special expeditions to quarries, and *indirectly* by exchange with other people. Which strategy was used is partly a matter of economics, depending on the availability of useful stone and how easily it could be obtained. It could also be socially determined by the relationships between people and the access they had to different territory.

The type of stone within sites and its distribution across the landscape can therefore show which regions were visited as part of seasonal movements or for specific purposes, as well as other social and economic relationships. Apart from everyday utility, some varieties of stone, and the quarries from which they were obtained, can have special significance and value in Aboriginal society. This is harder to show archaeologically, but ethnographic accounts give us some idea of this other dimension.

10.1
A silcrete quarry in Western Australia.

A QUARRY IN ARNHEM LAND

A quarry at Ngilipitji in Arnhem Land was an important source of stone used for spear heads and knives, which were distributed over a very wide area. In 1935 the anthropologist Donald Thomson wrote:

> That the quarry from which these spears came was remote, I had long known, for the very few, even of the oldest men on the northern coastline, who had told me about it, had even been there, although they knew and cherished, lovingly, the flint spearheads from it each wrapped in its sheath of fine soft paperbark tied with fibre string. (Thomson. D., 1983, p. 68)

It is possible to view control of this quarry as giving some people a monopoly over a scarce and valued resource, thereby increasing their personal power and status.

Larr-ngara clans are still held in some awe by their neighbours for their control of forces of Ngilipitji and their ability to hew artefacts of such exacting and death-dealing characteristics from the very depths of the ground.

10.2
Photograph by Donald Thomson of men at work at the Ngilipitji quarry in 1935. (Photo: Mrs D. Thomson/Museum of Victoria)

But, apart from an economic view of the significance of the quarry,

> there are planes of understanding about Ngilipitji, its ritual role, and its mythology which transcend . . . utilitarian precepts. Visits to the site were both utilitarian industrial ones to obtain armatures for weapons, and there were also mystical experience to re-unite the bonds between the place, the stone and its role in a broader religious system. (Jones, R., and White, N., 1988, p. 84)
>
> A film, *The Spear in the Stone* (Australian Institute of Aboriginal Studies, 1983), documents a visit to this quarry in 1981 by anthropologists and archaeologists, accompanying several senior Aboriginal men, including Diltjima, the senior member of the group owning the estate on which the quarry is situated, and Dhulutarrama, the 'manager' of the quarry charged with ritual and other responsibilities to look after the religious essence of the site, and the authority to control any activities carried out at it.
>
> As well as showing the techniques of quarrying stone, this film gives some idea of the power and danger associated with the site and the stone obtained from it. Equally importantly, it shows Aboriginal ideas and beliefs as important without (as Rhys Jones puts it) 'reducing Aboriginal attitudes to sanctimoniousness which does violence to their own often robust views'. (Jones, R., 1985, p. 23)

What can we learn from quarries?

Stone quarrying and knapping techniques. These show how material was extracted from the ground, and individual pieces prepared on the site and selected or rejected for later use.

Distribution of raw material. Where it is possible to trace stone from particular quarries we can map social connections across the landscape. Some of these may show the range of territory visited by individuals, or the extent of a trade or exchange network.

ITEMS EXCHANGED

James Dawson recorded some of the items exchanged at periodical large gatherings in western Victoria:

Stone for axes and wattle-gum adhesive from Geelong
Greenstone for axes from Goodwood
Sandstone for grinding axes from Lake Boloke
Obsidian or volcanic glass for scrapers from Dunkeld
Mallee saplings for spears from the Wimmera
Wood for spear shafts and fire-sticks from Cape Otway
Red clay pigment from Cape Otway
Marine shell from Warrnambool
(Dawson, J. 1881, p. 78)

ABORIGINAL STONE HATCHETS

After being roughed out at the quarry, axe 'blanks' or 'preforms' were taken away to be finished elsewhere. In most cases only the cutting edge of hatchets were given special treatment. Outcrops of sandstone were used to sharpen the axe by grinding the edge smooth. The cutting-edges were not sharp in the same way as modern steel axes are, but were long-lasting and more robust. Most stone hatchets were mounted on handles attached to the head; they were often bound in place with sinew and fixed with gum.

Hatchets of this sort were used primarily for woodworking, and especially for cutting bark slabs from trees to make bowls and dishes, shields or canoes. Hatchets were important in hunting; for example, for splitting open hollow logs to get at animals hidden inside, or for cutting toe-holes on the trunks of trees to climb up after possums.

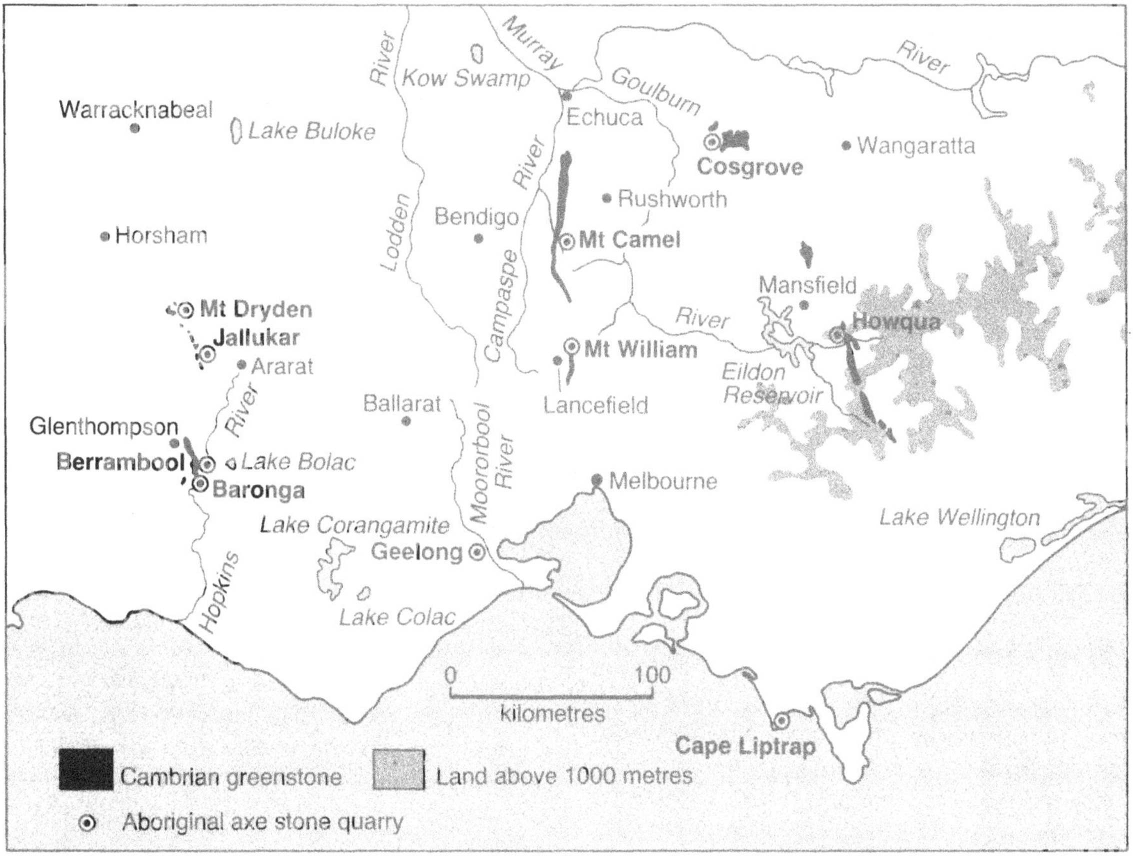

10.3
Location of stone quarries in the greenstone belts of Victoria. (After McBryde 1978, Figure 1)

10.4
Aboriginal men grinding the edges of hatchet heads. (Photo: T. Dick, Australian Museum)

10.5
Grinding-grooves on a sandstone outcrop near Mount Macedon, where the cutting-edge of hatchets were ground smooth.

Case study: Greenstone hatchets in Victoria

Greenstone (volcanic amphibole hornfels) suitable for making ground-edge hatchet-heads can be obtained from several quarries in central and western Victoria. Hundreds of greenstone hatchet-heads have been collected over the years from a very wide area. Isabel McBryde has been working on these for many years, with a particular interest in tracing the distribution of the stone from each quarry. This has involved a combination of historical, archaeological and geological evidence and has as its main aim the investigation of prehistoric social relationships.

The Mount William quarry

The Mount William site is the largest of the greenstone quarries in Victoria. The windswept northern slopes of a steep hillside are covered with scatters of chipped stone. These extend for over one kilometre along and down the ridge. In some sections greenstone boulders are surrounded by piles of stone chips. Here stone was levered or broken off outcrops projecting above the ground. In other places it was dug up from below the surface. Isabel McBryde has recorded over 250 shallow circular mining pits several metres in diameter. These are also surrounded by stone chips while some have larger blocks of stone originally used as anvils on which larger pieces were broken up. Other nearby heaps and scatters mark where the quarried stone was worked into shape.

Historical accounts

The social context of production

The Mount William quarry is discussed in many nineteenth century accounts. Many are derivative and second-hand, but others record information from knowledgeable Aboriginal people, such as William Barak.

The quarry lay within the territory of the Wuywurrung language group. Two senior men are recorded as having rights over and responsibilities for the site. One was Billibellary, a clan leader responsible for working the quarry. Ningulabul was the leader of an adjacent clan which inter-married with that of Billibellary and also had special rights over the site. The anthropologist A.W. Howitt, reporting Barak's opinion, noted that:

> Turnbull took care of the stone quarry where tomahawks were procured. He took care of it for all the tribe. Hence he was called Ningulabul — stone tomahawk (A.W. Howitt, unpublished notes on the Kulin in the La Trobe Library, Melbourne. Quoted in McBryde, I. 1984)

It is possible that, in keeping with a common practice among other Australian societies, Ningulabul and Billibellary, as senior men of allied clans, had complementary roles; one as the 'owner' of the quarry the other as the 'manager'.

10.6
Part of the Mount William stone quarry. Scatters of chipped stone mark where greenstone was quarried and roughly shaped.

> A.W. Howitt recorded the memories of William Barak about Billibellary and the Mount William quarry:
>
> When the neighbouring tribes wanted stone for tomahawks they usually sent a messenger for

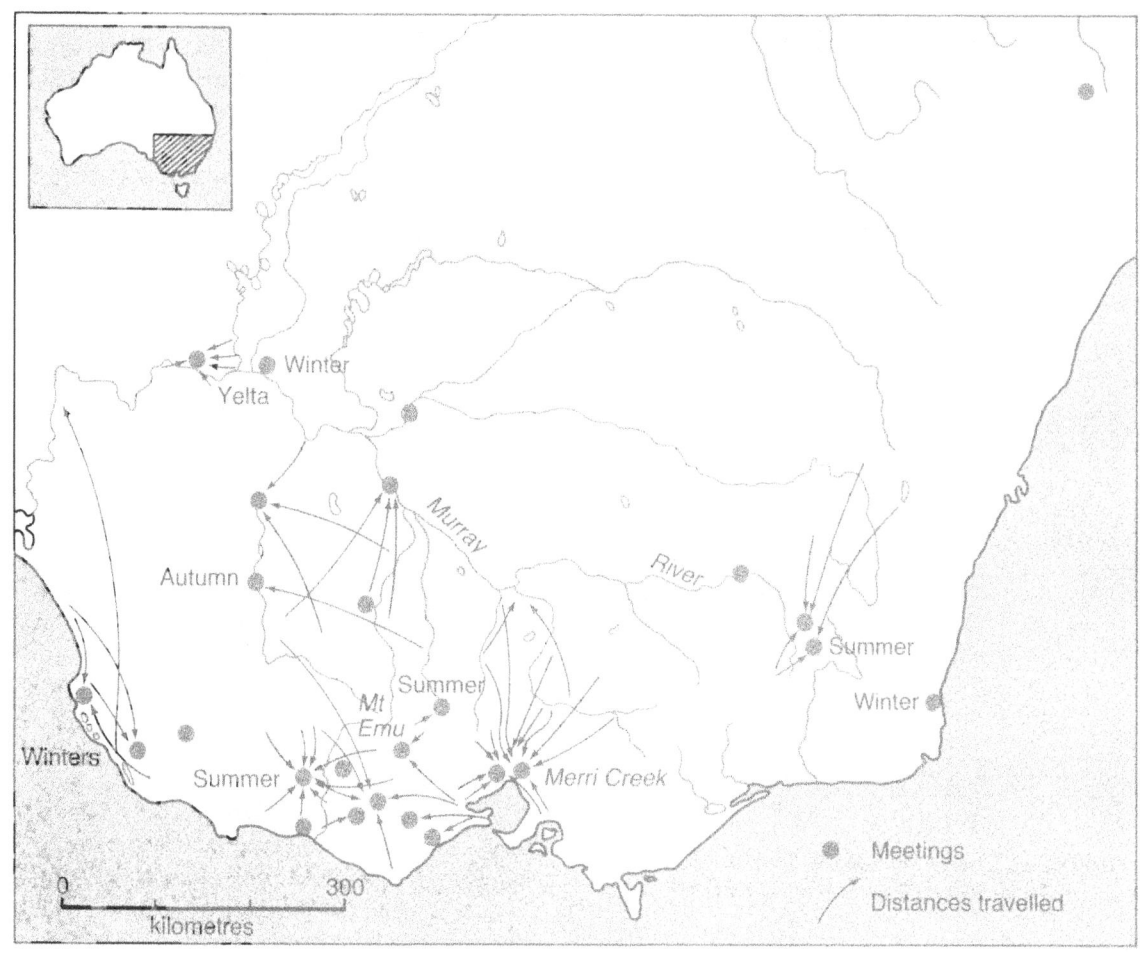

10.7
Documentary evidence for inter-group meetings and exchange in south-eastern Victoria. (After McBryde 1984, Figure 7)

Billibellary to say that they would take opossum rugs and other things if he would give them stone for them. When they arrived they camped around the place. Billibellary's father when he was alive split up the stones and gave it away for presents such as rugs, weapons, ornaments, belts, necklaces — three pieces of stone were given for a possum rug. People sometimes gave presents in advance to get stone bye and bye. I have heard Billibellary say to the people when they came 'I am glad to see you and I will give you all you want and make you satisfied, but you must behave quietly and not hurt me nor one another'. If however people came without giving notice there would be a row and a fight. Sometimes men came by stealth to steal the stone. (A.W. Howitt, unpublished notes on the Kulin, La Trobe Library, Melbourne. Quoted in McBryde, I., 1984, p. 272)

The context of distribution

Apart from local people who had immediate access to the quarry, others obtained stone directly from it, travelling long distances to do so. Some are known to have come over 100 km, from Geelong or beyond the Murray River. Other people obtained this prized stone indirectly, by exchange. Large-scale gatherings, often associated

10.8
Billibellary: a sketch by William Thomas. (R. Brough Smyth Papers, State Library of Victoria)

10.9
A roughly shaped hatchet head discarded with other stone debris at a greenstone quarry in western Victoria, shaped at the quarry.

with ceremonies (see Chapter 9), were also the occasion for the exchange of a wide range of goods. In this way stone from the Mount William and other quarries gradually moved long distances across the country.

In some cases locally unobtainable goods were obtained for basic utilitarian purposes — for example sandstone slabs for grindstones, or particular types of wood for spears. This does not apply to stone for hatchet-heads. Rock suitable for ground-edge hatchets is not uncommon and finer-quality greenstone, more-or-less indistinguishable from that from Mount William, could be quarried at many different places.

Despite the availability of equivalent material, a high value was placed on stone from the major quarries. The importance attached to Mount William stone is clear from the historical accounts describing the items given to Billibellary in exchange. These indicate that three pieces of stone were seen as equivalent in value to one possum-skin cloak, an item requiring considerable time and energy to manufacture. Why was this stone so much sought after, and distributed so widely?

It is not too inappropriate to apply the information that we have from Aboriginal societies elsewhere in Australia. We should see a non-utilitarian value for these items, which were desired not simply as items to use, but as items to have and to exchange. Although not hoarded as precious and never used, they must have had a social, rather than a simply economic and utilitarian value and significance.

Archaeological perspectives

Apart from providing details of the quarry itself, Isabel McBryde's work concentrated on the hundreds of greenstone hatchet heads found over a very wide area. This involved:

- the location and examination of as many stone hatchet-heads as possible in museums and other collections
- *petrographic analysis* of each hatchet to determine which quarry it came from

> ## TECHNIQUES OF SOURCING STONE
>
> *Examination by hand and eye.* Colour, hardness and texture can be used to identify some sources and specimens, but where rock is very similar, more sophisticated techniques of petrographic analysis must be used.
>
> *Thin section analysis.* An extremely thin slice of rock is cut and ground on a glass slide. Microscopic examination shows the characteristic shapes of different minerals present so that the composition of different samples can be compared.
>
> *X-ray diffraction.* X-rays passed through crystalline substances will be diffracted in standard patterns. The combination of reflections from all of the minerals present in a rock will produce a characteristic pattern, allowing comparison the mineral composition of samples, and identification of specific rock types.
>
> *Trace-element analysis.* Rocks and other substances contain extremely small quantities of some elements. The presence and relative proportions of these can be used to characterise samples. X-ray fluorescence, neutron activation and proton-induced x-ray emission are among the techniques now available for measuring these small variations in chemical composition, which can be used to compare samples and define groups.

Location of hatchets: problems of sampling

The vast majority of the hatchet heads collected over the last century come from casual finds, turned up by farmers or accidently picked up on the surface of the ground. Few come from archaeological sites or have any precise information on where they come from. Areas of the state with little agricultural activity or less intensive development are far less likely to be represented in the sample. Conversely, areas where an enthusiastic collector may have been at work may have an unusually large number of examples. The sample is therefore far from ideal and contains some unavoidable biases.

Petrographic analysis: problems of characterisation

There are two dimensions to these analyses: the definition of the rock-type characteristic of each of the quarries, and the sourcing of each individual sample. The greenstone from most of the quarries is very similar in composition and affected by similar geological processes. In some cases only very detailed analyses of trace-elements can differentiate between them. Some samples from Mount William and the nearby Mount Camel site cannot be separated at all. The identification of some quarries and the sourcing of some axes are, therefore, not always certain.

Patterns of distribution and relationships

The figures show some of the results of Isabel McBryde's sourcing programme. These can be looked at in several ways.

Direction of stone distribution

Figure 10.10 shows the overall distribution of artefacts from several quarries. Two things are immediately clear. One is the wide area over which material from many quarries is found, especially that from Mount William and Mount Camel. This clearly indicates the importance attached to stone from these two quarries. The second point is that the stone is not evenly distributed in all directions. Material from Mount William and Mount Camel travelled far to the west and north-west, but not so far in other directions.

This skewed distribution is also clearly seen in Figure 10.11 which plots the location of all hatchets sourced to the Mount William quarry. There is a comparative lack of greenstone artefacts from the semi-arid Mallee of north-western Victoria, where finds cluster near main rivers,

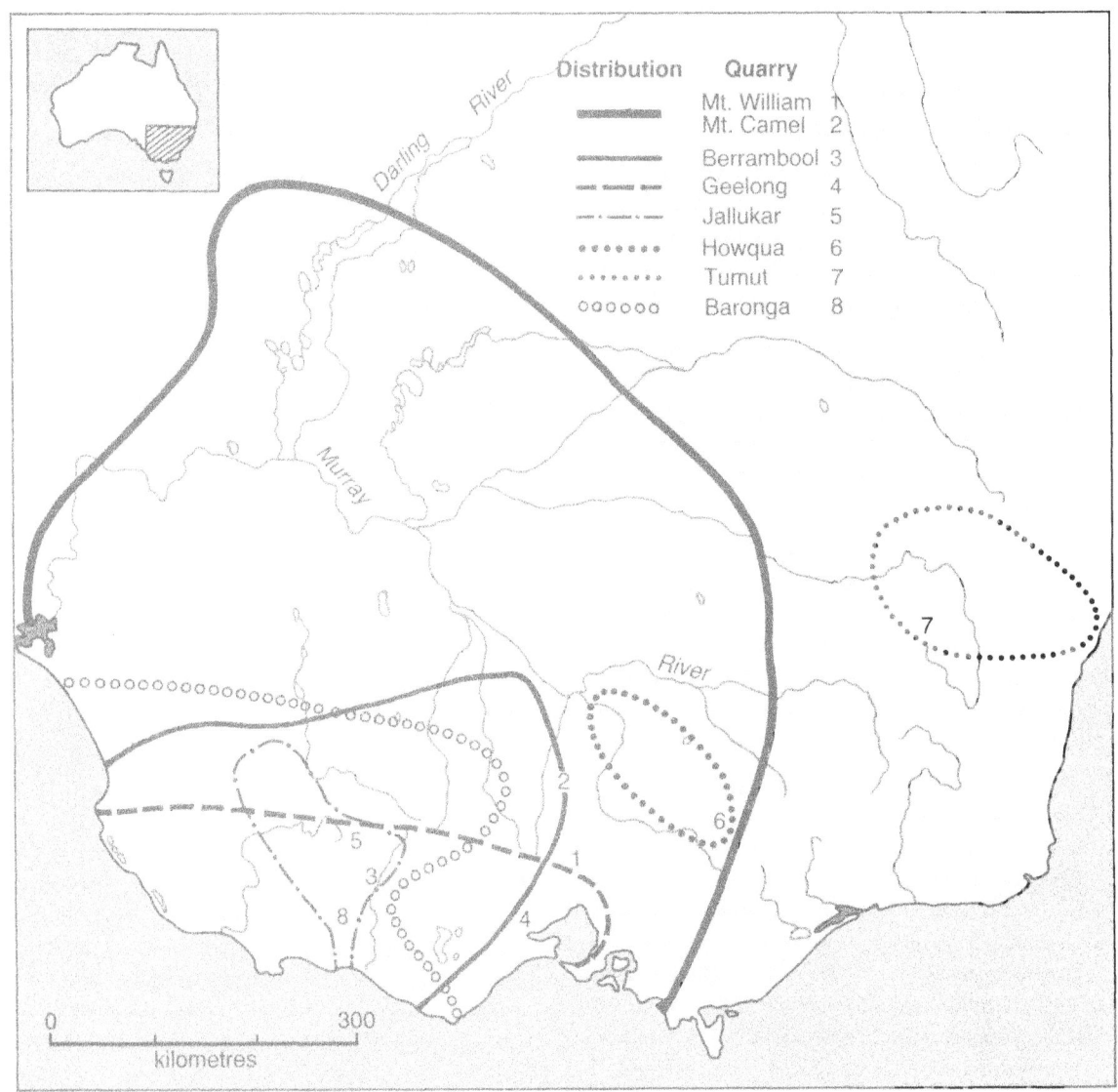

10.10

The areas over which stone from eight quarries was distributed, according to analyses by Isabel McBryde. (After McBryde 1986, Figure 6.1)

such as the Wimmera. We have two possible explanations for the lack of material in these areas. One possibility is that there were always fewer people living there compared with the far richer well-watered south-western regions of Victoria. If this were so, artefact concentrations reflect ancient population structures. Alternatively, the distribution of material may simply be the result of sample bias, reflecting the intensity of European development and collecting.

Other basic patterns, such as the comparative lack of material in Gippsland to the south-east, are less problematic. These tie in well with some fundamental structures in Victorian Aboriginal society, and provide McBryde with some of her most interesting explanations.

Both general historical evidence and studies of the languages of Victoria show that there was a major division between the Aboriginal people of Gippsland and those of central and western Vic-

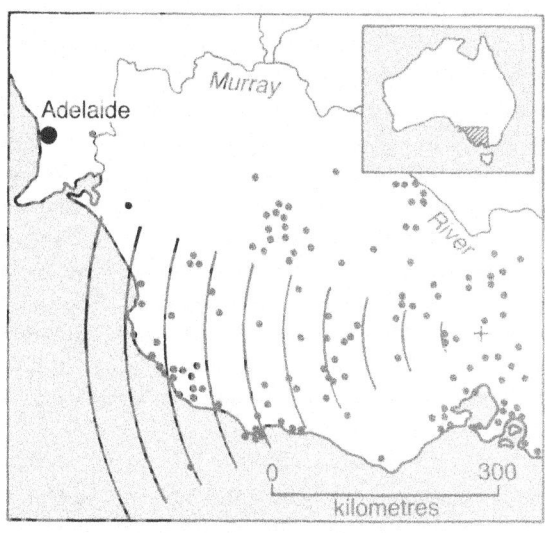

10.11
The find-spots for greenstone hatchet-heads identified by Isabel McBryde as coming from the Mount William quarry. The proportion of axes in each part of the western segment is shown in Figures 10.12 and 10.13. (After McBryde 1986, Figure 6.9).

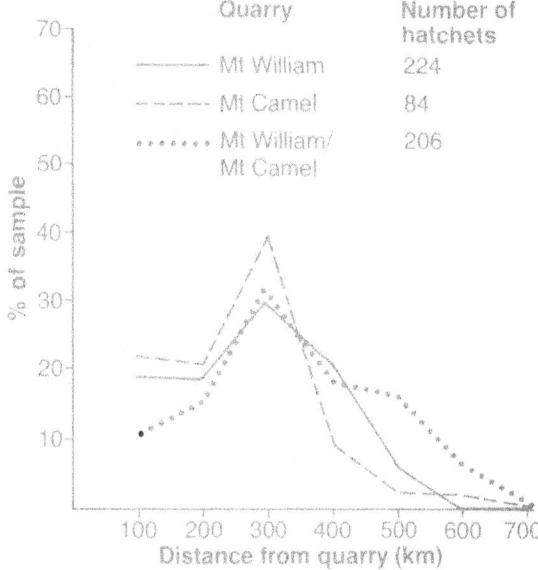

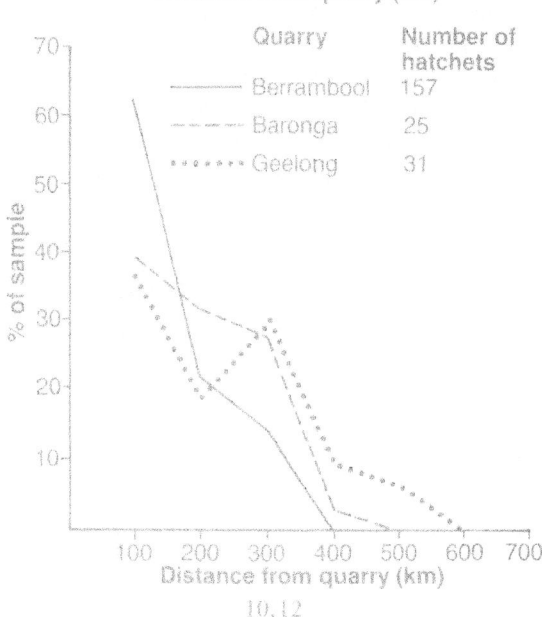

10.12
Distance decay curves showing the relative proportions of hatchets found at different distances from the source quarries. The Mount William/Mount Camel material has a different pattern of distribution, and travelled further from the source. (After McBryde 1978, Figure 3).

toria. There was little communication between the two areas and occasional serious conflict when they met. Although conflict observed in the middle of the nineteenth century may have been aggravated by pressures brought on by European settlement, the two groups were clearly antagonistic. Linguistic evidence confirms this pattern. The Ganay (or Kurnai) languages of Gippsland are distinct from the series of related Kulin languages spoken over much of central and western Victoria.

The social relationships linking and separating different regions are therefore neatly reflected in the pattern of distribution of greenstone hatchet heads.

Quantity and distance

Figure 10.12 shows the proportion of axes found at different distances from five quarries. These 'distance decay curves' may give an insight into the structure of the exchange system and the way in which hatchet heads were obtained or passed from one area to another.

Stone from the less important quarries at Berrambool, Baronga and Geelong shows a fairly steep, regular fall-off in quantity with distance, indicating an even process of distribution. The fall-off in quantity with distance for the Mount William and Mount Camel sites is different. Material travelled further, the slope is less steep and has an anomalous peak. The highest proportion of axes were not found close to the quarry, but between 200 and 300 km away. This may be due to several, perhaps related factors. McBryde suggests that there was a complex system of distribution, perhaps a redistribution centre away from the quarry itself. Historical accounts of exchange networks and tribal gatherings can be used to support this view.

It is interesting to explore this further. Once again part of the problem is how we count our data. Figure 10.13 compares two measures. These consider only the hatchets found west of Mount William, in the segment marked on Figure 10.11. This avoids distortions created by the asymmetrical distribution of material. In drawing her distance decay curve for this segment, McBryde followed the same procedure as in the previous graphs, counting the number of hatchets in each concentric 50 km band, and plotting the relative proportions in each. But these concentric bands do not, of course, all have the same area. The further that they are from the quarry, the larger they are. Is the pattern of more artefacts from more distant bands simply a product of their increased size? The second line on the graph tests this. It shows the number of hatchets per 10 000 km^2 in each band.

The patterns are not altogether dissimilar, but there are some interesting differences. The ratio of hatchets to area close to the quarry is far greater than the raw number, but the comparative lack of finds between 50 and 150 km is still clear. Further from the quarry the pattern is slightly different and a more even distribution is suggested. Although we can still argue for some complex redistribution of Mount William stone, it becomes harder to correlate high numbers of finds with specific meeting places.

It is, of course, also possible that these patterns are exaggerated by sample bias, with larger numbers of artefacts coming from the more intensively farmed areas of south-western Victoria.

Further discussion

The wide distribution of stone from these quarries testifies to their importance. As the rock

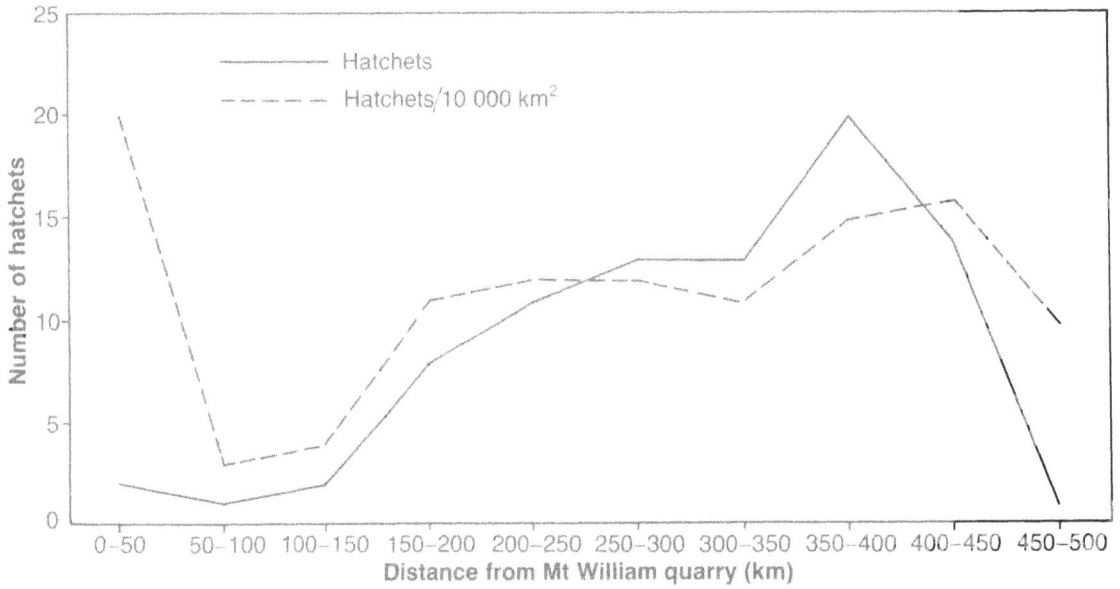

10.13
Distance-decay curves, showing the proportion of hatchets from Mount William found at different distances from the quarry in one segment (see Figure 10.11). Two curves are shown, one with the number of hatchets, the other compensating for the different area of each concentric ring. (Data from McBryde 1986, Figure 6.9)

from many sources was so similar, we must surmise that people knew where their greenstone came from. The value ascribed to them was not based on intrinsic properties, but on associated information passed on with the hatchet-heads. Although highly regarded, these tools were still used and, quite obviously, were also lost or otherwise discarded.

Studies of acquisition and use of axe-stone in Papua New Guinea show the high value placed on imported stone. This was partly a social, but also very much a utilitarian value. Axe-heads were continually resharpened and reused. They were not normally discarded until they were too small to be useful any longer. Victorian greenstone was not handled in the same way. There is no indication, for example, that the hatchet-heads found further from the quarries are smaller, and therefore might have had a longer use-life than others.

From this study, integrating ethnographic and linguistic evidence with scientific analysis of archaeological data, we can see how artefacts can serve social as well as economic functions. The exchange and distribution of raw material is affected by social relationships and connections, not simply the desire for a useful item. Although the archaeological material we observe today is the result of numerous individual transactions, the overall pattern reflects long-lasting structures in society. The linguistic and cultural areas of the nineteenth century must be as old as the exploitation and distribution of greenstone.

There are some suggestions that the distribution of greenstone can be seen as part of a wider growth of ceremonial activities, large-scale gatherings and exchange networks in the last few thousand years. There are however, two problems. One is that we have little idea of how old any of the greenstone hatchet heads are, or for how long Mount William and other quarries were used. Very few pieces of greenstone have been found in excavations, so that although the oldest fragments known at present are about 2000 years old, this cannot be used to indicate when greenstone began to be used and traded. The other problem is that stone was not the only item traded. Even if greenstone was only used in the recent past there may have been earlier exchange systems involving other goods.

POINTS FOR DISCUSSION

1 Do you know of any circumstances in your own society where gifts have symbolic or social rather than functional or commercial value?
2 If stone hatchet-heads were important and valuable, why were so many lost or discarded?
3 To what extent do you think the sample of hatchet-heads used by McBryde is affected by biases in discovery and collecting?

PICTURING THE PAST

1 Describe a journey from a distant region to Mount William to obtain greenstone from the quarry.
2 Trace the history of a piece of greenstone from the time it was quarried until the present.

References

Dawson, J., 1881, repr. 1981, *Australian Aborigines*, George Robertson, Melbourne.

Jones, R., 1985, 'New Research Aims, Aboriginal Liaison and Field Strategy' in *Archeological Research in Kakadu National Park*, ed. R. Jones, Australian Parks and Wildlife Service, Special Publication 13, p. 23.

Jones, R. and White, N., 1988, 'Point Blank: Stone Tool Manufacture in the Ngilipitji Quarry, Arnhem Land, 1981', in *Archeology with Ethnography: An Australian Perspective*, eds D. Meehan and R. Jones, Australian National University, pp. 51–87.

McBryde, I., 1978, 'Wil-im-ee Mooring: or, Where Do Axes Come From', *Mankind*, Vol. 11, pp. 354–382.

McBryde, I., 1984, 'Exchange in Southeastern Australia: an Ethnohistorical Perspective', *Aboriginal History*, Vol. 8, pp. 132–153.

McBryde, I., 1984, 'Kulin Greenstone Quarries: the Social Context of Production and Distribution for the Mt William Site', *World Archaeology*, Vol. 16, pp. 267–285.

McBryde, I., 1986, 'Artefacts, Language and Social Interaction: A Case Study from South-eastern Australia', in *Stone Age Prehistory*, eds G.N. Bailey and P. Callow, Cambridge University Press, pp. 77–93.

Thomson, D., 1983, *Donald Thomson in Arnhem Land*, (compiled by N. Peterson) Currey O'Neill, Melbourne.

Turpin, T., 1983, 'The Social and Economic Significance of the Movement of Edge-ground Hatchets in Australia', *Journal of Australian Studies*, Vol. 12, pp. 45–52.

11

Rock art sites

In common with all other peoples, Aboriginal people decorate a wide variety of items. Some of this art is casual but some is imbued with greater significance. This is especially so with rock art.

Rock art is found in many areas of Australia, but varies greatly in quantity, technique and style. It is possible to see some common elements throughout the continent and to regard art as serving a common function in all Aboriginal societies. Where Aboriginal people still paint or engrave scenes and signs on rock surfaces both the images and the activity itself are encompassed within a complex web of social and metaphysical meanings, with significance on many different levels. Scenes and symbols may be 'owned' or 'managed' by members of one specific group, but painted by members of another. Several different meanings may be ascribed to images, depending on the status of individual people. The full series of meanings may be known only to the most senior members.

Such knowledge is extremely important within Aboriginal society. From an external perspective, we can use rock art to explore a different set of questions. These may be relevant to us, but not necessarily relevant to the artists or owners of the art. We do not need to confine ourselves to investigating mythological 'meaning', but can explore other issues. Some of these are anthropological, looking at how art en-

11.1
Some of the major styles of rock art in different parts of Australia (see colour plates).

codes meaning and may symbolise relationships between different people, or between people and their natural and supernatural world. We may take an art-historical approach, concerned with styles, techniques, and aesthetics. Or we can use rock art in a way similar to other artefacts, to search for formal similarities and differences as clues to long-term developments and relationships in the past.

History and trends in rock art

A new, experimental *cation-ratio* dating technique has recently been used on several engraved motifs in the Olary region of South Australia. A series of dates from 30 000 years ago to the present have been obtained. If the technique proves to be reliable, then it demonstrates not only that art in Australia is extremely old (perhaps as old as human settlement) but also that the techniques and designs of rock engravings continued relatively unchanged in some areas for tens of thousands of years. Sites that we see today with hundreds of motifs are the cumulative products of generations of artists working in a similar style.

The earliest radiocarbon dates associated with rock art come from Koonalda Cave in the Nullarbor Plain. Here charcoal found far underground is dated to about 20 000 years ago. This charcoal must come from burning torches used by people to light their way deep into the limestone cave, and can therefore be used to date linear markings on the nearby walls of the cave. Similar finger markings have also been found in Orchestra Shell Cave near Perth, New Guinea II Cave beside the Snowy River in eastern Victoria and in several other caves, including Koongine Cave (Chapter 5) in south-east South Australia. None of these markings have yet been dated but some people have suggested that they belong to the same tradition as Koonalda Cave, and may be as old. This assumes that these widely separated sites were linked together as parts of a single early cultural tradition.

In a similar way it has often been suggested that there was a sequence of artistic traditions stretching across large areas of the continent with earlier non-representational engravings followed first by simpler and later by more complex paintings. As more research is done on rock art, such simple, broad models become more difficult to sustain. It is increasingly clear that local dated sequences of styles and motifs need to be established. Until then, broad models which assume a sequential development and continental-scale trends cannot be justified.

Advantages of working with rock art

- More than other items of material culture, rock art encodes symbolic meanings, and provides an insight into peoples' perceptions of their world.
- Rock art is very complex and so provides scope for detailed analysis of a wide range of variables.
- Unlike other items, rock art is fixed in place. There is no question about spatial patterning.
- The subjects depicted give clues to types of animals and artefacts in use at different times.

Disadvantages

- The very complexity of meanings in rock art that allows different and detailed analyses may also confuse any patterning that we try to abstract.
- Rock art can only rarely be dated, so that while it is fixed in space, even motifs within the same site cannot be regarded as being of the same age.
- Few sites are fully documented and the weathering of engravings or the fading and decay of paintings often make it difficult to identify all the images in a site, or to record them accurately.

Archaeological approaches to rock art

- Basic documentation of rock art sites – size, number of motifs, location

11.2
Koonalda Cave on the Nullarbor Plain. Wall markings far underground are 20 000 years old.

- techniques (e.g. pecking, engraving, painting)
- motifs (species of animals, items of material culture, abstract designs)
- styles
- Analysis of spatial patterning; local, regional and continent-wide similarities of various characteristics, and the definition of regional styles.
- Chronology of rock art: developments and change in local, regional and continent-wide styles.
- Developments in art as a reflection of social and environmental change.
- Artefacts and animals depicted can show change in technology and environment.

TECHNIQUES OF ROCK ART

Painting. Pigments made from ochres (yellow, red) pipe-clay (white) or charcoal (black) painted on with a brush.

Stencils. Pigments painted or sprayed from the mouth around objects or parts of the body to leave a negative image. Sometimes objects covered in paint can be pressed against the surface.

Pecking and engraving. Images pecked or cut into rock surfaces using a hammerstone or hard, sharp engraving tool.

Case study: Sturts Meadows, NSW

Sturts Meadows is in arid north-western New South Wales. In the winter the red flowers of Sturt's Desert Pea appear beside the flat rounded slabs of mudstone exposed in the low rises on either side of a creek-bed. These are covered with innumerable engravings. For several years John Clegg has been documenting and analysing these in an attempt to understand the structure of one major rock art site.

11.4
Rock outcrops at Sturts Meadows are covered with engravings.

Recording in the field

In his main field season in 1982 John Clegg worked with fourteen assistants at the site, locating and recording as many individual motifs as possible. He followed this sequence of activities, each of which had its own problems.

Sampling. The extent of the site, and the vast number of known motifs (over 130 000 have been counted) meant that some parts only of the site could be recorded in detail. Five sub-sites in different areas were selected, and even within these not all the rock exposures could be fully documented.

Definition of types. Here the problem was to define a set of standard types, deciding what degree of difference between two motifs was of minor or no significance, and what constituted a 'real' difference. Fifty-seven types were defined and recorded. In later analyses these can be combined into a smaller number of more general categories.

Recording. Large areas of the site were photographed, and many engravings were individually traced onto plastic film. Most of the recording was more simply a count of the number of each type of motif on each rock in each sub-site.

Dating

Five radiocarbon dates have been obtained from carbonate 'varnish' or coating built up on the surface of the rock and covering the engravings. These show that some engravings are as much as 10 000 years old, others are more recent.

Basic data

16 282 engravings were recorded on 214 rocks, with a total surface area of about 3377 m^2. The majority of engravings are bird and animal tracks, but there are many other more abstract designs. There are only a few rare examples which are recognisable representations of animals.

Uniformity within the site

Preliminary analyses used a smaller set of general types, combining the fifty-seven recorded types into sixteen more general ones. The proportions of these were compared within and between the sub-sites. This showed that at all scales (individual rock, groups of rocks or sub-sites) there was a fairly uniform proportion of major types of motifs. While the site is therefore remarkably homogenous, some separation between areas of the site is possible when rarer motifs are given special consideration.

Distribution

The numbers and density of motifs were plotted against the size and quality of rock surfaces. Not surprisingly the basic pattern shows that engravings normally occur on well-preserved rocks with smooth rather than rough surfaces.

Not all suitable rocks have the same density of engraving, but these tend to cluster into distinct sub-sites.

Use, and reuse of the site

Although we know some motifs are extremely old, we can still consider whether the art was produced during short periods of activity, or if the site represents a consistent, slow development.

When first pecked into the rock, engravings stand out as a lighter grey-blue against the dark grey-brown surface. Over time a patina develops,

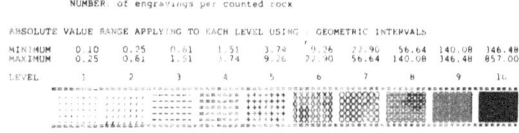

11.8

The relative density of engravings on rock exposures in different parts of Sturts Meadows. (After Clegg 1987, Figure 7)

DATING ROCK ART: IMPORTANT SIGNS AND TECHNIQUES

- *Motifs* buried by datable soil deposits within sites must be older than the material covering them.
- *Superimposed motifs*, where one is painted or engraved over another give a relative age for specific images within a site.
- *Animal species*, where these can be linked to the presence or absence of particular animals in a changing environment.
- Depiction of *other items of known age* (most obviously, recent European introductions such as ships or guns).
- *Weathering or fading* of paintings or engravings may give a rough estimate of relative age.
- *Radiocarbon dating* of organic material included in pigments or in overlying weathering of exposed rock surfaces. This is now increasingly feasible with recent developments in radiocarbon dating which allow it to be used with extremely small samples.
- *Cation-ratio dating* is a still-experimental technique which uses the ratios of potassium, calcium and titanium cations (positively charged particles) leached out of weathering rock surfaces.

and the engravings revert to the original rock colour. They then become difficult to see and may not have been noticed or were simply ignored by later artists who cut their own work across earlier engravings.

Clegg combined this idea with the information on the patchy distribution and uneven density of engravings to suggest that as each suitable rock was covered with engravings, people moved to another nearby one. In this way sub-sites, or local denser clusters built up. After a longer interval, when older engravings had lost the distinctive brighter colour, people returned to previously used rocks.

Clegg therefore favours a long-term development of the site, with periodic (every year? every decade?) gatherings in the area and renewed artistic activity. If this is so, what can we say about a stylistic tradition which continued over thousands of years?

Species and style in animal tracks

When is a particular design clearly a distinct motif, a regular (stylistic) variant of a motif, or an accidental minor variant? Josephine MacDonald investigated one aspect of this problem, looking at animal tracks recorded at Sturts Meadows. Her aim was to see if she could divide the representations of tracks into those of different species. To do this she first examined museum specimens of macropods (kangaroos, wallabies, etc) to show that different species had distinctively different feet, and then compared them with tracks engraved at Sturts Meadows.

This comparison allowed her to divide the engraved tracks into four main groups. Two of these can clearly be associated with particular species, such as red kangaroos or euros, and grey kangaroos. The artists who pecked these designs obviously had a clear idea of what they wanted to represent, and we can correlate our definition

11.9
McDonald's classification of engraved macropod tracks. (After McDonald 1983, Figure 6; Clegg 1987, Figure 11)

of these types with the artists' intentions. Differences within these types reflect a stylistic or individual variation in artists' execution rather than the intention.

Another category or group of tracks cannot be identified as those of any living animal. If tracks were all naturalistic representations, then these might be depictions of the tracks of the larger 'megafauna' (a range of animals that became extinct more than 15 000 years ago).

Style and tradition

If the 'stylistic' variation in macropod tracks was chronological, and if sub-sites or individual rocks were engraved at different times, then these differences should be evident. No such simple separation of different styles can be shown.

As noted above, the site is very homogenous, especially in terms of standard, basic forms. Any variation is minor and is at the more individual, accidental level. This may mean that there was a long-term continuity in the basic tradition of motif form and use.

Implications

Clegg's formal, numerical analysis of motif occurrence and distribution at Sturts Meadows does not consider the aesthetic aspects of Aboriginal art. Nor does it consider the symbolic meaning in the selection of what signs and scenes to depict. Instead it attempts to investigate the long-term social contexts within which large rock-art sites such as this developed. We can either see the uniformity within this and other similar sites as showing a simple copying by later artists of designs they saw on the rocks, or else regard it as showing a very long artistic tradition in this area of Australia lasting thousands of years. Whether this observed continuity can be carried over into other aspects of life (economic, technological, social and spiritual) remains a problem for future investigation.

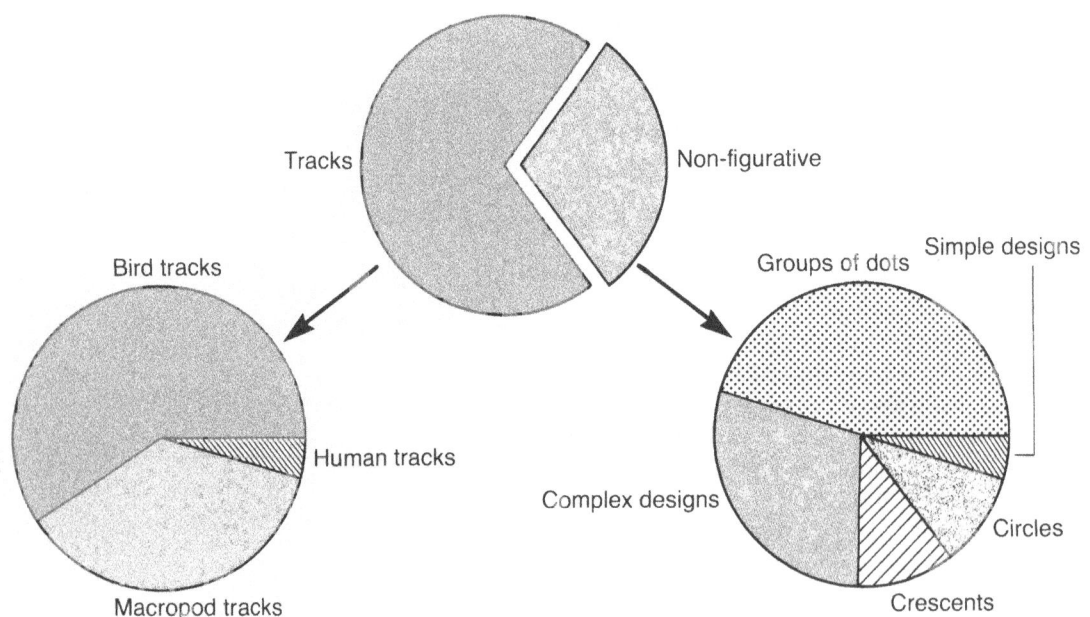

11.10
Proportions of main types of engraved motifs at Sturts Meadows. More than half are tracks, mainly bird and macropod tracks. Non-figurative designs take a variety of forms. (Data from Clegg 1983)

Najombolmi: An Artist in Arnhem Land

Prehistoric rock art is often seen as a highly traditional activity, with images produced by generations of anonymous artists following a closely defined style. The recognition of individual artists is uncommon. Najombolmi, a gifted and prolific painter in Arnhem Land is one painter whose individual impact on the rock art of the region can be documented.

Najombolmi was born about 1895 in the southern escarpment of what is now Kakadu National Park, inheriting his father's clan land, and so 'belonging' to Deaf Adder Creek. His life was typical of Aboriginal people in Arnhem Land in the first half of the twentieth century. He worked with buffalo shooters and later was associated with the developing tourist industry. Of greater importance was his involvement in Aboriginal ceremonial and social life; a powerful and active man, well travelled, skilled in bushcraft and hunting and knowledgeable in traditional lore. He died in 1967.

Over 600 paintings can be ascribed to Najombolmi, in forty-six rockshelters over a wide area both within and outside his own clan lands. Much of his painting was done when away from the European camps and economy, when travelling through and living off his land. Most of the sites where he painted were also lived in, and his paintings are often the latest in a long series of depictions on the shelter walls.

Najombolmi generally painted in a 'decorative X-ray' style. While some (perhaps earlier) X-ray paintings show internal bones and organs in naturalistic detail, Najombolmi divided the interior of animals into decorative zones, rather than representational features. This style of paintings, with animals in profile, and human figures full-face, is also relatively static, with little or no feeling of movement of figures.

Compared with other artists painting in the same tradition, Najombolmi showed a bias toward human figures, especially women, but he also painted many other subjects — animals, artefacts, plants, mythological figures, and, most commonly, fish. His paintings are especially brilliantly coloured, with use of red, white, black, yellow-green and probably also blue pigments. While some other aspects of his work fall within the general 'X-ray' tradition, his arrangement of figures into regularly composed scenes was a significant personal innovation. (See colour Figures 11.11 and 11.12.)

The frieze of humans and spirit figures in Anbangbang Shelter at Nourlangi Rock is the most famous of Najombolmi's paintings, produced a year before his death. Exceptional compositions such as this, together with his prolific and widespread output, make it clear that Najombolmi was an outstanding artist who made a major contribution to the rock-art of the region. We can trace the area over which he travelled, and see that as the focus of his life shifted, he painted more in certain areas than others. Although he worked for Europeans there is no sign of this in the subjects he chose to paint. Perhaps this was because he painted when living a more traditional life in the rocky escarpment during the wet season or perhaps because he saw the European world as less relevant to his creative work. People who knew him and were with him when he was painting explain that he painted because he liked to. As with other artists of the area, he chose his subjects, such as fish or animals, to record successful hunting or fishing expeditions. His preference for painting women is also said to reflect his personal interests. Some paintings, however, were done in a more formal context, as part of ceremonies.

The study of the work of an active artist like Najombolmi reminds us that although we cannot often see it in this way, rock-art *can* be the work of especially creative individuals, and not simply a formalised repetition of fixed forms. (Haskovec, I.P., and Sullivan, H. 1989. Chaloupka, G. 1982)

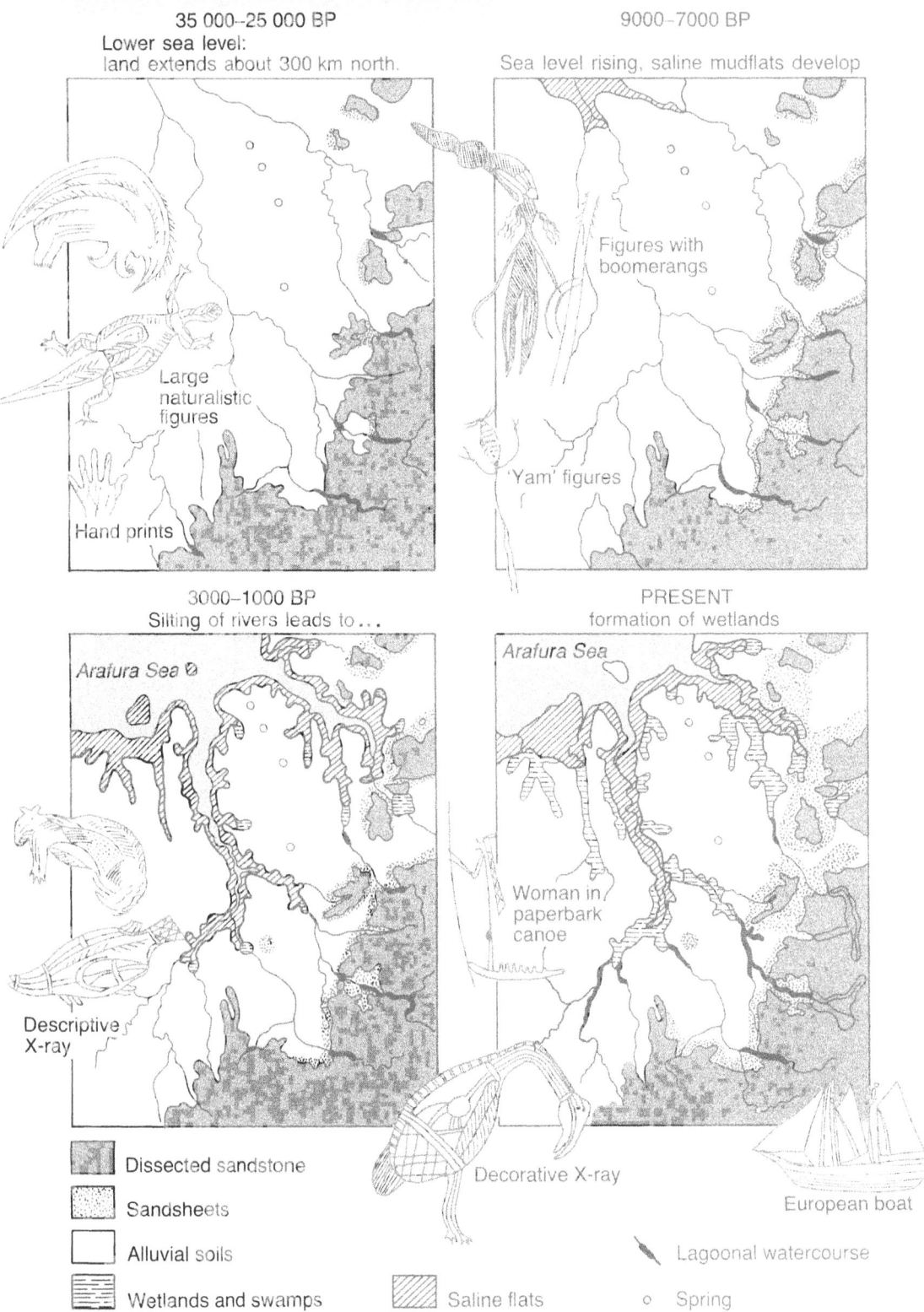

11.13 *Environment and artistic change at Kakadu. (Data from Jones (ed.) 1985)*

ENVIRONMENT AND ART AT KAKADU

Archaeological and geomorphological research in Kakadu National Park show major environmental changes as the sea level rose, initially forming saline mudflats. The freshwater swamps seen today are a very recent development. These changes in environment affected plants, animals and people. George Chaloupka has devised a sequence of art styles and motifs which run parallel to these environmental developments. (Data from Jones (ed) 1985)

Further discussion

Elsewhere in Australia changing styles and techniques can be seen in different areas. Not all regions have the same density or continuity of tradition as Sturts Meadows and other central Australian engraving sites.

There have been some suggestions that the quantity of rock art increased in the last few thousand years. Morwood, for example, argues that as shelters with art were first used about 4000 years ago in south-west Queensland this indicates not only more intensive occupation, but a development of a symbolic system related to more complex social relationships. Here art is regarded as carrying some social messages of group affiliation and relationship.

A similar development has been suggested for the simpler styles of art found in recently occupied shelters in the Grampians in western Victoria. Once again there is an assumption that the art on shelter walls must be contemporary with other uses of the site, and that all rock art carries significant social meanings.

Only rock art will survive archaeologically, and engravings will survive far better than paintings. The wide range of other modern Aboriginal art, using perishable materials like bark and wood, reminds us that most ancient art is probably lost to us if it, too, used these materials.

Simple attempts to measure the quantity of rock art as a measure of overall artistic production must therefore be treated with caution.

POINTS FOR DISCUSSION

1 What differentiates 'art' from 'craft' in present-day Australia?
2 Modern art favours individuality: to what extent is Aboriginal art different to modern art?
3 Should we apply the term 'art' or 'craft' to the following? Aboriginal:
   - rock-paintings and engravings
   - bark paintings
   - painted log coffins
   - body decoration
   - sand-sculpture
   - decorated spear-throwers
   - net bags and baskets
4 Should archaeologists treat rock-art differently from other artefacts because it had (or may still have) complex symbolic or mythological meanings?

References

Chaloupka, G., 1982, *Burrungay, Nourlangie Rock*, Northart, Darwin.

Clegg, J., 1983 'Correlations and Associations at Sturt's Meadows', in *Archaeology at ANZAAS 1983*, ed. M. Smith, pp. 215–235.

Clegg, J., 1987, 'Style and Tradition at Sturt's Meadows', *World Archaeology*, Vol. 19, pp. 236–255.

Haskovec, I.P. and Sullivan, H., 1989, 'Reflections and Rejections of an Aboriginal Artist', in *Animals into Art*, ed. H. Morphy, Unwin Hyman, London, pp. 57–74.

McDonald, J., 1983, 'The Identification of Species in a Panaramitee Style Engraving Site', in *Archeology at ANZAAS 1983*, ed. M. Smith, Western Australian Museum, Perth, pp. 236–272.

Watchman, A., 1989–90, 'New Clocks on Old Rocks: Dating Dreamtime Art', *Australian Natural History*, Vol. 23, pp. 242–247.

12

Regional prehistory

In the preceding chapters we have looked at a range of site-types, concentrating on individual sites and the information derived from them. Small-scale problems of method, approach, measurement and analysis affect the conclusions drawn in each case. Discussion of site-specific detail is not enough. It is also necessary to develop broader ideas on the history of larger regions or the continent as a whole, or to consider how hunter-gatherer societies functioned and developed. Here, following the geographical bias in our case-studies, we will look at the last 10 000 years or so in south-eastern Australia. Similar issues and problems, although different suites of sites, may be seen in other parts of Australia.

South-eastern Australia before 10 000 BP

Although we have little evidence of early occupation in Victoria or south-east South Australia we know that people were living by the shores of inland lakes a few hundred kilometres north by 36 000 years ago. We must assume other areas were also occupied from that time, especially the better watered regions which always provided a richer resource-base. As the resources of the inland lake-systems became less reliable after about 24 000 BP, before the lakes finally dried up altogether about 18 000 BP, local populations had to adjust to changing circumstances. While there was not a total abandonment of the area, there must have been a gradual drop in population density and the slow development of new patterns of settlement, mobility and technology. During the harsh windy dry period between about 18 000 and 15 000 years ago the main focus of settlement must have shifted south and east, away from the more arid parts of western New South Wales toward the better watered woodland fringe.

The sea was far lower at that time so that a wider coastal plain was exposed in all areas, including the area which is now Bass Strait, so that Victoria and Tasmania were linked by land. Some of this territory, with rivers meandering through it, must have become an important focus for settlement. With rising sea levels the evidence for this is, of course, lost.

An ancient cemetery at Kow Swamp together with other burials in the Murray Valley demonstrates that by at least 13 000 years ago there was a high density of population in that region. The physical form of these populations can be taken to indicate that relatively closed patterns of intermarriage, analogous to those of later periods, were already established.

After 10 000 BP

After about 10 000 years ago we have an increasing quantity of evidence, some of which has already been described. Wooden items such as one-piece spears and boomerangs were certainly in use by 10 000 years ago in the swamp and wetland regions of south-east South Australia, and presumably elsewhere. At that time a variety of stone tool industries can be identified. Although often lumped together under a broad umbrella category (Core Tool and Scraper Tradition) characterised by large, steep-edged tools, there were distinct local industries and styles. These include the Kartan tools of Kangaroo Island and the adjacent mainland, and the Gambieran industry of the lower south-east of South Australia, tools quite different in character from one another and from tools made in the central Murray Valley. These indicate clearly a regional diversity in technology at this time.

After about 4000 years ago a range of new tool-types appear in many sites in most areas of Australia. These include smaller, often more finely made items, particulary backed microliths and a variety of points, many of them used as barbs in composite spears. They are not found in all sites, and do not appear at the same time, or in similar proportions. The significance of their introduction is very unclear. At about this time dingoes were introduced to Australia, and spread into all areas except Tasmania. This has led some people to argue for a link between the two new elements and to seek an origin for backed microliths outside of Australia. Even if this new technology did originally come from outside the continent, this does not explain its widespread adoption within it. Did these barbs make spears more efficient? Were they simply a fashion? Can we use them to show some interaction between groups of people across the continent?

The physical form of populations developed into those of modern Aboriginal people. An earlier diversity in physical appearance gave way to a greater degree of uniformity. The more robust, larger boned people in some early populations (as at Kow Swamp) were no longer seen. This reflects a general pattern of evolution in human populations in all parts of the world, but may also have been affected by the arrival in Australia of new immigrants or a change in the degree of interaction between previously more isolated populations.

As discussed in earlier chapters, there are changes in types of sites, and within some individual sites. The greater quantity of information on more recent periods means that more detailed analyses are possible. Some of these will be considered in greater detail below.

A fundamental difficulty, of course, is that there is still too little data available at present. Future surveys, excavations and analyses will provide the basic information for testing current ideas or developing new ones. But the acquisition of data is not enough. Our regional prehistories do not develop simply by the slow accumulation of more facts. Equally important are overall concepts and attitudes. These determine which facts are selected as appropriate, and which patterns in the data are regarded as significant.

Changing questions and answers

As the data from sites mean nothing on their own, we need to understand the diverse approaches used to give them meaning. In south-eastern Australia we can identify several broad changes to archaeological explanation over the last hundred years. These are not simply local changes, but often reflect issues seen as significant by international researchers.

In the latter half of the nineteenth century one major issue was the link between social and biological evolution and the relative ranking of races. In Europe anthropologists attempted to correlate brain size and intelligence, weighing the brains of ('less intelligent') lower classes, and also enthusiastically dissecting each other when they died (as examples of highly intelligent individuals). The bodies of other peoples were also needed. The Tasmanian Aborigines were a prime target, leading to a sorry saga of grave-robbing. They were interesting to scholars of that time because of their isolation and a perceived difference from other Australian groups, while their simple technology placed them at the bottom of the ladder of social and technological evolution. Although these attitudes and research questions were later abandoned, a related problem remained — where did the Tasmanians come from? Here archaeology could contribute, and early excavations on the mainland were directed toward tracing links between local stone tool industries and those of Tasmania.

This fitted in with a broadly accepted view in archaeology of the early twentieth century that cultural or racial groups could be identified by their distinctive material culture. The origins and relationships between peoples could therefore be traced by studying their tools. A version of this view underpinned Norman Tindale's original analysis of the sequence of stone tools from Devon Downs and nearby sites in South Australia. The typological series he defined was interpreted as representing a succession of 'cultures' from the earliest Kartan people, using large core tools and choppers, through the Pirrian, characterised by small finely made points, to the later Mudukian, when bone tools were more important, and stone tools inferior in quality. This succession of cultures could be broadly correlated with ideas of population movements, especially those of Joseph Birdsell, who divided modern Aboriginal populations into three broad types, representing three waves of migration into the continent.

In a later analysis of material from Fromms Landing (a shelter near Devon Downs) and the sequence in a midden deposit at Glen Aire in Victoria, John Mulvaney could identify a similar sequence, but understood it differently. He saw these changes as technological innovation and not as representing different 'cultures'. He coined the term 'Adaptive Phase' for the most recent period of Australian prehistory, in order to indicate a dynamic system with regional variations. This technological definition met with little approval, and never gained widespread use, particularly as many archaeologists preferred to see a more important role for the environment and economy.

As briefly described in the chapters on middens and rockshelters, Roger Luebbers identified and explained change in south-east South Australia in relation to a changing environment. The emphasis in his research was on the distribution of sites and not on individual sequences. He regarded changes in stone tool technology (the replacement of earlier larger 'Gambieran' tools by the more finely formed microlithic blades and later less uniform types) as less important than the shifts in settlement pattern and economy brought about by a changing coastline and the drying up of inland swamps. Readjustment of economy and society in conjunction with this relocation created the systems destroyed by nineteenth century European settlement.

More recently still Harry Lourandos provided a new framework for discussion, emphasising the social above other aspects. Although the environment may be important in providing a stimulus for change or a limit to population density, he sees the organisation of social relationships as of crucial importance. Technology is significant but only as it affects the efficiency or productivity of economic activity following rather than causing social developments. Lourandos' model of an intensification of social relationships, of productivity and of production in the last 4000 years has been adopted by many other archaeologists both in Victoria and elsewhere. It provides one overarching framework into which much archaeological data can be fitted.

Case study: Intensification in western Victoria

In developing his model of social evolution in western Victoria, Harry Lourandos made use of three elements:

- *theoretical* concepts of social organisation and change
- *historical* data on nineteenth century Aboriginal society
- *archaeological* evidence

Theoretical concepts

Lourandos explicitly sets out his theoretical perspective. Firstly, most models of Aboriginal

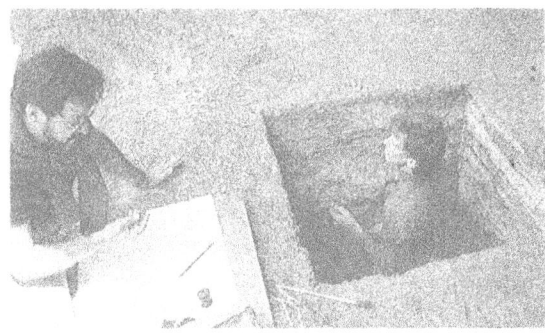

12.1
Harry Lourandos excavating at Narcurrer Shelter in south-east South Australia.

society emphasise regulatory mechanisms that operate to keep things as uniform and unchanging as possible. This assumption imposes an overall view of continuity, stability or minimal change. Lourandos prefers a freedom to look for more revolutionary change, particularly the increasing intensity of economic production.

Secondly, the most important key to identifying and explaining change is in the area of social relationships. While an increase in population may require more efficient productivity and increased production (or reliability of production) the economic strategies are socially determined, and are not simply a matter of technological innovation.

Historical reconstruction

Basing his analysis primarily on the journals of George Augustus Robinson, Lourandos developed a model of Aboriginal society in the early nineteenth century. Two main elements are of greatest importance: density and structure of population and the extent of social interaction.

Lourandos plotted the distribution of Aboriginal 'bands' named by Robinson during his travels through south-western Victoria. He argued that these 'bands' were land-using units, with a fluid membership as people moved from area to area or associated themselves in different groups. The average size of a band is suggested to be in the range of 30 to 60 people.

Population size is difficult to estimate. Population density varies from one region to another, depending on local and seasonal productivity, while historical accounts of numbers of people are subject to numerous distortions. It is not certain that the 'bands' described and named by Robinson were really groups of people; they may, for example, have referred to geographical associations or kinship affiliation. The 'average' size may also be misleading, as some regions (or bands) might have very few inhabitants in one season, and many in the next. That is, bands are not all equivalent units of population.

Lourandos combined several lines of argument to estimate population size. Using his estimate of average band-size, the number of recorded bands, and the relative size and productivity of different areas, he calculated an overall population density of one person per 3.6 km^2 for the whole Western District, giving an approximate population size of about 7900 people altogether. This is nearly twice as high as any previous estimates, which range from 1800 to 4000.

Some aspects of larger 'tribal' (that is, language) grouping and ceremonial and exchange networks have already been described in Chapters 9 and 10. Evidence of this sort is also used by Lourandos to build a picture of the complexity of social interaction.

In summary, on the basis of the historical evidence, Lourandos argues for:

- a very high density of population
- sizable semi-permanent settlements
- a complex system of smaller and larger-scale group affiliation
- regular gatherings for ceremonies and exchange

Archaeology

If we really do have such a high population density and complex social system in the early nineteenth century, how did this come about? Lourandos regards it as a recent development occurring within the last 4000 years. In order to demonstrate this we need to show linked changes in several areas, such as:

- increased population density (more sites, more intensive use of sites, use of marginal environments)
- greater degree of sedentism (i.e. staying in one location)
- the investment of energy in facilities such as fish-traps
- the development of alliance networks and exchange systems
- increased ceremonial activity

Harry Lourandos excavated three sites (the fish-traps at Toolondo, a rockshelter, Bridgewater Cave South and a large midden, Seal Point). Following and elaborating his work, Elizabeth Williams concentrated on mounds. Some of their archaeological work has already been considered separately in earlier chapters, but can now be considered together within this specific framework.

Intensity of site usage

On the basis of the density of cultural material in Bridgewater Cave South, Lourandos argues for an earlier period of less intensive use, followed very much later by an intensive occupation within the last few hundred years. From his excavations at the Seal Point midden he suggests a similar pattern. The Seal Point midden is unusually large, with evidence of 'hut depressions'. Lourandos' analysis of the sequence shows an initial exploitation of seals, later replaced by fish and land-animals. He argues that about 1500 years ago people first penetrated the rugged, inhospitable marginal area of the Otway ranges and established an 'extensive semi-sedentary basecamp'. Nearby seal colonies were severely depleted by human predation, and people later used more of the other resources of the area. If these two sites are typical, then we could argue for a greater intensity of site-use, intensive overexploitation of resources, and the use of more marginal areas, previously neglected.

Sedentism

A degree of sedentism or permanent settlement can be suggested for the Seal Point midden. Elizabeth Williams also argues that Western District mounds indicate 'villages', once again showing a reorganisation of society and settlement in the last 2500 years.

Energy investment and resource management

Lourandos argues that fish-traps, such as the one he examined at Toolondo, demonstrate resource management strategies and enhanced productivity. These signal a new order of social organisation with the potential for supporting large numbers of people, especially the major gatherings associated with ceremonies.

Alliance networks and exchange systems

These can be indirectly demonstrated from the development of facilities for providing large quantities of food. The distribution of stone for hatchet-heads from major quarries archaeologically illustrates long-distance alliance networks and exchange systems.

Population density

Figure 12.2 was prepared by Elizabeth Williams, following an earlier version by Lourandos. It shows the number of newly established sites in each 500-year-long period, using the earliest radiocarbon date for each site. They both argue that the dramatic increase in the number of new sites in the last few thousand years seen in this figure indicates a significant population increase.

Explanation

It is always easier to describe than to explain. Some suggest that environmental factors were responsible for initiating and structuring change; others argue that a population increase preceded and led to more complex social relationships. For Lourandos the key to the transition from an earlier less intensive, more nomadic pattern to a later intensive semi-sedentary one is to be found in increasingly complex and competitive social networks. Environments may shape the form of developments, population increases may accompany them, but the fundamental forces are social.

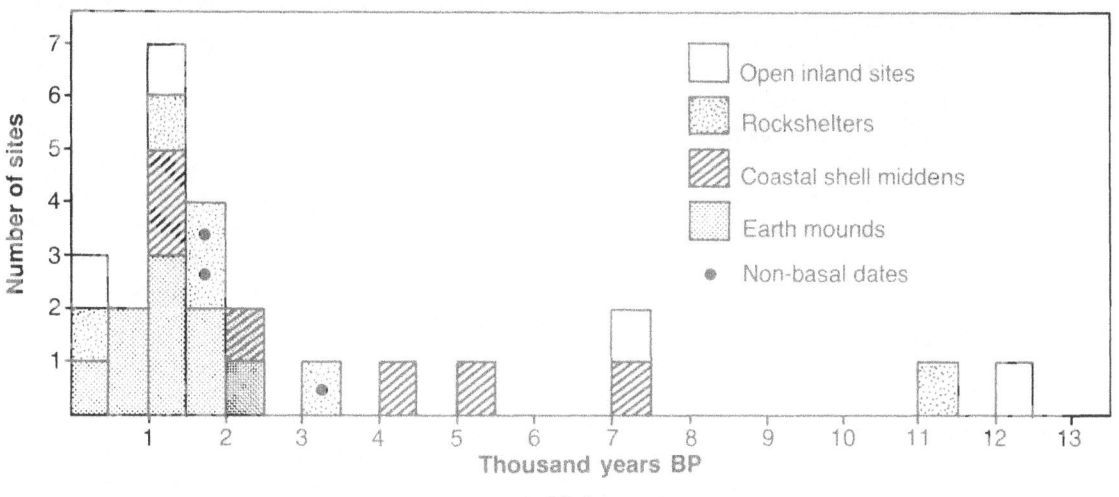

12.2
Basal radiocarbon dates for sites in south-western Victoria presented by Williams. (After Williams 1988, Figure 10.1)

The evidence set out by Lourandos, Williams and others clearly illustrates aspects of the recent prehistoric record, and fits well with historical accounts. The broad concept of 'intensification' is both interesting and satisfying. It gives a structure to otherwise unrelated evidence, and suits a view of historical cultural development. It has therefore been adopted as a framework elsewhere in Australia, where equivalent patterns and processes are sought. These models of culture change have stimulated much further research and consideration of the nature of past Aboriginal society. But they are not necessarily correct.

Problems of scale and intent

As we have seen in earlier chapters prehistoric archaeology cannot deal well with individual people or specific events. We still, however, lack an ability to understand and explain the longer-term patterns with which we have to deal. Models such as 'intensification' operate at a very large all-encompassing scale. The intention is to identify long-term trends and to give them a coherent meaning. Broad overviews of 'what happened in history' are interesting, and necessary. But it is equally interesting to seek understanding of behaviour and explanations for change at a smaller scale. We can focus our attention on specific points in prehistory and attempt to determine how societies functioned and changed in each circumstance. That is, to understand patterns of behaviour and adaptation rather than of broad historical development. These two approaches cannot be totally separated, and the difference between them is partly a matter of deciding which is the most appropriate scale for handling our current data-base and satisfying our current interests. It is also a matter of understanding the limits and problems of our data.

Case study: A radiocarbon sequence, and a critique

Caroline Bird and I have recently attempted an alternative approach to the data from western Victoria and south-east South Australia. Our aim was to critically assess the evidence for regional chronology. To a large extent this involves a critique of earlier theories, particularly those of Lourandos and Williams. The basic question we asked was: what can we really say about the numbers and ages of sites, or the development of new technology and site-types?

The data-base

Although radiocarbon dates form the basis of archaeological chronology they are not always as well published, or as easily available as they might be. Our first, somewhat tedious task was to find all the dates from the area — some published, others not. Eventually we tracked down 184 reliable dates (others were so out of sequence that the excavators reject them as incorrect). These come from 87 sites.

Dates are not always reliable, but when there are only one or two from a site we have no way of checking them. Unfortunately more than half the sites have only one date, three-quarters have one or two. In addition there are biases in the distribution of dates. Sixty-five per cent of the dated sites are coastal shell middens. This means that simple counts of dates is heavily biased toward this one type of site — which, as we have seen in Chapter 4, were not necessarily very important. In all our analyses we must remember these basic structural problems in our data.

Patterns through time

There are several different ways to portray the numbers of sites in different time-periods. Only one is illustrated in Figure 12.3, an estimate of the number of dated sites occupied in each 500-year long period. Several patterns are obvious:

- mounds appear in the last 2500 years BP
- there are some shell middens from 9000 years ago, but the number of dated examples increases in the last 4000 years
- there are two periods of rockshelter use, before 7000 and after 5000, with an increase in numbers from about 4000 years ago

Superficially these patterns seem to support the idea of more occupied sites, and therefore a greater intensity of land use and higher population density in the recent past. But closer consideration shows that this is not so.

Middens

As discussed in Chapter 4, middens are very vulnerable to destruction by erosion and the movement of dunes. Older middens will rarely survive, and if they do will be badly damaged. Archaeologists seldom excavate such poorly preserved sites, which have little potential for answering questions about economy or society. Instead they excavate the well-preserved ones. We have a two-fold bias. Low survival of older sites and an archaeological selection for more recent ones. We cannot, therefore, use this increase in dated sites as a measure of original site numbers.

Rockshelters

Unlike middens, the deposits in caves and rockshelters are not so vulnerable to erosion. They therefore may show periods when sites were used or neglected. The lack of occupation in rockshelters between about 7000 and 5000 years ago may therefore be real, but what does it mean? In Chapter 5 two conflicting ways of interpreting sequences in these sites were discussed, and a general question posed — when is it appropriate to interpret changes within individual sites as part of broad trends, and when as of local significance only?

If rockshelter use reflects local conditions and strategies then this, too, need not show a fundamental change in social organisation.

Mounds

Here certainly the current evidence is unequivocal. Mounds are a recent phenomenon. But do they really indicate sedentism and larger settlements? Once again, as discussed in Chapter 6, mounds may result from a new seasonal form of housing (solid winter camps), rather than a significant, fundamental shift in settlement structure. They may be a local response to changing climatic conditions.

Other site types

Only three types of site are shown in Figure 12.3, but other elements are important in models of social reorganisation, especially the development of facilities such as fish-traps to enhance productivity, the development of alliance networks and large-scale ceremonies which brought people together and served as the focus

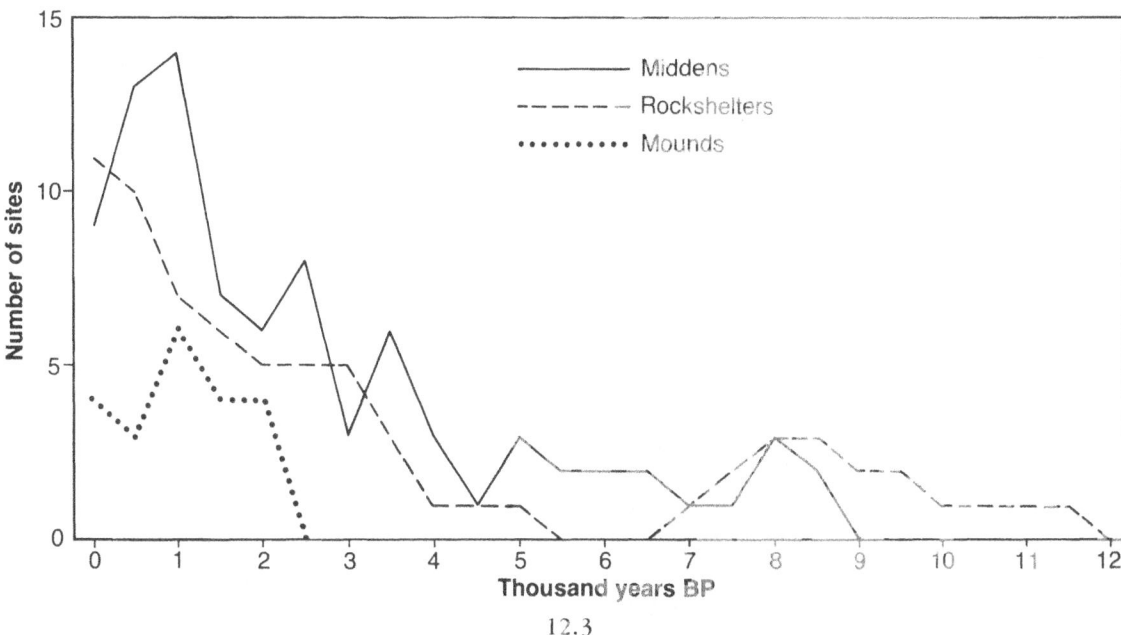

12.3
A different compilation of the number of dated sites in western Victoria and south-east South Australia (After Bird and Frankel 1991)

of new exchange systems. As discussed in earlier chapters, there is no direct evidence for the antiquity of any of these. They are assumed to develop at the same time that other changes are interpreted as taking place.

In other words, the special explanation of intensification requires the selection of certain data and the assumption of associated changes. It makes a good, coherent story, but has little foundation in our current data. We can illustrate the nature of recent prehistoric society, but we cannot so easily say how or when it developed its characteristic form.

It is, of course, easier to criticise than to create an acceptable alternative. If we do not accept the view of cultural development proposed by Lourandos, Williams and others, what do we put in its place?

Changes, environments and responses

We may start from a different premise. Instead of attempting to link sites into an overall historical process, we can see changes within sites or regions as largely independent, and taking place at a local, short-term or even individual scale. We can therefore do away with the need to explain a single process of intensification, separating recent Aboriginal societies from earlier ones. Instead we may attempt to explain particular archaeological evidence independently, without an all-encompassing model.

One possible way to understand the observed patterning is to refer to changes in the environment. While the environmental context does not determine what people do, it may provide a stimulus for developments. This can be seen at several levels. Broad climatic changes, affecting large areas and taking place over hundreds or thousands of years, provide the background for long-term cultural trends and developments. Short-term local fluctuations rapidly affect individual sites and circumstances.

Evidence from geomorphological studies of lake levels in western Victoria and south-east South Australia show an increase in water availability after about 10 000 years ago. Lakes were at their highest levels about 6000–7000 BP. Later it became drier, and from about 2500 years ago there was a return to wetter conditions. People may respond to changes such as these either by readjusting settlement patterns and demography or by developing new technology.

As far as we can tell at present, the wettest conditions in inland Victoria (6000–7000 BP) were accompanied by a decline in the number of sites, while site numbers increase in the later drier times. By contrast, the more recent increase in water availability saw the development of mounds. It is possible that we have two different responses to similar environmental changes. Earlier, there was redistribution of people as a consequence of the expansion of open water at the expense of more productive swampland. People may have shifted northward, toward the more arid areas of the Mallee. The later response to wetter conditions was the development of more solid, winter housing, seen archaeologically as mounds. Seen in this way, these sites do not signal a special form of change in settlement pattern or permanency of occupation, but a particular response at a specific time.

On the coast, sea levels rose until about 6000 years ago, and have continued to fluctuate slightly ever since. These changes had a varied impact on local productivity, both of the foreshore and immediate hinterland. The patchy occupation of coastal caves and rockshelters (such as Koongine and Bridgewater Cave South) might simply reflect changing local conditions. This may also be so for other changes seen in the numbers and contents of middens.

Whether or not one assumes an important role for the environment, we can still argue for a view of prehistoric change as a series of limited alterations to basic patterns rather than as all related and cumulative. There are developments, inventions, alterations, but they do not necessarily tend in any single direction. What life was like at any one time can be seen as the product of local factors, and any combination of developments was accidental rather than purposeful. From this perspective earlier Aboriginal society is not seen as any less dynamic or with less complex social networks than in later times.

Our future task now becomes one of clarifying these local patterns and developments and exploring the variety of social, technological and environmental responses.

In conclusion

In this book we have seen different archaeological approaches to a selection of sites from a small part of Australia. The differences of opinion on small issues and on large show that we are still only at the beginning of our search for an understanding of the Australian past.

Our examples show how archaeologists provide structure to their data, by choosing which areas to survey and which sites to study. Not only can the interpretations of data vary, but the data themselves are not absolutely fixed. Just as a sculptor extracts one statue out of many possible forms in a block of stone, so archaeologists give a particular shape to the archaeological record that they find, excavate and classify. In a very real way we create not only images of the past, but also the evidence on which those images are based. To understand the value of our conclusions we must understand why we prefer certain types of problems, and critically assess how we go about solving them.

It is often said that archaeology is like a detective story. But this is a little misleading. The fictional detective has a set of clues leading to a single, correct solution. And we know the form the solution should take. Our clues are harder to find, we can have different views on what the solution should be like, and even then, different solutions are possible. Our task is harder, but therefore all the more interesting — the open-ended exploration of alternative past worlds.

POINTS FOR DISCUSSION

1 List different types of sites and note what types of material you would expect to find in each.
2 Is it possible to show change in social relationships and economy on the basis of archaeological evidence?
3 What sort of changes *did* take place in the past?
4 Do changes in the environment *cause* or *influence* change in human behaviour?
5 Aboriginal people are often described as hav-

ing 'the oldest culture in the world'. What do you think this means?

PICTURING THE PAST

Write an account of a year in the life of an Aboriginal group living in the Western District of Victoria. At different seasons people may be on the coast or inland, living in rockshelters or in the open, repairing fish-traps and harvesting eels, separating into small units or gathering in large numbers for ceremonies.

EXERCISE: DATES AND DENSITY OF OCCUPATION

The numbers of dated sites give a basic view of developments in the past. A selection of radiocarbon dates from sites in western Victoria and south-east South Australia is given in Table 12.1. Draw a diagram following the model illustrated in Figure 12.4 and plot these dates on it. Using this as a base, estimate how many sites are known to have been occupied in different periods.

- What do you mean by 'occupied'?
- What do you mean by 'periods'?
- Were sites 'continuously' used?

DEBATES: ARCHAEOLOGY AND SOCIETY

The type of research that archaeologists do and the problems they select to study often reflect general attitudes and interests in society as a whole. They write about people, and often about other peoples' ancestors. What they say can have some influence on how people perceive themselves and how they think of others. Some archaeological research, such as the demonstration of our common ancestry, has a more profound effect, but even relatively minor issues can be significant. Some archaeologists go so far as to suggest that archaeologists should not only recognise their role in forming social perceptions and attitudes, but should consciously set out to transform society.

150 years ago most people in Europe believed that the world was created about 6000 years ago and that each species was created in its present form. What ideas about the origins of humanity, and about ancient societies and civilisations do you have, and take for granted?

How important is archaeology in forming or changing our ideas about ourselves and about other people?

Consider the following four statements. What do you think about the style, concepts and attitudes expressed?

> If there have remained anywhere up to modern times man whose condition has changed little since the early Stone Age, the Tasmanians seem to have been such a people. They stand before us as a branch of the Negroid race, illustrating the condition of man near his lowest known level of culture. (E.B. Tyler in Roth, H.L., 1890, p. v)

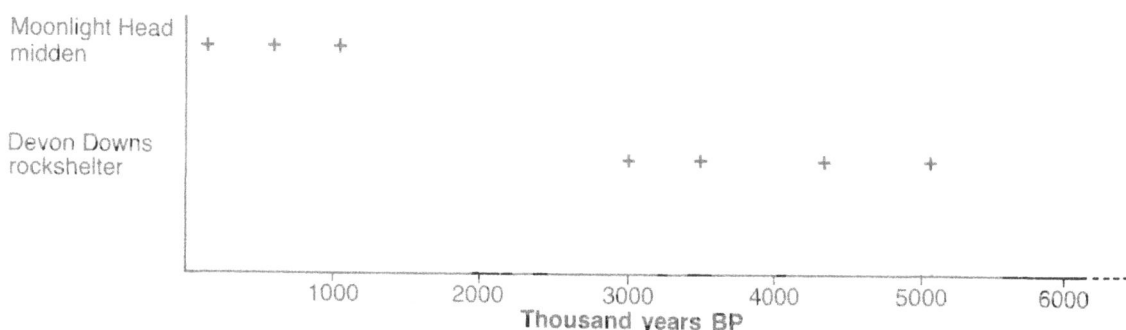

12.4

Table 12.1 Radiocarbon dates from selected sites in western Victoria and south-east South Australia

Site	Context	Sample no.	Age BP
Moonlight Head Midden	Bottom of site	GAK 9011	1030 ± 120
Moonlight Head Midden	Middle of site	GAK 9008	590 ± 110
Moonlight Head Midden	Top of site	GAK 9007	180 ± 90
Seal Point Midden	Bottom of site	SUA 552	1420 ± 130
Glen Aire Shelter II	Bottom of midden	R 728	370 ± 45
Nobles Rocks 3/3 Midden	Midden	Wk 1136	5320 ± 60
East Monbong 4/1 Midden	Midden	Wk 1105	7960 ± 90
Dura Midden	Bottom of site	ANU 6451	1100 ± 70
Bridgewater Cave South	Base of upper unit	Beta 3922	450 ± 40
Bridgewater Cave South	Top of lower unit	Beta 8464	8350 ± 130
Bridgewater Cave South	Top of lower unit	Beta 8465	10760 ± 110
Bridgewater Cave South	Lower unit	Beta 3923	11390 ± 310
Koongine Cave	Top of site	Beta 21540	150 ± 70
Koongine Cave	Upper occupation	Beta 14858	700 ± 70
Koongine Cave	Lower occupation	Beta 14859	8270 ± 400
Koongine Cave	Lower occupation	Beta 21541	8900 ± 110
Koongine Cave	Base of site	Beta 14861	9710 ± 180
Mt Talbot 1 Shelter	Lower unit	Beta 18888	5710 ± 80
Mt Talbot 1 Shelter	Middle unit	Beta 18886	3800 ± 80
Mt Talbot 1 Shelter	Middle unit	Beta 18887	3690 ± 90
Montrose Mound 1	Base of mound	ANU 3758	1270 ± 100
Montrose Mound 2	Upper unit	ANU 3759	410 ± 100
Montrose Mound 2	Base of mound	ANU 3757	1600 ± 220
FM/1 Mound	Base of mound	SUA 574	2350 ± 150

(For a complete listing see Bird and Frankel 1991)

Let us end with Tasmania and consider the trauma which the severance of the Bassian bridge delivered to the society isolated there. Like a blow above the heart, it took a long time to take effect, but slowly but surely there was a simplification in the tool kit, a diminution in the range of foods eaten, perhaps a squeezing of intellectuality. The world's longest isolation, the world's simplest technology. Were 4000 people enough to propel forever the cultural inheritance of Late Pleistocene Australia? Even if Abel Tasman had not sailed the winds of the Roaring Forties in 1642, were they in fact doomed — doomed to a slow strangulation of the mind? (Jones, R., 1977, p. 203)

Prehistoric Tasmanians may have had a simple toolkit and limited ceremonial life, but they survived more than 20 000 years on their rugged island, they successfully weathered the glacial cold further south than any other people, they produced some of the finest rock engravings in the world, and they achieved a successful balance between hunters and land and a population density equivalent to that on the Australian mainland. (Flood, J., 1983, p. 178)

I make no judgement on Tasmanian society. Some in the past have made a negative moral assessment of it in terms of primitiveness. Others in recent times, reacting to these views have wandered into the realm of neo-idealistic virtues of Tasmanian life expressed in terms of perfect adaptation and ecological purity. (Jones, R., 1987, p. 41)

References

Bird, C.F.M. and Frankel, D., 1991, 'Chronology and Explanation in Western Victoria and Southeast South Australia', *Archaeology in Oceania*, Vol. 26.

Flood, J., 1983, Archeology of the Dreamtime, Collins, Sydney.

Jones, R., 1977, 'The Tasmanian Paradox', in *Stone Tools as Cultural Markers*, ed. R.V.S. Wright, Australian Institute of Aboriginal Studies, Canberra, pp. 189–204.

Lourandos, H., 1977, 'Aboriginal Spatial Organisation and Population: South Western Victoria reconsidered', *Archaeology and Physical Anthropology in Oceania*, Vol. 12, pp. 202–225.

Lourandos, H., 1983, 'Intensification: a Late Pleistocene/Holocene Archaeological Sequence from Southwestern Victoria', *Archaeology in Oceania*, Vol. 18, pp. 81–97.

Lourandos, H., 1985, 'Intensification and Australian Prehistory', in *Prehistoric Hunter-gatherers: the Emergence of Cultural Complexity*, eds T.D. Price and J.A. Brown, Academic Press, pp. 385–423.

Roth, H.L., 1890, The Aborigines of Tasmania, F. King, Halifax.

Williams, E., 1987, 'Complex Hunter-gatherers: a View from Australia', *Antiquity*, Vol. 61, pp. 310–321.

Glossary

analytical units parts of a site or sequence treated separately in analysis and for comparative purposes. They may be single excavation units or a composite of several of the original units.

artefact an item made or modified by people.

BP years before the present. With radiocarbon dating the 'present' is fixed at 1950.

blade a long, narrow stone flake, at least twice as long as it is wide.

core a piece of stone from which pieces are struck to be used as tools.

excavation unit a part of a site or sequence defined and separated during excavation. They may be discrete layers, built features or arbitrarily defined spits. They are the basic unit of analysis, but are often grouped into larger analytical units.

flake a piece of stone struck off a larger piece (core) which may be used as a tool either immediately or after further modification or retouching.

material culture the items made or used by people, all the material goods of a society.

microlith small stone tool. The most common microliths are small blades, backed or blunted along one edge and probably used as spear-barbs.

midden a rubbish dump. In Australian archaeology the term is most commonly used for accumulations of discarded shell.

MNI Minimum Number of Individuals. An estimate of the smallest number of animals represented by the bones or shells found.

NISP Number of Identified Specimens. The number of bones or shells which can be identified according to animal species.

retouch modification of the working-edge or back of a stone tool.

section the exposed face of a cutting through accumulated archaeological deposits or sediments.

spit an arbitrary unit of excavation, in many Australian sites set at about 5 cm depth.

stratigraphy the superimposed layering of deposits, with older material overlain by later deposits.

stratigraphic excavation excavating each identifiable layer in turn, starting with the uppermost and working downward through the sequence.

waste, waste flake unmodified or unused pieces of stone discarded during the process of manufacture of tools.

Government archaeological authorities

Aboriginal communities in several states have legal rights and responsibilities over sites. They and the appropriate state government body should be contacted before any archaeological research is undertaken. Permits may not be required for non-destructive surveys but local Aboriginal communities still need to be informed or consulted. Excavations can only be carried out by qualified archaeologists, with appropriate permission and official permits.

Many state archaeological authorities publish information leaflets about sites or more detailed reports of research. Access to information in Site Registers is normally restricted, but may be available to bona fide researchers.

Commonwealth: Australian Heritage Commission, 53 Blackall Street, Barton ACT. (PO Box 1567 Canberra ACT 2601). (062) 71 2111.

Northern Territory: Museum and Art Gallery of the Northern Territory, Darwin. (PO Box 4646 Darwin NT 5794). (089) 82 4211.

New South Wales: National Parks and Wildlife Service, 43 Bridge Street, Hurstville. (PO Box 1967 Hurstville, 2220). (02) 585 6444.

Queensland: Heritage Section, Department of Environment and Conservation, 100 Ann Street, Brisbane. (PO Box 155 North Quay 4002). (07) 227 6491.

South Australia: Aboriginal Heritage Unit, Department of Planning and Environment, 55 Grenfell Street, Adelaide. (GPO Box 667, Adelaide 5001). (08) 216 7777.

Tasmania: Department of Parks, Wildlife and Heritage, 134 Macquarie Street, Hobart. (GPO Box 44A, Hobart 7000). (002) 30 6596.

Victoria: Victoria Archaeological Survey, 29–31 Victoria Avenue, Albert Park. (PO Box 262 Albert Park 3206). (03) 690 5322.

Western Australia: Department of Aboriginal Sites, Western Australian Museum (Francis Street, Perth 6000). (09) 328 4411.

Further studies and career prospects

Most Australian universities teach archaeology as part of an Arts or Humanities degree. For information consult university calendars where courses may be listed under 'archaeology', 'prehistory', or 'anthropology'. If you want to major in archaeology it is useful to discuss your overall enrolment with university staff, who can recommend other appropriate subjects (such as anthropology, history, geology or geography). Those interested in a career in archaeology need to complete a four-year Honours degree, rather than the normal three-year pass degree.

Many Honours graduates continue in archaeology. Some undertake higher degrees and may later teach in universities. Some find work in museums (a postgraduate Diploma in Museum Studies is becoming more necessary). Others are employed in public archaeology or cultural resource management. They may be on the staff of government archaeology departments or work as freelance consultants doing environmental impact assessments. Further details can be found in a pamphlet, *Careers in Archaeology*, which may be obtained from The Graduate Careers Council of Australia, PO Box 20 Parkville, Vic., 3052.

Annotated bibliography of general works

Binford, L.R., 1983, *In Pursuit of the Past*, Thames and Hudson. An important series of essays on key issues in archaeology by one of the more influential American archaeologists.

Blainey, G., 1975, *Triumph of the Nomads*, Sun Books, Melbourne. A very readable but somewhat general and romantic view of Australian prehistory and Aboriginal life.

Connah G., (ed), 1983, *Australian Field Archeology: A Guide to Techniques*, Australian Institute of Aboriginal Studies, Canberra. A more technical set of papers on practical aspects of Australian archaeology.

Coutts, P.J.F., 1981, *Readings in Victoria Prehistory. Volume 2: The Victorian Aboriginals 1800 to 1860*, Victoria Archaeological Survey, Melbourne. A useful compilation of information and particularly of illustrations. Unfortunately, not as well organised or designed as it could have been.

Dingle, T., 1988, *Aboriginal Economy: Patterns of Experience*, McPhee Gribble/Penguin, Melbourne. A very useful short, neat and clear account of Aboriginal economy and technology.

Fagan, B.M., 1985, *In the Beginning: An Introduction to Archaeology*, 5th edition, Little, Brown, Boston. A good introduction to the methods, problems and techniques of archaeology.

Flood, J., 1989, *Archaeology of the Dreamtine*, 2nd edition. Collins, Sydney. A general overview of Australian prehistory. A fairly uncritical account but contains basic information on most of the more important sites and issues.

Flood, J., 1990, *The Riches of Ancient Australia*. University of Queensland Press, Brisbane. Contains descriptions of sites in all parts of Australia open to visitors. Useful for touring and for reference.

Haigh, C. and Goldstein W., (eds), 1982, *The Aborigines of New South Wales*, Parks and Wildlife Vol. 2 No. 5, National Parks and Wildlife Service, NSW, Sydney. General articles dealing with a range of issues, problems and regional studies of Aborigines and archaeology in NSW.

Kirk, R.L., 1981, *Aboriginal Man Adapting*, Oxford University Press. An authoritative introduction to Australian Aboriginal population biology.

Maddock, K., 1982, *The Australian Aborigines*, 2nd edition. Penguin Books, London. A clear introduction to traditional Aboriginal society and culture

Mulvaney, D.J. and White, J.P., (eds), 1987, *Australians to 1788*, Fairfax, Syme and Weldon, Sydney. A valuable general reference work, with specialist contributions covering key aspects of Australian archaeology and Aboriginal society.

White, J.P. and O'Connell, J.F., 1982, *A Prehistory of Australia, New Guinea and Sahul*, Academic Press, Sydney. A more academic and critical approach to major problems in the Australian region.

Current research is published in Australian journals, the more important of which are:

Archaeology in Oceania (116 Darlington Road H42, University of Sydney, NSW 2006)

Australian Aboriginal Studies (Australian Institute of Aboriginal and Torres Strait Islander Studies, GPO Box 553, Canberra, ACT 2601)

Australian Archaeology (Australian Archaeological Association, c/o Department of Prehistory and Anthropology, The Faculties, Australian National University, Canberra, ACT 2601)

Rock Art Research (Australian Rock Art Research Association, PO Box 216, Caulfield South, Vic., 3162)

Films

Many films and videos are available about Aboriginal life, past and present. The list here is of films most relevant to topics covered in this book.

The Spear in the Stone (Australian Institute of Aboriginal Studies, 1983, 35 mins, VHS, Umatic or 16 mm). Documents a visit to Ngilipitji quarry in 1981. Shows Aboriginal attitudes to an important and 'dangerous' source of stone.

Unconsidered Trifles (Bass Strait Videos, La Trobe University, 1989, 2 × 35 mins, VHS). Two films on the history and prehistory of Erith Island in the Bass Strait. Designed for schools, they give a basic introduction to techniques and the nature of changing environments.

Waiting for Harry (Australian Institute of Aboriginal Studies, 1980, 57 mins, VHS, Umatic or 16 mm). Funeral ceremonies in Arnhem Land. Important for showing the social context of burial customs and one method of delayed disposal using a painted log coffin.

People of the Australian Western Desert (Australian Commonwealth Film Unit and Australian Institute of Aboriginal Studies, Vol. 1, 173 mins, Vol. 2, 126 mins, VHS). A basic series of documentaries although dealing only with the specialised adaptation to arid environments, and so not typical of Aboriginal life elsewhere. Some parts (tool-making and hunting and gathering) are more relevant than others.

Out of Time, Out of place (Film Australia, 1986, 16 mm, 60 mins, VHS). The origins of the Australians. A useful film, but presents only one of the alternative views of Aboriginal population history.

Discovery: Out of Darkness (Independent Productions, 1984, 55 mins). Covers some important excavations and archaeological theories, particularly on the earlier periods of Australian prehistory.

The Coming of Man (Opus Films, 60 mins, VHS). Now somewhat dated, but covers major sites, excavations, archaeology and art with reference to historical and ethnographic material.

Sacred Sites (Rainbow Serpent Episode 4, SBS, 1985, 24 mins, VHS). Examines the significance of sacred sites to Aboriginal communities today and in the past.

Additional references

Only a very few the many specialist studies which have appeared over the last twenty years have been inlcuded here. Apart from the more general books these are limited to ones which deal most directly with the specific sites, areas or issues discussed in each chapter.

General

Australian archaeology

Hiscock, P. 2008, *Archaeology of Ancient Australia*, Routledge, London. A convenient summary of the broader issues in Australian archaeology.

Holdaway, S. and N. Stern, 2004, *A Record in Stone. The Study of Australia's Flaked Stone Artefacts*. Aboriginal Studies Press, Canberra. An essential basis for understanding the archaeological use of chipped stone artefacts.

Lourandos, H., 1997, *A Continent of Hunter-Gatherers,* Cambridge University Press, Cambridge. An important statement of a particular perspective on Australian archaeology.

Mulvaney, J. and J. Kamminga, 1999, *Prehistory of Australia*, Allen and Unwin, Sydney. A substantial text dealing with the major issues in Australian archaeology.

Murray, T. (ed.), 2004, *Archaeology from Australia*, Australian Scholarly Publishing, Melbourne. A series of essays on a wide variety of research carried out by Australian archaeologists locally and abroad.

Films

First Footprints (Bently Dean and Martin Butler, 2013). 4 x 56 minute videos giving insights into the long history of Aboriginal accupation and adaptation from a current archaeological and Indigenous perspective.

Organisations and websites

The Australian Archaeological Association
http://www.australianarchaeologicalassociation.com.au/

Archaeological and Anthropological Society of Victoria
http://aasv.org.au/

Australian Association of Consulting Archaeologists
http://www.aacai.com.au/

Australian Rock Art Research Association
http://home.vicnet.net.au/~auranet/

Australian Institute of Aboriginal and Torres Strait Islander Studies
http://www.aiatsis.gov.au/

Individual chapters

2. Prehistory as society

Gammage, B., 2011, *The Biggest Estate on Earth: How Aborigines Made Australia*. Allen and Unwin, Crows Nest.

Hiscock, P., 2012, 'The arrival of humans in Australia', *Agora*, Vol. 47, pp. 19–22.

O'Connell, J.F. and J. Allen, 2004, Dating the colonization of Sahul (Pleistocene Australia-New Guinea): a review of recent research, *Journal of Archaeological Science*, Vol. 31, pp. 835–853.

4. Shell middens

Hall, J. and I. McNiven (eds), 1999, *Australian Coastal Archaeology*. Research Papers in Archaeology and Natural History No. 31, Department of Prehistory, Research School of Pacific Studies, Australian National University, Canberra.

5. Rockshelters and caves

Bird, C.F.M. and D. Frankel, 2001, Excavations at Koongine Cave: lithics and land use in the terminal Pleistocene and Holocene of South Australia. *Proceedings of the Prehistoric Society*, Vol. 67, pp. 49–83.

Bird, C.F.M. and D. Frankel, 2005, *An Archaeology of Gariwerd. From Pleistocene to Holocene in Western Victoria.* Tempus 8. (Archaeology and Material Culture Studies in Anthropology) University of Queensland, St Lucia.

8. Fish-traps

McNiven, I.J., T. Richards, N. Dolby, G. Jacobsen and Gunditj Mirring Traditional Owners Aboriginal Corporation, 2012, Dating Aboriginal stone-walled fishtraps at Lake Condah, southeast Australia, *Journal of Archaeologcal Science,* Vol. 39, pp. 268–286.

11. Rock art

Flood, J. 1997, *Rock Art of the Dreamtime*, Angas and Robertson, Sydney.

Morwood, M.J., 2002, *Visions from the Past; The Archaeology of Australian Aboriginal Art.* Allen and Unwin, Sydney.

12. Regional prehistory

Frankel, D., 1991, First-order radiocarbon dating of Australian shell-middens, *Antiquity,* Vol. 65, pp. 571–4.

Bird, C.F.M. and D. Frankel, 1991, Problems in constructing a prehistoric regional sequence: Holocene South-East Australia, *World Archaeology,* Vol. 23, pp. 179–192.

Bird, C.F.M. and D. Frankel, 1998, Pleistocene and early Holocene archaeology in Victoria. A view from Gariwerd, *The Artefact*, Vol. 21, pp. 48–62.

Frankel, D. and C.F.M. Bird, 2013, Integrating hunter-gatherer sites, environments, technology and art in western Victoria. In D. Frankel, J.M. Webb and S. Lawrence (eds), *Archaeology in Environment and Technology: Intersections and Transformation.* Routledge, New York and London, pp. 69–83.

Godfrey, M.C.S., C. Bird, D. Frankel, J.W. Rhoads and S. Simmons, 1996, From time to time: radiocarbon determinations on Victorian archaeological sites held by Aboriginal Affairs Victoria, *The Artefact*, Vol. 19, pp. 3–51.

Lourandos, H., 1997, *A Continent of Hunter-Gatherers*, Cambridge University Press, Cambridge.

Index

Allambie (Vic), 88–93
Anbarra, 22, 42
animals, 3, 23, 46, 49–51, 62, 63–5, 91, 135, 136
arid zone, 1, 17, 29–33
Arnhem Land (NT), 15, 16, 19, 22, 42, 54, 119, 137
art, 131–9

Bailey, G., 55
Barak, W., 9, 122–3
Barham (NSW), 77–82
Bass Point (NSW), 54
Beaton, J., 53, 115, 117
Berryman, A.J., 77–82, 85
Beveridge, P., 9, 76
Bird, C.F.M., 145–8, 151
birds, 23, 136
Bluff Cave (Tas), 16, 17
bora grounds, 107, 112, 115
Bowdler, S., 54, 55
Brewarrina (NSW), 96
Bridgewater Cave (Vic), 70, 72, 144, 148, 150
Bunurong, 54

Caramut (Vic), 82–5
Carnarvon Range (Qld), 116
Central Australia, 1, 29–33
ceremonies, 20–1, 23–4, 95, 100, 106–17, 123–4, 139, 143, 144
Cheetup Cave (WA), 116
Clegg, J., 133–7, 139
Collarenebri, 37–8

colonisation, 1, 15, 17, 24, 26, 141–2
Condah (Vic), 75, 88, 89, 92, 101–3
conservation, *see* heritage
Coutts, P.J.F., 88, 93, 102, 104, 155
Cranebrook Terrace (NSW), 16
Crown Lagoon (Tas), 27
culture contact, 9–10, 39, 87, 93, 138–9, 142, 149–50

dating, 1, 7, 10–12, 15–16, 46–7, 58, 61–2, 67, 72–3, 97, 132, 134, 135, 144
Dawson, J., 9, 76
desert, *see* arid zone
Devon Downs (SA), 58–66, 70, 71, 72–3, 142
diet, *see* economy
disease, *see* health

economy, 3, 18–23, 29–31, 41, 42, 47–53, 54–5, 62, 63, 70, 94–5, 97, 115–16, 143, 144
eels, 97, 99–100, 102
Egloff, B., 114–15, 117
environment, 3, 17–18, 53–4, 65, 69–70, 85, 102–3, 138–9, 140, 144, 147–8
ethnographic sources, *see* historical accounts
excavation, 7–9, 14, 42–5, 57–8, 66–7, 79–80, 108–9

exchange, 1, 23, 106, 118–20, 123, 124–9, 144

fish, 23, 50–1, 54, 77, 94–5, 116, 144

Gambieran tools, 25, 68, 69, 141, 142
gathering, 18, 19, 22–3
Gaughwin, D., 5, 55
Gidjingarli, 42
Gippsland, 113
Glen Aire (Vic), 142

hatchet, 25, 118–29
Head, L., 102–3, 104
health, 29–33
heritage, 2, 4, 6, 7, 28, 33, 39, 104–5, 116–17, 153
historical accounts, 4, 9 10, 42, 75–6, 99–100, 110–13, 114–15, 116–17, 142–3
Howitt, A.W., 9, 113, 122–3
hunting, 18, 19, 22–3, 38, 139
Huon Peninsula (PNG), 16

Jones, R., 120, 129, 137–8, 151

Kakadu (NT), 137, 138
Kartan, 141–2
Koonalda Cave (SA), 132
Koongine Cave (SA), 66–70, 132, 148, 150
Kow Swamp (Vic), 140–1

Lake George (ACT), 15
Lake Mungo (NSW), 16
Langford, R., 39
languages, 126–7
Lindsay Island (Vic), 33–7
Little Swanport (Tas), 27
Lourandos, H., 26–7, 70, 73, 97–101, 104–5, 142–5, 146–7, 151
Luebbers, R., 53, 142

Malakununja II (NT), 15, 16
Matenkupkum (PNG), 16
Mathews, R.H., 9–10, 112
McArthur Creek (Vic), 83–4
McBryde, I., 120–9
Meehan, B., 27, 42, 55
microlith, 10, 24, 25, 141, 142
Momega Outstation (NT), 19, 20, 22
Moonlight Head (Vic), 42–53, 150
Morwood, M.J., 116, 117, 137
Mount William (Vic), 23, 122–9
Mulvaney, D.J., 27, 39, 54, 117, 142, 155
Mumbulla Mountain (NSW), 114–15
Murray River, 7, 29–38, 58, 74, 75, 77, 123, 140–1

Najombolmi, 137
New South Wales, 16, 17, 23, 54, 55, 77, 95, 106, 112, 114, 133, 140
Ngilipitji (NT), 119

origins, see colonisation
Otways (Vic), 43, 120, 144

Papua New Guinea, 16, 17, 99, 129
Pardoe, C., 33–9
Phillip Island (Vic), 54

plants, 3, 4, 18–19, 22–3, 77, 102–3, 112, 115–16
pollen analysis, 4, 102–3
population density, 5, 18–19, 32–3, 38, 53, 54, 57, 70, 85, 116, 141, 143, 144, 149–50

Queensland, 23, 33, 106, 110, 115, 137

radiocarbon dating, 1, 11, 16, 61, 67, 72–3, 84, 98, 135, 145–7
Richmond River (NSW), 55
Robinson, G.A., 9, 74–5, 87, 97, 99–100, 143
Roonka (SA), 35

sacred site, 24, 106, 114–17, 119–20, 131, 139
sampling, 5, 43, 57, 125, 133
Satterthwaite, L., 115
scraper, 25
sea level, 17, 69–71, 138–9, 140–1, 148
Seal Point (Vic), 144, 150
seals, 144
seasons, 2, 19, 20–1, 26, 55, 62, 65, 77, 80–2, 85, 91, 95, 97, 100, 101, 115–16, 143
settlement pattern, 4–5, 18–19, 38, 53–5, 70–2, 80–2
shellfish, 2, 23, 41–55, 77
Smith, M., 95, 105
Smith, M.A., 60–6, 73
Smyth, R.B., 10
South Australia, 33, 48, 58, 66, 132, 141–51
stone tools, 3, 10, 12, 24–5, 26–7, 46, 49, 57, 62, 63–5, 84, 90–1, 108–9, 118–29, 141–2

stratigraphy, 8, 10–11, 43–5, 46–7, 57, 58, 61, 66, 67, 83–4, 89, 108–10
Sturts Meadows (NSW), 133–6
Sunbury (Vic), 106–14
survey, 4–5, 14, 33, 54–5, 78–9, 88
Swan Point (WA), 94–5

Tasmania, 1, 16, 17, 18, 23, 27, 41, 140–41, 151
thermoluminescence dating, 11, 15, 17
Thomas, W., 54–5, 75
Tindale, N.B., 58–66, 73, 142
Toolondo (Vic), 97–101, 144
trade, see exchange

Upper Swan (WA), 16

Vanderwal, R.L., 43, 45, 55
Victoria, 7, 23, 33, 41, 42, 43, 48, 54, 66, 70, 74, 77, 82, 83, 87, 88, 90, 97, 106, 112, 118, 120, 132, 137, 141–51
Victoria Archaeological Survey, 7, 88, 89, 92, 102

Wakool River (NSW), 77–82
Webb, S., 29–33, 38, 40
Wesson, J.P., 88–93
Western Australia, 16, 23, 66, 95, 116, 132
Western Port (Vic), 5, 54–5
Willandra Lakes (NSW), 16, 17, 18, 82
Williams, E., 82–4, 86, 93, 144–5, 146–7, 151
wooden tools, 2–3, 53, 54, 69, 140–1
Wyrie Swamp (SA), 53, 54, 69

11.1A Rock engravings at Mount Cameron West, Tasmania. (Photo: Robert Edwards)

11.1B Paintings at Glenisla Shelter, Grampians, Victoria.

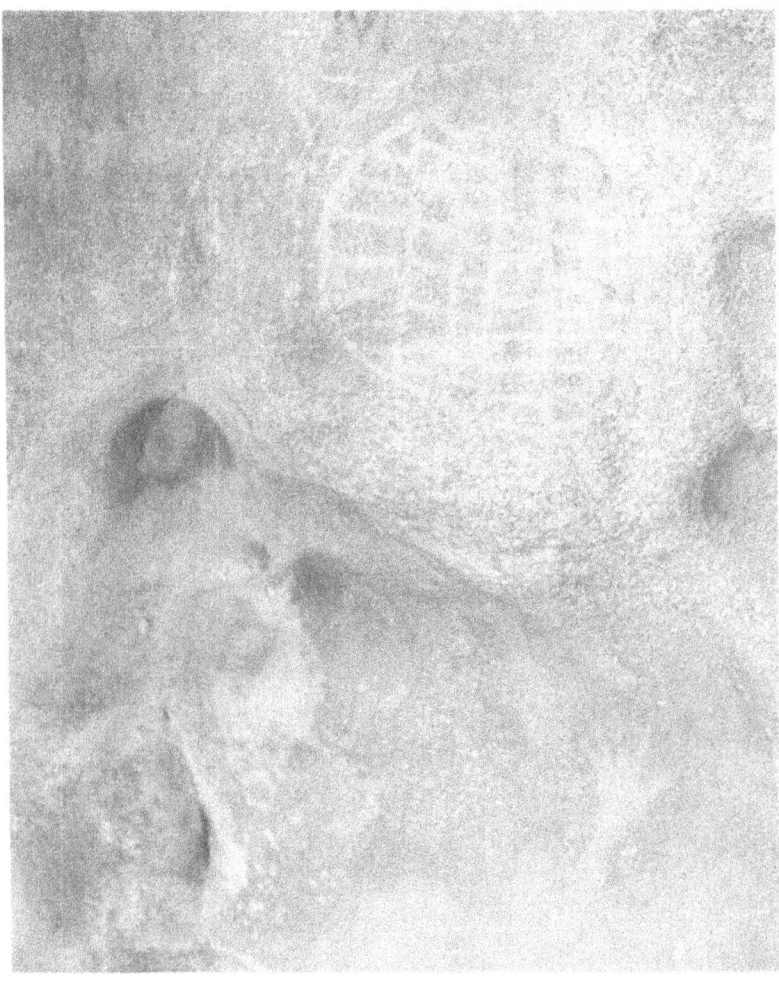

11.1C Rock engravings in Chambers Gorge, Flinders Ranges, South Australia.

11.1D Paintings and stencils at Dales Cave, Western Australia.

11.1E Paintings at Walga Rock, Western Australia.

11.1F Pecked ibis, Gum Tree Valley, Dampier, Western Australia.

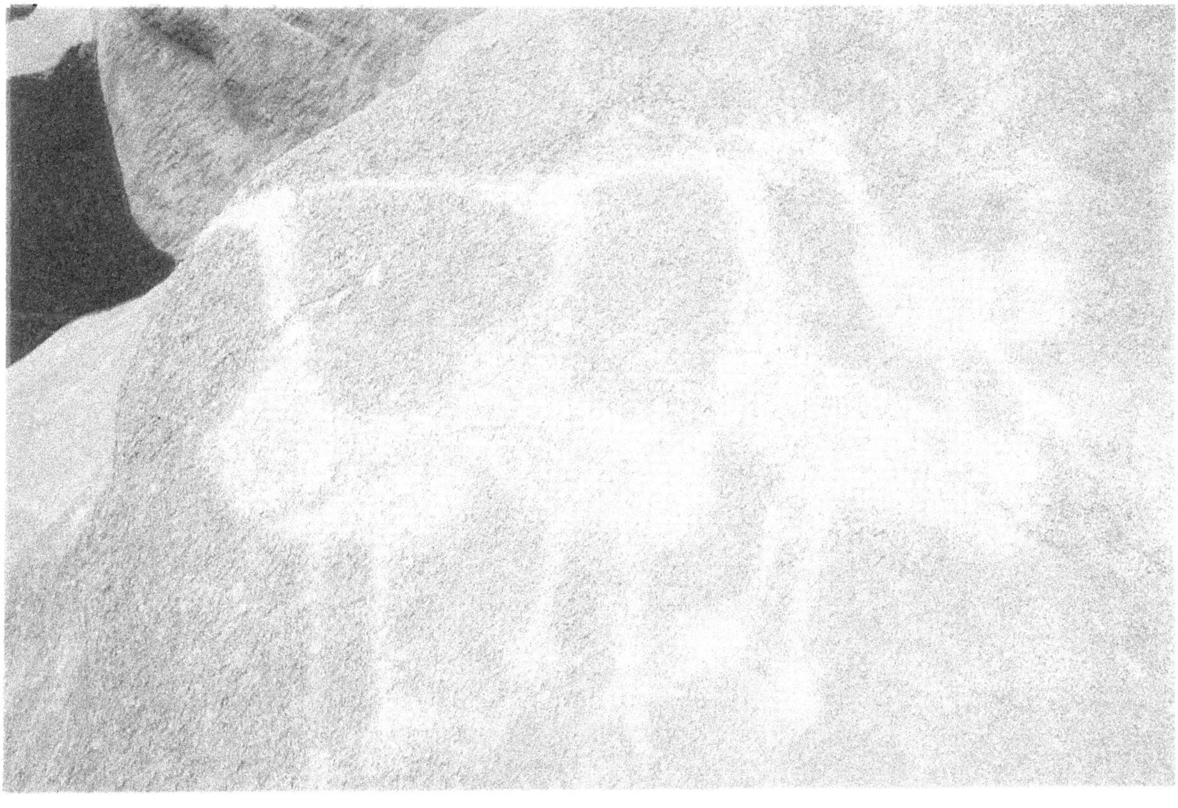

11.1G   Painted crocodile and other figures, Kununurra, Western Australia.

11.1H   X-ray paintings of fish, Kakadu, Northern Territory.

11.1I Rock engravings at Ewaninga, Northern Territory.

11.1J Quinkan figure at Guguyalanji, Laura, North Queensland.

11.1K Stencils of hands, boomerangs and other items at Cathedral Cave, Carnarvon Range, Queensland.

11.1L Outline engraving of a human figure in the Sydney district, New South Wales. (Photo: John Clegg)

11.3 Markings on the wall of Koongine Cave in south-east South Australia are similar to the 20 000 year old markings found in Koonalda Cave.

11.5 Rock engravings at Sturts Meadows.

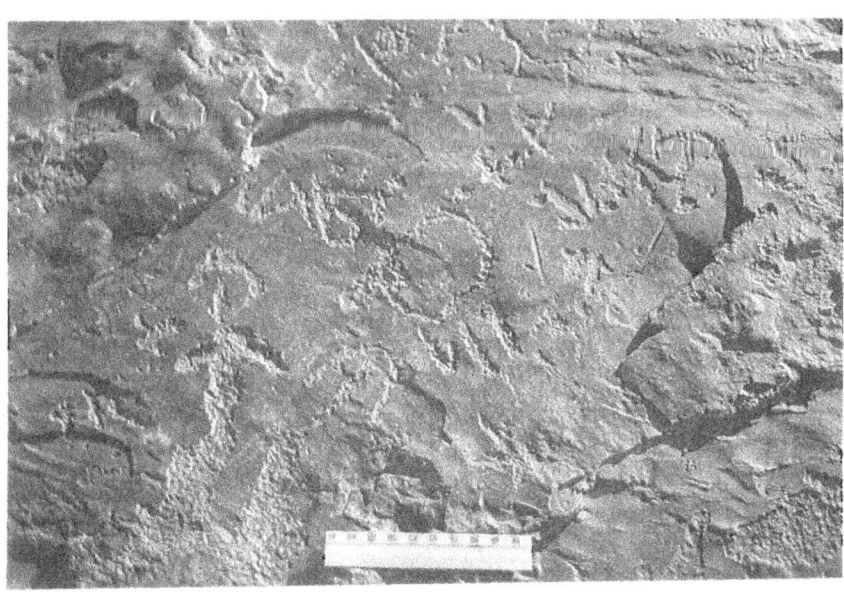

11.6 Rock engravings at Sturts Meadows. (Photo: John Clegg)

11.7 Engraved animal tracks at Sturts Meadows.

11.11 A major composition of people and mythic beings painted by Najombolmi in 1964 at the Anbangbang Shelter, Kakadu.

11.12 Paintings of fish and other figures by Najombolmi, at Kakadu.

www.ingramcontent.com/pod-product-compliance
Lightning Source LLC
Chambersburg PA
CBHW081329090426
42737CB00017B/3062